Feminism and Criminal Justice

Feminism and Criminal Justice

A Historical Perspective

Anne Logan
University of Kent, UK

First published 2008 by
PALGRAVE MACMILLAN

Palgrave Macmillan in the UK is an imprint of Macmillan Publishers Limited, registered in England, company number 785998, of Houndmills, Basingstoke, Hampshire RG21 6XS.

Palgrave Macmillan in the US is a division of St Martin's Press LLC, 175 Fifth Avenue, New York, NY 10010.

Palgrave Macmillan is the global academic imprint of the above companies and has companies and representatives throughout the world.

Palgrave® and Macmillan® are registered trademarks in the United States, the United Kingdom, Europe and other countries.

ISBN-13: 978-0-230-57254-6   hardback
ISBN-10: 0-230-57254-5   hardback

This book is printed on paper suitable for recycling and made from fully managed and sustained forest sources. Logging, pulping and manufacturing processes are expected to conform to the environmental regulations of the country of origin.

A catalogue record for this book is available from the British Library.

Library of Congress Cataloging-in-Publication Data

Logan, Anne, 1957–
    Feminism and criminal justice : a historical perspective / Anne Logan.
        p. cm.
    Includes bibliographical references and index.
    ISBN 978-0-230-57254-6 (alk. paper)
      1. Criminal justice, Administration of—Great Britain—History.
        2. Women prisoners—Great Britain—History.   3. Female
        offenders—Great Britain—History.   4. Feminism—Great
        Britain—History.   I. Title.

HV9960.G7L64 2008
364.41082—dc22   2008029940

10   9   8   7   6   5   4   3   2   1
17   16   15   14   13   12   11   10   09   08

Printed and bound in Great Britain by
CPI Antony Rowe, Chippenham and Eastbourne

Contents

Acknowledgements

During the last ten years of research that has led to this book, I have incurred a great many debts of gratitude. Thanks are due first and foremost to Angela V. John who suggested that the early women magistrates might be a suitable subject for research and then co-supervised my PhD on that topic, out of which this project has developed. I am also very grateful to my other supervisor, Mick Ryan, for introducing a 'born-and-bred' historian to the discipline of criminology. More recently, during the process of undertaking further research and writing this book, I have been encouraged to pursue the project by the Head of the School of Social Policy, Sociology and Social Research at the University of Kent, Chris Hale, and helped financially by a small research grant from the university's Faculty of Social Sciences. I would also like to thank my Medway campus colleagues, particularly Kate Bradley for help with information technology, and Simon Shaw and Jo O'Mahoney for reading draft chapters, and Philippa Grand at Palgrave for her interest in my project.

I am very grateful to Daniel Grey, Elizabeth Seal and Mari Takayanagi for sharing with me their recent research findings. The high standard of their work suggests that the future of historical research on gender and the law is very bright. I have also benefited from many conversations with other historians, especially at the Institute of Historical Research women's history seminar, the University of Greenwich history research seminar and various events organised by Women's History Network. I wish to thank Lucy Bland especially for kindly supplying me with some references concerning the execution of Edith Thompson. I am also indebted to John Minkes for information about the probation service in Wales before 1945.

I have visited many archives and libraries during the course of my research but would especially like to thank Pauline Adams, librarian at Somerville College, Oxford, for her help with the Margery Fry papers and her enthusiasm and interest in my project. Some years ago the Magistrates' Association were kind enough to supply me with coffee and biscuits while I worked through their annual reports. Many thanks are also due to Jane Wynne Willson and her family for not only providing me with much information about Jane's mother, Theodora Calvert, but also for entertaining me so well at their home.

Finally, a great deal of gratitude is due to my husband, Brian, and daughters Clare and Ruth for all the support they have offered over the last decade and for putting up with me while I completed the research and writing. I wish to dedicate the book to the memory of my parents, Jack and Frances Catford.

Anne Logan
University of Kent

Abbreviations

ACTO	Advisory Council on the Treatment of Offenders
AMSH	Association for Moral and Social Hygiene
DPAS	Discharged Prisoners' Aid Society
GWMS	Gloucestershire Women Magistrates' Society
HLPR	Howard League for Penal Reform
HWMA	Hampshire Women Magistrates' Association
JBS	Josephine Butler Society
JP	Justice of the Peace
MA	Magistrates' Association
NAPO	National Association of Probation Officers
NCADP	National Council for the Abolition of the Death Penalty
NCW	National Council of Women
NFWI	National Federation of Women's Institutes
NSPCC	National Society for the Prevention of Cruelty to Children
NUSEC	National Union of Societies for Equal Citizenship
NUTG	National Union of Townswomen's Guild
NUWSS	National Union of Women's Suffrage Societies
NUWW	National Union of Women Workers
NVA	National Vigilance Association
NWCA	National Women's Citizens Association
PRL	Penal Reform League
PSMC	Public Service and Magistrates' Committee (of NCW)
QC	Queen's Council
SJCIWO	Standing Joint Conference of Industrial Women's Organisations
SPG	Six Point Group
WCA	Women's Citizens Associations
WCG	Women's Co-operative Guild
WFL	Women's Freedom League
WILPF	Women's International League for Peace and Freedom
WSPU	Women's Social and Political Union

Introduction

> I think the wisest course for an MP who wants to be of
> use is to acquire as much knowledge as possible on
> some one subject . . . I am much interested in crimi-
> nology and penal reform, and I should try to make a
> study of that subject.

These words (which appeared in an interview given by the former
suffragist and Labour parliamentary candidate Clara Dorothea Rackham,
to the feminist newspaper, *The Vote*, in 1928)[1] clearly exemplify one
woman's commitment to the politics of criminal justice and penal
reform. In 1920, Mrs. Rackham, along with over 200 other women,
became one of the first of her sex to take her place on the magisterial
bench as a Justice of the Peace (JP) following the Sex Disqualification
(Removal) Act, itself a consequence of the partial enfranchisement of
women two years before. Further appointments were made in the years
that followed. Although the Act also allowed women to become solicitors and barristers, its impact on the magistracy was far more immediate and numerically significant.[2] Many of the new women magistrates
had been active in the suffrage movement; a few had even experienced
first-hand the criminal justice system in courts and prisons during the
struggle for women's votes. They fully appreciated that their appointment as JPs was an important indicator of their new status as citizens
but recognised that there was far more to the job of magistrate than the
glory conferred by this 'poor man's knighthood'. Therefore, over the
years that followed, many of these women, and the organisations to
which they belonged, were to make their 'study' of penal reform and
take a profound, and often critical, interest in the workings of the criminal justice system.

The appointment of the first women JPs was a landmark in the history of British justice but it represents neither the beginning nor the end of women's, and feminists', interest in the system. While there has been some recognition from scholars that 'first wave' feminists were involved in specific campaigns related to criminal justice (especially for the appointment of women police), there is less understanding of their distinctive contribution to penal reform and to the emerging discipline of criminology during the middle years of the twentieth century. Ngairie Naffine, for example, begins her 'history' of feminist criminology in the 1970s.[3] However, historians have indicated that 'first wave' feminists expressed similar concerns about the criminal justice system to those of their late twentieth-century counterparts, for whom problems such as rape and domestic violence loomed large. The work of Josephine Butler's Ladies' National Association in confronting the double sexual standard inherent in the regulation of prostitution by the Contagious Diseases Acts (in force between 1869 and 1886) has long been recognised.[4] Similarly, late Victorian feminist-inspired campaigns against wife-beating and child abuse have received a good deal of coverage, although in the latter case, some discussion has arguably come more from the perspective of the history of sexuality than of criminality.[5] Perhaps surprisingly, there has been rather less attention given to the feminist critique of criminal justice and of the penal system which emerged at the height of the struggle for women's votes (despite the fact that suffragette memoirs often described their authors' court appearances and incarceration in some detail)[6] and the longer-term influence of that critique.

Therefore there are still many missing pieces before a more complete understanding of the engagement of feminism with the criminal justice system in England and Wales over the last century or so can be achieved; not least, the period c. 1920–70, which is the main concern of this book. Once regarded as the 'intermission' between the first and second 'waves' of the women's movement,[7] the middle years of the twentieth century have more recently been found to be a fruitful, if subdued, period for historians of feminism to analyse. It is now understood that the so-called first wave feminists did not vanish from the political stage but, by and large, continued campaigning after the First World War, while unsurprisingly abandoning the attention-grabbing tactics of the suffragettes in favour of other low-key, but vitally important, methods, such as parliamentary lobbying. Clearly too, the goals of the movement were to alter, as circumstances changed.[8] There has also been some recognition of the extent of the success of feminists in their parliamentary strategy (which was not new, but a reversion to an older campaign style) in getting 'women-friendly' legislation onto the statute book, especially in the immediate post-war years.[9] The varied forms that feminism took in the mid-twentieth century have also been analysed minutely, although the contrast formerly drawn between the so-called new or welfare feminism and the 'old', equalitarian type is now recognised to have been overemphasised.[10] Importantly, there has been some recognition that the health of the feminist movement cannot be measured simply by counting the number of branches affiliated to the former suffrage societies such as the National Union of Societies for Equal Citizenship (NUSEC). Instead, historians have started to research the wider women's movement, the many and varied associational contexts (including Women's Institutes, Women's Citizens Associations, the Mothers' Union and the National Council of Women) that mobilised hundreds of thousands of women across the country during this period and have debated the extent to which they can be regarded as 'feminist'.[11]

Inevitably, once women had won the vote in 1918 and 1928, there was some reordering of priorities among feminists. While some (most notably the leader of NUSEC, Eleanor Rathbone) focused on improving the welfare of working women, others had their sights set more on the widening of professional opportunities or reforming family law. Helen Jones has surveyed a range of policy areas that engaged the attention of women in the interwar years, including poverty and its gendered impact, education, health and foreign affairs. However, criminal justice is notably absent from Jones's survey.[12] Similarly Jill Liddington has shown that the peace movement above all other causes attracted a great deal of feminist energy both during and after the First World War, unsurprisingly since the course of international relations was one of the greatest political challenges of the early and mid-twentieth century.[13] The argument of this book is that criminal justice also continued to be a major political concern for some of the women who had fought so hard for women's suffrage, but that their activity in this sphere has been hitherto neglected or underestimated both by historians and criminologists, not least because of a tendency to define women's involvement in criminal justice as 'welfare' orientated, rather than as concerned with the apparently 'masculine' domain of law and order. Interestingly, this artificial, gendered bifurcation has persisted despite the identification of 'penal welfarism' as the dominant strand in crime control and criminal justice policies between the 1890s and the 1970s and the recognition of the close relationship between penal policy and the development of the Welfare State during the period.[14]

As has been already mentioned, the main focus of this book is on the period between 1920 and 1970, in which the feminist engagement with the criminal justice system has been largely neglected in the historiography, except with regard to two key aspects: the history of women police and the treatment of prostitution.[15] However a central argument of this book is that this period cannot be seen in isolation, but in the context of a longer time span, including the eras of the so-called first and second 'waves' of feminism and beyond to the twenty-first century. Indeed, there is a case for arguing that it is no longer useful or appropriate to see a social movement as culturally embedded as feminism is in Britain as a passing phenomenon subject (to extend the oceanic metaphor) to occasionally flowing, but mostly ebbing, tides. A comparison between the agenda items of women magistrates' organisations in the 1920s and the section headings of the 2004 report of the Fawcett Society Commission on Women in the Criminal Justice System suggests the need for a longer-term perspective.[16] This is not to deny the reality of historical change (a very striking transformation has occurred in the proportion of women entering the legal profession in recent years, for example) but to suggest that fundamental social change takes place more slowly than we sometimes suppose and that shifting political and social contexts account for the more superficial variations in the apparent success and visibility of social movements such as feminism. Consequently this book will argue that even the period 1945–59 was not so much 'the nadir of feminism'[17] as an era when the women's movement had to adapt to the cautious, conservative and constitutional culture of the time as well as cope with the passing of the suffrage generation, and that, given the extent of the challenges it faced, the women's movement stayed relatively buoyant.

Feminism in twentieth-century Britain

Firstly, however, it is necessary to establish the definitions of 'feminist' and 'feminism' that will be employed in this book. In keeping with many other authors, my intention is to employ a fairly broad definition of these terms, with the controversial consequence that a few individuals who actively refused to describe themselves as 'feminist' will earn that label as well as a larger number who merely sought to play down their feminist inclinations. That such a term can be applied in retrospect is not an uncommon occurrence: the words 'feminism' and 'feminist' were neologisms of the late nineteenth century, yet the latter word is often used to describe Mary Wollstonecraft, who died before the end of the eighteenth century. However, in this book the term 'feminist' will mostly be applied only to people (not necessarily women) whose words or actions indicate that they perceived gendered inequalities in social relationships and in access to power,[18] and who consciously decided to take some action, however small, to improve the status or condition of women. Thus the term can be fairly broadly applied to activists in a range of women's organisations in the early and mid-twentieth century, including, most importantly for this study, the National Council of Women (NCW). Caitriona Beaumont has persuasively argued that mainstream women's organisations such as the NCW chose to emphasise citizenship rather than feminism in their public pronouncements during the decade after the achievement of full suffrage in 1928.[19] Yet equal citizenship was at the core of liberal feminist thinking during that period, so any separation would be hard to achieve, however keen activists may have been to play down their feminist sensibilities. Antipathy to the term 'feminist', even among individuals who clearly espouse feminism's main tenets, has anyway been widely documented. Therefore, it is more tenable to view organisations such as the NCW as 'prudently' feminist, regardless of their alleged avoidance of feminist ideology.[20]

'Feminism' is not one monolithic ideology but a dynamic concept that can take many forms at any one time, adapting to changing social conditions and cultural mores, while retaining its core values of equality and citizenship. Nowadays it is widely recognised that, in theoretical terms at least, the plural form 'feminisms' is often more appropriate than the singular.[21] With regard to the theoretical perspectives of the early twentieth century, debate has focused largely upon the 'new' versus 'old' feminism debate which culminated with a split in NUSEC in 1927 over the question of whether to support protective factory legislation which applied only to women workers.[22] While the so-called old or equalitarian feminists hoped to carry further the progress of middle-class women into male professional enclaves, the 'new', or 'welfare' feminists arguably were more interested in advancing the economic status, and by implication, the citizenship, of working-class women and mothers in particular. However, it is important to stress that the debate took place within the overall context of liberal feminism. All sides in the debate were striving for greater equality and believed that it could be achieved through constitutional and parliamentary action. Some scholars have linked 'welfare' feminism to the older tradition of 'maternal' feminism – the belief that women have special, superior qualities as mothers and nurturers. There have also been suggestions that feminism was in retreat in the interwar years that witnessed a restoration of the pre-war gender order.[23] But the contention that support for family allowances, birth control and protective legislation (espoused, for example, by some socialist women in the twentieth century) was a pragmatic strategy rather than a capitulation to patriarchal ideology is more tenable.[24]

The organisation at the centre of the division over 'New Feminism', NUSEC, was just a part of the wider women's movement in the early decades of the twentieth century for which the consolidation of women's citizenship was, regardless of the precise conception of the female citizen's role, a key objective. This loosely networked women's movement and its involvement in criminal justice will be explored fully in Chapter 1, and the term is taken to encompass not only the direct descendants of the suffrage societies, but also bodies with less overtly feminist credentials (including Women's Institutes, the Women's Co-operative Guild (WCG) and Women's Citizens Associations) that nevertheless helped to form the rich, feminist-influenced associational culture of the period. In these groupings, individual women were able to express group identity and consider the collective needs of themselves and of other women as women. But gender was not the only element in the construction of British women's identity: class distinctions in many ways dominated social analysis for most of the twentieth century and strongly impacted on individuals' sense of self. It is a truism that feminism was (is?) a middle-class social movement and the women's movement's leaders were mainly (but not exclusively) drawn from a few, well-defined, social elites whose members had both the time and the seriousness of purpose to devote to public work.[25] But leaders are only part of the story. Sadly, although the activity of some working-class women in the suffrage movement has fortunately been documented,[26] we can only guess about the opinions of the majority of women due to a paucity of sources. However, it would not be entirely safe to assume that the early-twentieth-century women's movement was completely middle class or that working-class women utterly lacked feminist sympathies or a willingness to serve. The WCG was particularly significant in this respect because of its large rank-and-file membership of working-class women – mainly wives of manual high wage-earners – in the early twentieth century who were actively encouraged to meet to discuss political and social issues, including criminal justice matters, and to put their names forward for civic office. While they almost certainly did not have domestic help to support their forays into public life, Guildswomen were arguably just as enthusiastic about their citizenship and as engaged with social welfare as their middle-class counterparts. Therefore the WCG became an important source of working-class nominees to the magisterial bench in the 1920s and 1930s with the result that, by 1937, 137 of its members had become JPs.[27]

This book argues that feminist women, mainly, but not exclusively, from the middle and upper classes, and working through the complex network of the women's movement and penal reform pressure groups, took a greater interest in and exerted more influence over criminal justice policy than is usually understood. Although they were largely confined to voluntary activities (most obviously and pertinently the magistracy and the network of interest groups associated with it), feminists used their influence to carry forward some clear objectives, including better employment opportunities and benefits for women workers in criminal justice, improved care of victims and more humane penal treatment for women and children (and also for men). Although success was by no means total, and progress at best gradual, generations of women in the twentieth century focused their attention upon an area of policy that was traditionally regarded as a masculine sphere.

Throughout the book there will be emphasis on the interdependence of feminist theory and practical politics and of policy analysis and active campaigning. Politically active feminists could not afford to be dogmatic or have one-track minds; they had multiple identities, interests and commitments to a range of causes, not all of which were straightforwardly 'women's issues'. In practice, the women's organisations of mid-twentieth-century Britain desired *both* better employment opportunities for women *and* improved conditions for mothers in a twin-track approach to the achievement of social equality. It was not for them an 'either-or' matter, in fact sometimes the two could be neatly combined, for example by stressing the 'social motherhood' capabilities of middle-class women to fill supervisory roles in disciplinary institutions. Their pragmatism is clearly visible in the context of criminal justice. Feminists saw nothing incompatible in encouraging more women to become lawyers *and* arguing that imprisoned mothers should keep their babies with them. Feminist ideology, as expressed through the network of women's organisations, was anyway not static throughout the period concerned and clear differences can be ascertained between the approaches of different groups and individuals in different decades. The women's movement could not remain hermetically sealed from the cultural forces all around it, including (to use shorthand, rather generalising terms) the domesticity of the 1950s and the permissiveness of the 1960s. However, the core principle of equal citizenship remained central, despite the multiple interpretations put upon it. Moreover, on certain key points with regard to criminal justice, the stances adopted by the leaders of the mainstream women's movement were remarkably consistent.

Within the 1920–70 period as a whole, what might be called the 'long 1950s' – the time between the end of the Second World War and the beginning of the 'real' 1960s that coincided with the arrival of the Beatles and of the Wilson government in 1963–4 – poses a particular problem for historians of the women's movement, having been memorably dubbed 'the nadir' of British feminism (albeit with a question mark).[28] Stephanie Spencer's recent work has thankfully begun the task of reappraisal of the 'forgotten generation' of the 1950s,[29] a process I hope this book will continue. Periodisation (and any associated generalisations) is probably the most hazardous part of the historian's enterprise as the last but one sentence exemplifies. For the history of feminism the publication of Betty Freidan's *Feminine Mystique* in 1963 might seem a more significant signpost than either Wilson or the Beatles. But the full impact of such an important work on its readers cannot have been instant whereas de Beauvoir's *Second Sex* had been available in an English translation since the early 1950s and was selling well.[30] The stereotypical view of the 1950s as a time of all-pervasive, culturally repressed, anti-feminist conservatism requires greater scrutiny than it has received hitherto. A political analysis of the relationship between feminism, moderate conservatism (with a small 'c') and the liberalism with which feminism is more conventionally linked, in the context of criminal justice policy, is therefore one of the themes of this book.

The records of some of the organisations that make up the women's movement provide much of the source material of this book, together with the records of other pressure groups operating in the criminal justice policy area in which feminist women played an important role, principally the Howard League for Penal Reform (HLPR) and the Magistrates' Association (MA), both of which were established immediately after the introduction of the first women JPs. Personal papers, memoirs and other biographical materials have also been examined, in full recognition of the problematic and partial nature of such sources. Behind the few well-known individuals at the centre of the feminist-criminal-justice reform network was an extensive group of women JPs whose biographical details have been gathered in a list of over 600 women magistrates appointed between 1920 and 1950, together with their affiliations to women's organisations, pressure groups, political parties and so on.[31] From a mass of scattered evidence it was, therefore, possible to build a picture of the complex networks – both formal and informal – that supported feminist activism in criminal justice. While many of the key campaigners and organisations were based in London, they were supported by a network of affiliated bodies and branches spread throughout England and Wales.

To balance the views of campaigners, who necessarily portray their efforts in the best light possible, the book also draws on evidence in public records, mainly those of the Home Office, and of national and local newspapers, for example *The Times*, which throughout the period studied was regarded as the newspaper of record, as well as serving as a forum for debate for individuals and organisations interested in the criminal justice system, including the aforementioned pressure groups and individuals. Debates over issues such as youth justice, penal conditions and (in the 1950s and 1960s) criminal injuries compensation regularly took place in its columns, providing stimulating material for any researcher seeking insight into the social and moral attitudes of the past.

The remainder of this introduction is devoted to a brief survey tracing the nineteenth-century origins of feminist activism in criminal justice matters. Chapter 1 maps the network of women's groups and other organisations that campaigned actively on criminal justice and penal reform in the twentieth century, which I have collectively, if inelegantly, named the 'feminist–criminal–justice reform network'. The book then deals thematically with their campaigns, which can be divided conveniently into matters concerning children (the formation of juvenile courts and so on), advocacy for women in the courts, the employment of women in the criminal justice system (including in a voluntary capacity) the treatment of women offenders, the punishment of women and the care of victims. The conclusion probes further the themes of continuity and change.

Feminism and criminal justice before 1920

It is generally understood that individual women have made important contributions to criminal justice policy during its development over the last 200 years. Most strikingly, the name of Elizabeth Fry is still widely recognised nearly two centuries after she first visited Newgate Prison, if only because of her appearance in recent years on a banknote. Mary Carpenter, the pioneer of reformatories in the 1840s, is less well known, although she is often acknowledged as the major figure in the development of juvenile and youth justice in the nineteenth century.

But it was not only a few exceptional women who got involved in the criminal justice system. Lucia Zedner's excellent study *Women, Crime and Custody in Victorian England* highlights Elizabeth Fry's legacy in the creation of the role of the Lady Visitor of prisons, to whom there was apparently no male equivalent, at least before the twentieth century.[32] Elizabeth Fry's work also had an international impact as she inspired

North American women to visit jails and penitentiaries in Canada and the US, some of whom, as Estelle B. Freedman shows, applied a feminist analysis to the penal problems they encountered.[33] She also was an inspiration to the workhouse visiting movement in Britain (which did much to legitimise the involvement of women in social welfare, and therefore, ultimately, in the political life of the country) and indirectly to the many women 'rescue' workers of the late nineteenth century who concentrated their efforts on the reform of prostitutes and prevention of prostitution. Mary Carpenter did not invoke as reverential a response as Elizabeth Fry (perhaps because her ideas often conflicted even with those of other reformatory enthusiasts)[34] but she was nevertheless famed for her pioneering work with delinquents and was even consulted by parliament as an expert on the subject, an exceptional achievement for a woman in the 1850s. So it is clear that even in the nineteenth century a number of women – more, perhaps than just the few near-legendary figures that entered the public memory – played a significant role in an area of policy which, second only to war and peace, was perceived as a quintessentially masculine domain, even in the days when women were denied any opportunity of formal roles in the legal system.

It is a moot point whether these early campaigners can be considered feminists, particularly in the years before there was any properly organised movement in existence. Although it is clear that Elizabeth Fry strongly advocated the notion of 'women's mission' to other women and insisted that female staff should be employed with female prisoners,[35] it is not evident that this stance was prompted by nascent feminism. Mary Carpenter's attitude towards the emerging feminist movement of her day was equivocal at first and she rebuffed approaches from both Anna Jameson and John Stuart Mill to back calls for the vote. However, Carpenter eventually came to support actively both the campaign for women's suffrage and the movement in opposition to the Contagious Diseases (CD) Acts, serving as a vice-president of the Ladies' National Association for Repeal (LNA) and signing a petition for the right to vote as well as speaking on behalf of the latter cause in 1877.[36]

By then the outline of a feminist critique of the criminal justice system was taking shape as the women's movement developed. Legal discourse anyway lay at the heart of the Victorian women's movement as feminists sought to challenge and change unequal laws concerning property, voting rights and access to professions. Pressure on parliament was of fundamental importance in facilitating legal change and arguably the centrality of the suffrage campaign to the women's cause in the 50 years from 1866 was merely a reflection of the reality that progress on all the other issues would remain slow until women themselves could influence the outcome of elections to the House of Commons. Yet campaigns for other, not unrelated, 'causes' continued to be fought, sometimes successfully, as in the case of the repeal of the CD Acts, achieved in 1886. It was during the course of this campaign that specific and strong doubts were raised and articulated about the behaviour of the all-male agents of criminal justice towards women, specifically the police and magistrates.

The CD Acts repeal campaign itself is generally understood to have been feminist influenced and led, and there was considerable overlap between the membership of the LNA and of suffrage societies.[37] As Judith Walkowitz has shown, there were two distinct strands in the feminism of the repeal campaign's charismatic leader, Josephine Butler: on the one hand, the assertion of equality of the sexes and on the other, of the distinctiveness of women.[38] Like Elizabeth Fry, Butler's influence was pervasive and women social activists, especially middle-class 'rescue' workers, continued to revere her and follow her example during her lifetime and after. Although, as Walkowitz points out, not all of them were committed to feminism in the fullest sense, many of them did share the critique of the criminal justice system that Butler and the movement she headed had generated and articulated.

This critique, which later became commonplace among feminist activists in the social purity movement, was of alleged male bias in the criminal justice system operating to the detriment of (female and/or child) victims. Roused initially by tales of the rough handling of prostitutes (and suspected prostitutes) by police in garrison towns under the CD Acts, feminists soon widened their attack to include allegations that physical assaults on wives by their husbands were taken insufficiently seriously by the courts. This cause was espoused most famously in Frances Power Cobbe's 1878 article 'Wife-Torture in England' and in the *Women's Suffrage Journal*, edited by Lydia Becker. Martin J. Wiener has drawn attention to earlier comments by the press on this matter (including some by John Stuart Mill and Harriet Taylor) in the late 1840s and argues that concerns of this nature were part of a longer-term 'reconstruction of gender'.[39] But as the network of reforming, female-dominated pressure groups grew in the last quarter of the century, their concerns about criminal justice became more widespread and vocal. The new purity organisations of the 1880s broke new ground by raising the question of sexual assault on young persons; their campaign memorably culminated in the *Pall Mall Gazette's* controversial articles headed 'The Maiden Tribute of

Modern Babylon' and the subsequent raising of the age of consent to sexual intercourse to 16 by the Criminal Law Amendment Act of 1885.[40]

Also, by the 1880s, activists were taking the next logical step in arguing that young and/or female victims would be better served if adult women were able to play some part in the administration of criminal justice, or at least if the latter were permitted to remain in court when the former's assailants were tried. As the feminist campaigner Henrietta Muller tellingly commented, after refusing to leave a court hearing concerning a 15-year-old girl made pregnant by her uncle, ' a woman was not tried by her peers'.[41] Furthermore, a common practice at the time was for a judge or magistrate to order the court to be cleared of all women (not men) if the evidence was likely to be of the type 'unsuitable' for mixed company, even if the testimony was to be given by a female victim: as Muller's stance indicates, this procedure was anathema to feminists. In 1886 the National Vigilance Association (NVA) advocated a proposal to enshrine in law the 'right of any woman or girl concerned in a trial to have some friends of her own sex in court when the assumed right to exclude women is exercised'.[42] Increasingly too, demands were made for police matrons to take care of women held in police custody. The NVA petitioned the Home Secretary to that effect in 1887 and subsequently circularised police superintendents for their views.[43]

By the Edwardian era the belief that the scales of justice were weighted against working-class women, and that only the involvement of their middle-class sisters in the legal system would redress the balance, had become firmly embedded in the discourse of the women's movement. Some progress had been made on the appointment of police matrons, but the removal of women from court hearings continued to be an irritant – in fact, it was to remain so as late as the 1920s, when, on occasions, women magistrates were asked to leave their bench, while judges were allowed to order the formation of all-male juries for many decades to come, even when women were empanelled. Specific demands for the appointment of women as JPs were being articulated by 1910, for example, in the columns of *Common Cause*, the newspaper of the National Union of Women's Suffrage Societies, where a correspondent demanded the presence of a woman on the magisterial bench 'in all cases brought before the Police Courts in which girls and children are the victims and men the offenders'.[44]

This campaign gained ground in the years leading up to and during the First World War, during which suffrage papers, including the Women's Freedom League organ, *The Vote*, and *Votes for Women*, run by the United Suffragists, continued to publicise examples of what they perceived to be rampant misogyny in the courts. The former ran an ironically titled column, 'How Men Protect Women' in which Nina Boyle and Edith Watson exposed lenient sentences on abusers and encouraged their readers to monitor the courts by attending hearings and refusing to leave if attempts were made to remove them.[45] *Votes for Women*, which during the War was edited by the former suffragette, Evelyn Sharp, regularly displayed comparisons between the punishments awarded to men found guilty of violent assaults on girls with the (frequently heavier) sentences handed out for property crimes. For example, in May 1917 two cases in Plymouth were featured. In the first, a man was cleared of indecent assault and found guilty of common assault for which he received a sentence of three months in the second division. In the second case, two offences of housebreaking were punished by ten months' imprisonment with hard labour. Another issue of the paper compared two bigamy cases tried in the same court by the same judge. The first defendant, an army officer, was imprisoned for one day while the second, a working-class woman, was sentenced to six months in jail.[46]

With the onset of war, women's organisations stepped up their campaign for the appointment of women police to patrol women workers and keep girls out of trouble in railway stations and near military camps. But even before the war, the women's suffrage movement had refocused feminist anxiety about the criminal justice system by highlighting conditions in Britain's jails. That the treatment of the country's prisoners was so unbefitting a nation that prided itself on its 'civilisation' must have been a shock to some of the ladies imprisoned for taking part in suffragette protests, even though in fact they often received preferential treatment. It certainly raised their consciousness of 'the common bond of womankind' and the necessity to seek a wide range of reforms, including to the penal system.[47] Suffragette law-breakers, such as Lady Constance Lytton, quickly wrote accounts of their experiences and expressed some sympathy with the 'ordinary' prisoners they encountered.[48] Accordingly in 1907 a new pressure group, the Penal Reform League (PRL), was set up as a direct result of an account given by the suffragette Mrs Cobden Sanderson of her prison experiences to an audience at a ladies' club called the Sesame. This led to a correspondence with Captain St John who had recently spoken about penal conditions at a vegetarian restaurant and who soon became the League's first secretary.[49] The PRL soon gathered an impressive roster of well-known people as its vice-presidents, many of whom were active suffragists, including the Earl of Lytton, his sister (Lady Constance) and the Metropolitan magistrate Cecil Chapman.[50] Active members also included Gertrude Eaton, a suffragist, and a Quaker humanitarian, Edith Bigland, both of whom worked devotedly for the PRL and its successor, the HLPR, for many years to come.

In his account of the history of penal reform, Gordon Rose argued that the PRL had little to do with the suffrage question after its formation.[51] This was not the case: the evidence strongly indicates that the PRL remained close to the women's movement in general and engaged with the problems of suffragette prisoners in particular. In its annual report for 1913, the League took pains to point out that it was not a suffrage society, and that it did not 'defend the crimes of suffragists [*sic*] any more than it does those of other persons who find their way into prison',[52] but nevertheless the PRL retained close links to the women's movement, especially the 'law-abiding' suffrage societies, purity organisations and professional women's groups. The controversy regarding the treatment of hunger-striking suffragettes was anyway impossible to ignore. In 1913 in response to the 'Cat and Mouse Act' the PRL demanded the unconditional release of hunger-striking prisoners of conscience whose lives were in danger.[53] In addition, several combined lobbying and discussion activities with women's organisations took place during the League's lifespan of around 14 years, including a conference entitled, 'Girls' Moral Danger: Punishment or Re-Education?' in 1912, chaired by Cecil Chapman and jointly convened by the PRL, the Ladies' National Association, the Church Army, the Girls' Friendly Society, the Salvation Army and the National Union of Women Workers' Rescue and Preventive Committee.[54] In 1919 a PRL-organised deputation to the Home Office included representatives from about 20 other organisations including the Association of Headmistresses, the Federation of Uniformed Women, several Suffrage societies, the Women's Co-operative Guild, the Royal British Nurses Association and the National Union of British Nurses. Under discussion on this occasion were the deputation's demands for the appointment of women governors and women medical officers for women's prisons, trained women nurses in all prisons and changes to the disciplinary regime including 'the discontinuance of dietary punishment, unnecessary humiliation in dress (especially for women), and the spy-hole'.[55] The PRL therefore seems to have taken a particular interest in women prisoners, even though they represented only a small minority of the total prison population. It was also concerned about measures to combat juvenile delinquency, including the development of special children's courts (first sanctioned by legislation in 1908), the appointment of probation officers and the introduction of women magistrates. Again, joint deputations with women's organisations were held (see Chapter 2). Thus the modus operandi of penal reformers working in close collaboration with women's groups was well established before the feminist Margery Fry took over as PRL secretary in the early 1920s and engineered its merger with the Howard Association.

By 1920, therefore, a network of women's organisations and penal reformers was already in place, energetically pressing for change in the criminal justice system from a feminist perspective. A clear agenda had emerged of interconnected demands: female victims to be better cared for, female defendants and prisoners to be safeguarded and to have more appropriately gender-specific treatment, special arrangements for children – be they victims or culprits – and greater employment opportunities for women in the system, particularly as professionals (the latter often justified by reference to the special needs and vulnerability of one of the other two groups). Even before women won the parliamentary vote and were admitted to the House of Commons, the magistracy and the legal profession, their organisations had shown a profound interest in the criminal justice system and individual women were actively engaged in penal reform campaign groups. As women's rights to citizenship expanded with the acquisition of the parliamentary franchise and the removal in 1919 of sex disqualification in the legal profession and the magistracy, women's groups were able to advance this agenda, which continued to form the basis of their demands for the next 50 years. The next chapter examines in greater detail the organisations active in this field of policy during that half-century.

1
Feminism and Criminal Justice Reform

On 27 July 1920 a deputation of representatives of organisations jointly lobbying over the government's proposals for reform of juvenile courts in London met the Lord Chancellor and the Home Secretary. The government's bill (which aimed to concentrate the handling of cases involving young people in a few specially established juvenile courts in the capital where they would be heard by lay men and women Justices of the Peace [JPs] accompanying the stipendiary magistrates) was facing opposition in parliament and from the Metropolitan (stipendiary) magistrates, a group of qualified barristers who were employed to adjudicate in the capital's busy courts of summary jurisdiction. The deputation included representatives of the Howard Association, the Labour Party, the National Council of Women (NCW), the Penal Reform League (PRL), the Standing Joint Committee of the Industrial Women's Organisations (SJCIWO), the State Children's Association, Wage-Earning Children's Committee and the Women's Local Government Society.[1]

What brought together this coalition of women's organisations, penal reform groups and children's welfare lobbyists? Clearly all parties had an interest in the improvement of juvenile justice and were broadly 'progressive' in nature. Some, perhaps, were more concerned about the citizenship rights of women to sit as magistrates while for others the main priority was the protection of children. Schuster, the permanent secretary in the Lord Chancellor's Office, was certainly of the opinion that the deputation's motives were mixed and claimed that Lord Lytton of the State Children's Association (who led the deputation) was 'far more interested in the Children's Court idea than the women idea'.[2] But despite these apparent differences of emphasis this was in fact a remarkably cohesive lobby group supported by a close network of individuals and overlapping organisations. Lytton had, of course, been a strong advocate of women's rights before the First World War, serving as president of the Men's League for Women's Suffrage. He was also a backer of the Penal Reform League. Margery Fry, one of the speakers of the deputation, took part in her capacity as PRL secretary, but she was also associated with the NCW and with the Labour Party, and, as a newly appointed magistrate in London, could expect to play a part in the new children's courts the government was planning. The connections between the women's movement and penal reformers were evidently already very strong.

As the introduction to this book pointed out, this coalition was not a new phenomenon, although the network undoubtedly had been strengthened by the controversies surrounding the treatment of suffragette prisoners and, more generally, by the heightened interest in women's rights in the second decade of the twentieth century. This chapter will map the feminist–criminal–justice reform network, which continued to be significant during the next 50 years and in which women magistrates (and to a lesser extent, other female volunteers working in criminal justice) were to play a major part at a time when the number of women lawyers remained low and academic criminology was in its infancy. The network brought together the explicitly feminist successors and survivors of the women's suffrage movement such as the Women's Freedom League (WFL) and the National Union of Societies for Equal Citizenship (NUSEC); mainstream women's organisations such as the NCW and the National Federation of Women's Institutes (NFWI); labour women's organisations (for example the Women's Co-operative Guild); the Magistrates' Association (MA) and local magistrates' groups (including women-only ones); and penal reform groups, notably the Howard League for Penal Reform (HLPR) and the National Council for the Abolition of the Death Penalty (NCADP). Through this network, reformers were able to pursue a range of objectives that connected feminism to the reform of the criminal justice system, by promoting the deployment of women in both voluntary and professional capacities, lobbying parliament for legal reform, encouraging more consistent application of the law in courts across the country and providing training for women (and, eventually, for men) JPs for 40 years before the introduction of the official government scheme for training lay magistrates. The chapter will also introduce some of the leading feminist women who placed criminal justice policy among their main interests and made significant contributions to its development in the twentieth century. For some of these women the criminal justice system became the main focus of their public work, the principal expression of their citizenship and a vital outlet for their feminist energy in the decades after the vote was 'won'. But such outstanding women as Clara Rackham, Margery Fry, Florence Keynes and Charis Frankenberg, were actually connected to, and representative of, a much wider network of organisations whose individual membership included a large propor-tion of the women JPs of England and Wales as well as many voluntary social workers.

Organisations featured herein range from national bodies, some of which had a local branch network, such as the National Women's Citizens Association (NWCA) and the NCW, to purely local clubs, such as the Gloucestershire Women Magistrates' Society. Some were pre-existing groups, for example the two former suffrage societies that remained in business after 1918, whereas others were new organisations. Many of the bodies featured in this chapter were women-only, although some of the local women magistrates' societies invited men to their meetings, albeit often with little response.[3] The MA was mixed-gender, but is included because its inception in the year following the appointment of the first women magistrates was no coincidence and because its individual membership in the early years was about one-third female. The HLPR was also a mixed body, but its female activists were of cru-cial importance in the running of its campaigns and not infrequently formed a majority of its executive attendees until the 1950s. Some of the women's organisations have been traditionally regarded as 'feminist', while others, most obviously the NCW, have been viewed as insuffi-ciently radical for such a description. The precise rationale of these organ-isations varied but they all played a part in lobbying and disseminating information on criminal justice matters, in organising conferences and training activities for magistrates and locating potential recruits for the bench.

Membership of the organisations naturally overlapped, so that personal friendship networks of feminists and reformers were also established. These networks were to be found within, but also were transcendent of, political allegiances. Because of personal ties, relationships between the organisations were often quite harmonious and joint ventures were organised both nationally and locally: for example, both the WFL and the HLPR were affiliates of the NCW.

To a large extent the activities of some of the groups in the network can only be guessed at due to the lack of detailed evidence. This is particularly true in the case of local women magistrates' societies, only two of which, Gloucestershire and Hampshire, have extant records, although there are clear indications that similar bodies existed in other parts of the country including East Kent, Middlesex and the North East of England. More local research would doubtless reveal other examples, as well as details of less formal gatherings of JPs and other interested parties. Where the less specialised women's groups are concerned, evidence is again patchy. Only a few NCW branches or women's citizens associations have extensive archives, although their activities can be traced through local newspaper reports and other sources, such as private papers. For example, there is a good deal of material on the Tunbridge Wells branch among the papers of its long-time secretary, Amelia Scott. Fortunately a full set of minutes of the NCW Public Service and Magistrates' Committee (PSMC) covering the period from 1913 to the 1970s in the London Metropolitan Archives provides a great deal of insight into the perspectives and activities of its members. Likewise, there is a complete set of HLPR minutes from 1927 to 1955 in the Warwick University Modern Records Centre. However 'national' records such as these do evince a great deal of metropolitan bias.

Perhaps because of the relative paucity of primary sources, not all the women's organisations of the twentieth century have received thorough historical analysis. There are, however, important exceptions, notably Maggie Morgan's work on the Women's Institute movement, Sue Innes on the Edinburgh WCA, and Caitriona Beaumont, whose research covers six organisations including the National Union of Townswomen's Guilds (NUTG) and the NCW. The historiographical debate centres on whether the 'mainstream' women's groups of the post-suffrage era can justifiably be interpreted as 'feminist' in inclination. Morgan argues that the NFWI was part of a 'continuum' of organisations that included the more 'overtly politicized' women's groups and Innes contends that the activity of some local women's citizens' groups also demonstrated the continued vibrancy of feminism. Beaumont, on the other hand, perceives a distinction between the support that the mainstream women's organisations gave to the notion of citizenship and a more explicitly feminist stance.[4] I have argued that the key goal of liberal feminism, equality, remained a major priority for groups such as the NCW, and agree with Innes that the divisions and tensions between 'old' and 'new' feminists were less visible in the context of the practical strategies adopted by women in pursuit of their key objective of equal citizenship.[5] Furthermore, the role performed by early and mid-twentieth-century women's organisations effectively as feminine 'mutual improvement societies' should not be underestimated.[6] A knowledge and understanding of the criminal justice system was just one aspect of citizenship around which feminist consciousness could be raised.

The Suffrage Societies 1: The Women's Freedom League (WFL)

The former suffrage societies played an important role, particularly in the 1920s, in maintaining the network of women activists. Once their original objective of votes for women was obtained (in 1918 and 1928) they turned their interest to other aspects of equal citizenship, among which equality in the legal system featured prominently. This helped to perpetuate their members' interests in criminal justice which had been promoted by their focus on the treatment of women in courts of law at the height of the suffrage campaign. Although the membership of both the WFL and the NUSEC was falling, both organisations produced journals throughout the 1920s and beyond, respectively *The Vote* and the *Woman's Leader*, which regularly featured articles concerning women and the criminal justice system.

A reading of editions of *The Vote* published between 1913 and November 1933 (when it was replaced by a more cheaply produced publication, the *WFL Bulletin*) would suggest that the work of the courts was of utmost interest to League members who perceived involvement in it to be a vital expression of women's citizenship. For example, the inclusion of three WFL members in the Lord Chancellor's List of appointments to the magistracy (1920) was celebrated with full, front page profiles.[7] In the 1920s hardly a month went by without the announcement in *The Vote* of the appointment of more women to a Commission of the Peace somewhere in the country. By the 1930s the appointment of women to key justices' committees was also being noted.[8] The progress of women in the legal profession was highlighted as well:[9] its importance was indicated by the fact that the call for the appointment of women as judges, barristers and solicitors was the third point in the WFL manifesto, preceded only by the vote on equal terms and the election of women MPs. The reportage of the achievements of women in the legal system was in keeping with *The Vote's* desire to celebrate women's successes, especially when achieved in traditionally masculine spheres, but it was also connected to broader concerns about the treatment of women by the criminal justice system. Hence issues such as infanticide, sexual assault, the deployment of women police and even the use of the death penalty on women were also raised. Magistrates held a central place in the coverage of the justice system; there were features in *The Vote* on the work of women JPs,[10] news items about magistrates' conferences, reports of Home Office Committees and commentary on penal reform and practice. To an extent the appointment of women to the magistracy was seen as a panacea by the WFL in that a strong female presence on the bench would, the League hoped, reduce the potential for the abuse of male privilege in the justice system.

Why did the WFL take such an interest in criminal justice? Commenting on the character of the WFL towards the end of its life, Elizabeth Wilson alleged that its emphasis was on equality, rather than a special role for women[11] and it undoubtedly took an equalitarian stance where the legal system was concerned, for example by demanding that there be equal numbers of male and female JPs and objecting forcefully to the exclusion of women from the bench or jury box. But WFL interest in criminal justice went far beyond the question of citizenship and its newspaper strongly promoted penal reform, even to the extent of sometimes adopting arguments that appeared to support different treatment for women. Elizabeth Knight, who largely financed *The Vote*, and the League Secretary, Florence Underwood, were keen supporters of penal reform and worked with the HLPR as well as supporting the abolition of the death penalty. However, their dominance of the WFL in the 1920s[12] is not alone a sufficient explanation of the prominence that the group attached to such matters or of the progressive positions adopted. The League's stance was democratically agreed at its Annual Conference by the adoption of formal resolutions: for example in 1923 it demanded reform of 'the entire penal system of this country'.[13] There is also evidence that local branches expressed support for the reform of criminal justice.[14] Ultimately, opinions expressed in the pages of *The Vote* must have resonated with a majority of its readers. The flurry of correspondence following the removal of a woman JP and volunteer social workers from a court in Southport in 1925[15] indicated that the publication was read by quite a few of the country's women magistrates and that they strongly supported the League's policies.[16]

Although WFL membership declined in the interwar period, it remained a feminist pressure group of some significance, and one that took a special interest in criminal justice. Its pronouncements in the 1920s (both in formal resolutions and through the editorial stance of its paper) demonstrate the continuing close relationship between feminism and 'progressive' attitudes towards penal reform. Leading WFL personnel continued to feature prominently in criminal justice campaigns, notably its president, the former suffragette leader Emmeline Pethick Lawrence, who was also a member of the HLPR council and, alongside her husband, Fredrick, a prominent supporter of the National Council for the Abolition of the Death Penalty.

The Suffrage Societies 2: the National Union of Societies for Equal Citizenship (NUSEC)

Like the WFL, The National Union of Women's Suffrage Societies (NUWSS) had to adopt a new agenda in the 1920s. However, unlike the WFL, the NUWSS had to find a new, more relevant name once the parliamentary franchise had been won. It therefore became NUSEC, the National Union of Societies for Equal Citizenship, thereby retaining its branch network and federal structure. The quest for equality in the legal system was of fundamental significance within the overall goal of equal citizenship and NUSEC naturally welcomed the opening of the legal profession, the magistracy and the jury box as a result of the Sex Disqualification (Removal) Act in 1919. Many leading NUSEC figures were among those nominated to the magistracy in 1920, including the former and current presidents, Millicent Fawcett and Eleanor Rathbone. Like *The Vote*, NUSEC's paper, the *Woman's Leader*, (succinctly described by Margery Fry as a 'little magazine [which] circulates among the most respectable constitutional suffragist-of-the-past circles')[17] reported on these and other appointments in its columns. But NUSEC made two further, special contributions to the construction and maintenance of the informal network of women JPs and therefore to the promotion of criminal justice reform as a key feminist objective. Firstly, it pioneered the organisation of conferences and training schools specifically for women magistrates. Secondly, between 1923 and 1931 the *Woman's Leader* contained a regular feature entitled 'The Law at Work'. Together the conferences and the column provided a valuable source of information and education in law and justice to NUSEC members during the 1920s.

The first women magistrates' summer school held in 1922 at St Hilda's College, Oxford was a hitherto unheard of innovation, although the NUSEC had organised its first conference for women magistrates as early as November 1920 and suffrage summer schools had been an established fact for some years.[18] The 1922 event even attracted attention in the House of Commons when an MP asked the Attorney General if similar arrangements could be made for male magistrates, clearly indicating that the suggestion that magistrates should be educated or even prepared for their task was still a novel one.[19] The *Women's Leader* reported that the summer school was marked by an 'eager thirst for knowledge' by the participants 'evidenced by attendance at lectures, raids on bookstalls and not least by snatches of earnest conversation overheard in the garden or common room'.[20] Co-operation with the penal reform lobby was close: Margery Fry was one of the main organisers. The event seems to have been successful: one participant, Miss Sessions of Gloucestershire, was so thoroughly inspired by it that soon after she formed a discussion society for women magistrates to replicate in her home county these opportunities for mutual improvement and discussion.[21]

'The Law at Work' column in the *Woman's Leader* (officially edited by Mrs Rackham JP, Miss Fry JP and Mrs Crofts – one of the first women solicitors – but in practice mainly written by Mrs Rackham) also performed an educative function. A former NUWSS executive member, Mrs Rackham appears to have put much of her formidable feminist energy into her work as a magistrate, enhancing her understanding of criminal justice and disseminating knowledge and opinion to others. For Mrs Rackham, and presumably some of her readers, a keen interest in criminal justice was not a diversion from their commitment to the women's movement but a direct expression of it. 'The Law at Work' articles were mainly of interest to actual or potential women JPs and social workers. Their publication suggests that NUSEC continued to attach great importance to criminal justice matters throughout the 1920s. The column's subjects were not restricted to items directly relevant to JPs: topics covered included fairly predictable themes (such as the juvenile courts, police court visiting and the probation service) and less obvious items (such as prisons in Australia and capital punishment). Mrs Rackham's column also featured reviews of books of interest to magistrates and social workers (for example Cyril Burt's *The Young Delinquent*) and provided useful summaries of lengthy official documents such as the annual reports of the Prisons Commission. Innovative schemes such as the 'League of Honour' experiment in Nottingham Prison (see Chapter 4) and a new liquor-licensing regime in Carlisle also received good coverage.[22]

Close co-operation with the HLPR was evident as early as 1923 when 'The Law at Work' recommended the latest edition of the *Howard Journal* to readers. The two organisation's interest in each other's campaigns was close and mutual: the first issue of the *Howard Journal* had reported on the NUSEC conference for women magistrates as well as commenting on the need for women police and separate facilities for women held in police cells.[23] Much of this closeness may be ascribed to Mrs Rackham's personal friendship and association with Margery Fry at the hub of the feminist–criminal–justice reform network. The two women worked together for many years on the Executive Committee of the HLPR and supported each other's campaign initiatives, for example in favour of legal aid for poor prisoners. For example, Fry's influence was probably at work in 1931 when Mrs Rackham used her column in the *Woman's Leader* to publicise the work of Mrs Le Mesurier with young

male offenders in Wormwood Scrubs. (Fry was at the time on the management committee that was trying to find more funding for Mrs Le
Mesurier's project.)[24] Later, in 1937, the pair travelled to Eastern Europe
together to visit prisons in Rumania, Bulgaria, Yugoslavia and Hungary.[25]
All available evidence suggests that they enjoyed a close friendship as
well as a similar political outlook and shared goals.

The suffrage societies, not unnaturally, played a less significant role in
the feminist–criminal–justice reform network as time went on,
although individuals connected with them continued to use other
organisational bases for their campaigning activities, particularly the
NCW, the MA and the HLPR. The death of Elizabeth Knight was a blow
to the WFL and necessitated the introduction of the less expensively
produced *WFL Bulletin* in place of *The Vote* while the *Women's Leader*
underwent a facelift in 1931 when a new editorial policy caused the cessation of Mrs Rackham's 'Law at Work' column, and replaced it with
more domestically orientated features such as the 'home page' and 'children's page'. NUSEC was anyway visibly weaker following the split of
the late 1920s and in 1932 it was replaced by two separate bodies, the
National Council for Equal Citizenship (NCEC) and NUTG. The former,
according to Harrison, 'faded out after the Second World War', although
the latter retained a lively branch network as the urban equivalent to
the NFWI.[26] Nevertheless, another offshoot of NUSEC, the London
Society for Women's Service, survives to this day as the Fawcett Society,
while the WFL was only wound up in 1961.

The Six Point Group (SPG)

One new, post-1918, national feminist group is particularly worthy of
mention. Sometimes regarded as the true successor to militant suffragism,[27] SPG was founded in 1921 by the Welsh businesswoman,
Lady Rhondda. Its aim was to campaign on a range of feminist issues,
although it is surely significant that the very first of the eponymous six
points was a criminal justice matter – 'to secure satisfactory legislation
for child assault'.[28] One of the Group's first campaigns was in support of
the bishop of London's Criminal Law Amendment Bill which aimed to
raise the age of consent for indecent assault to 16 and abolish the
defence of 'reasonable cause to believe' that a girl was over 16 under the
1885 Act.[29] Leading supporters of the SPG included a number of women
who took a great interest in the criminal justice system (for example,
Cicely Hamilton) and Lady Rhondda was herself one of the first women
magistrates appointed in Wales. Yet commentators on the group tend to

associate them far more with the struggle for equality in the workplace and with married women's rights[30] rather than with criminal justice campaigns.

Nevertheless, in the 1950s and 1960s under its final president, Hazel Hunkins Hallinan, the SPG again turned its attention to the position of women in the criminal justice system. Hallinan took practical steps both to encourage the appointment of women magistrates by suggesting names to the Lord Chancellor and to promote the employment of women in professional legal capacities. She also played a leading part in the campaign for reform of the law on jury qualification in order to enable more women to exercise the rights and duties of citizens in the courtroom.[31]

The National Council of Women's (NCW) Public Service and Magistrates' Committee (PSMC)

The NCW was crucial to the network of feminists and penal reformers for several reasons. Its PSMC was pre-eminent in promoting the appointment of women JPs and in circularising those appointed with detailed information. The vibrant NCW branches organised practical assistance for women caught up in the criminal justice system[32] and gathered evidence in support of campaign objectives, as well as furthering them through local action, for example by pressing for the employment of women police through watch committees and putting forward the names of women willing to serve as magistrates. The Moral Welfare Committee carried into the twentieth century the concern over the treatment of prostitutes in the criminal justice system that had occasioned the establishment of its forerunner, the Rescue and Preventative Committee, and it continued to collaborate with the Association for Moral and Social Hygiene (AMSH) in articulating feminist concerns over the solicitation laws.[33] Importantly, the NCW was also at the forefront of campaigns for women police for over half a century.[34]

The NCW, which acted as an umbrella for a diverse collection of women's groups, has often been portrayed as a 'conservative' organisation[35] and has not always been acknowledged as 'feminist'. In 1897 Beatrice Webb memorably described the forerunner of the NCW (the NUWW) as 'dominated . . . by bishops' wives' and its members as 'a good sort' in contrast to what she unsympathetically termed the 'screeching sisterhood' of the suffragists.[36] However, conservatism was by no means inimical to feminism even at the height of the struggle for votes for women.[37] Furthermore, the NUWW was not as impervious to feminism as Webb supposed. The broad base of the NCW, the main reason for its apparent conservatism, was a weakness, in that policy development was retarded by the need to get as many of the groups in agreement as possible, but it was also a strength. When the NCW backed a campaign, it did so with the authority of organised, middle class, female opinion. As Patricia Hollis explains, NUWW conferences were 'the women's movement in council'[38] and its well-connected leaders, though sometimes regarded by the male establishment as 'dangerous agitators for the feminist cause',[39] were the sisters, wives, daughters and cousins of politicians, judges, bishops and lords. Therefore the Council commanded some respect, or at the very least a polite hearing, in government circles. Their power as a feminist lobby group was thus second to none, as were their networks, both nationally and locally. NCW members belonged to any one of the county's three main political parties, or, in many cases, to none. However, despite some association with the WCG, in the main, working-class NCW members were a rarity.

The PSMC was one of a number of specialist 'sectional' committees of the NCW, each of which was concerned with a particular interest.[40] It originated as the Public Service Committee, founded in 1913 'to watch the administration of the law in the Courts of Law and the administration of existing Acts of Parliament, to endeavour to secure their efficient working, and to suggest improvements',[41] hardly modest objectives at a time when women still lacked any formal influence over the law either as voters or legislators. It was by no means an insignificant committee; over the years its membership included some of the most formidable NCW activists. The first secretary was Amelia Scott of Tunbridge Wells, a poor law guardian and borough councillor, who led what surely must have been one of the country's most dynamic NCW branches. The first chairman was Mrs Edwin Gray of York, a leading suffragist who was later appointed as a JP. Mrs Rackham, by 1913 already a poor law guardian and activist in the Cambridge branch, was an early member.

The appointment of women magistrates appears to have radically altered the committee's direction. By 1918 the PSMC was lobbying prospective MPs for the appointment of women as magistrates and in 1920 it organised the submission of lists of nominees to the Lord Chancellor's Advisory Committee on Women Justices. In 1921 a conference on juvenile offenders was held at which it was agreed that a sub-committee of JPs be formed to meet one hour before the main committee meeting.[42] The sub-committee already had 52 members and soon a larger venue had to be found to accommodate all the women magistrates who attended. Four years later the sub-committee and its parent body merged under the leadership of Florence Keynes but criminal justice matters, if anything, received even more attention than previously (except perhaps in the late 1920s when the government's proposed changes to the poor law dominated the agenda), occasioning complaints from time to time that the local government side of the committee's work was neglected. During her period in charge Mrs Keynes combined the compilation of a list of women JPs with a recruitment drive so that by 1927 there were 555 magistrate members,[43] approximately one-third of all women who had been appointed to the Commission of the Peace. Although by no means all of these were able to attend the meetings in London (about 40 women, mainly from the southeast of England did come) each member received a copy of the printed minutes, including verbatim accounts of guest's speeches. Therefore, at a time when training for new JPs was non-existent and diligent novices were merely advised to obtain a copy of 'Stone's Manual for Justices', the PSMC provided its members with detailed and readable information on important aspects of the administration of justice.

The interests of women magistrates were not the only criminal justice-related concern of the PSMC. Major campaigns were launched in favour of a woman's right and duty to be called for jury service in the 1930s and again in the 1960s.[44] The PSMC also conducted surveys and canvassed members for their views or for information about the local practices of justice agencies, for example over supervision arrangements for women held in police cells, subsequently using the information they had gathered to lobby the Home Office for the appointment of women police and police surgeons.[45] Details were circulated in the PSMC minutes and may have helped to spread best practice. Whether any of this information reached women magistrates in the remoter rural districts (if there were any) is open to question since NCW members appear to have been mainly concentrated in larger cities and prosperous towns. However, women JPs in the PSMC network were at least as well – and probably better – informed as their male colleagues about Home Office recommendations and the latest criminological research. It should be noted too, that although some historians and contemporaries failed to characterise the NCW as a feminist body, the PSMC surveys were strongly focused on securing enhanced rights for women under the law, whether they be legal professionals, prisoners, separated wives, unmarried mothers or even prostitutes.

In the late 1920s and 1930s the PSMC under Mrs Keynes concentrated much of its attention on the appointment of more women as magistrates and as members of the local advisory committees that were responsible for recommending potential JPs to the Lord Chancellor. However, the PSMC also kept a watching brief on government enquiries (to which many of its representatives gave evidence and on which some NCW members served) and on legislation such as the 1933 Children and Young Person's Act. Mrs Keynes wrote NCW-published pamphlets on the need for both women jurors and women magistrates.

By the late 1930s the committee's leadership had passed to Elizabeth Kelly JP, a social worker and Chairman of the Portsmouth Juvenile Court who was also active in the MA. She appears to have been another very formidable lady, obviously fond of plain speaking.[46] However, I have been unable to find any evidence of her involvement in feminist activity prior to her membership in the PSMC.[47] During Miss Kelly's period in charge, speakers at PSMC meetings included Madeline Symons JP,[48] a member of the government's enquiry into court social services, Lady Ampthill JP, from the Home Office committee on corporal punishment and Mr Turton, an MP who spoke about the law regarding prostitution. The inclusion of a talk about 'the scientific treatment of delinquency' on the agenda in 1937 suggests that PSMC members continued to be in the forefront of the movement for 'modern' methods in dealing with offenders. Certainly this seems to have been Miss Kelly's position.[49] In evidence to the Committee on the Treatment of Young Offenders she expressed strong support for psychoanalytic assessment of offenders, the abolition of the requirement to record a conviction against young people put on probation, the renaming of reformatories and the improvement of probation services – all items that featured prominently on the penal reform agenda.[50]

PSMC attendance was badly affected by the outbreak of War in 1939 but had recovered to around 40 by 1948. Its wartime agenda was predictably dominated by the effects of evacuation and other emergency measures. In the post-war years equal rights for men and women JPs continued to be a cause for concern[51] along with the volume of female appointments to the bench and the treatment of women in prison. Despite its alleged conservatism, the NCW continued to support 'progressive' penal methods, including the use of probation and the rejection of corporal punishment. By the 1960s the PSMC was able to welcome the appointment of 'Mister Justice' Elizabeth Lane[52] and to look forward to the replacement of the Victorian prison at Holloway by a new, state-of-the-art women's prison.

NCW's progressivism on criminal justice matters was probably reinforced by the maintenance of strong ties with the HLPR at least until the

1950s. The League was officially represented on the PSMC (and the NCW Executive) for many years by its secretary, Cicely Craven, who repeatedly ensured that HLPR-inspired resolutions found their way onto the NCW Annual Conference agenda. Mrs Holman, a London JP who was first secretary and later chairman of the PSMC during the 1940s, was another HLPR Executive member. Margery Fry and Clara Rackham attended PSMC meetings from time to time and when Craven retired Miss Brophy took her place as the HLPR delegate. In the 1950s and 1960s the dominant character in the PSMC was Charis Frankenberg, a member of the Institute for the Study and Treatment of Delinquency (ISTD) as well as of the Howard League and the Council of the Magistrates' Association. Born in 1892, Frankenberg had attended suffragette meetings in Hyde Park with her mother to hear what she later recalled as the 'stirring speeches by the magnetic Pankhursts'.[53] Frankenberg combined involvement in several feminist organisations, including the Manchester and Salford WCA, with voluntary social work and helped establish a local family planning clinic alongside fellow feminist and JP Mary Stocks in 1926.[54] In 1967, on her retirement from the Salford bench, the *Guardian* profiled this 'ubiquitous committee woman', the reporter remarking that 'one can hardly imagine a National Council of Women annual conference without her'.[55] Frankenberg was as strenuous in her support of women police as she was in her opposition to corporal punishment, and in the 1960s she headed the NCW campaign for change in the law regarding jury service.

Frankenberg's continued commitment to feminist politics, and her use of the NCW as a forum for it, underlines the continued significance of the organisation in the pursuit of women's rights. The NCW was less affected by the passage of time than the former suffrage societies, which had depended largely upon the support and commitment of members of a single generation, and therefore it probably had even greater significance in the 1950s and early 1960s, a period when many of the old feminist groups were experiencing declining levels of support and an aging membership.[56] The NCW proved itself capable of continued relevance in the face of changing political circumstances and social mores: its ability to renew itself is exemplified by the transformation of the Rescue and Preventative Committee (dedicated to tackling the evils of prostitution and sex trafficking) into the Moral Reform Committee, then into the Social Welfare Committee, and eventually (in 1993) into the Social Issues Committee.[57] However, since the 1950s the NCW has inevitably suffered from a reduced level of voluntary social activism among middle-class women, a trend undoubtedly related to increased labour market participation and the widening of career opportunities for women that the organisation itself had naturally supported. In the 1980s even formerly dynamic and well-supported branches, such as the one in Tunbridge Wells, were forced to close as the active membership aged and eventually dwindled. Nevertheless, in 1995, its centenary year, the president, Daphne Glick (a solicitor by profession) reported that branches still contained many members engaged in voluntary activities, especially the magistracy, as well as professional women.[58] The most recent data (2007) shows the NCW has 21 branches and still operates as an 'umbrella group' for 43 affiliated organisations. Among other topics, the 2007 Annual Conference discussed domestic violence, and although there is no longer a magistrates' committee or a formal relationship with the HLPR, NCW policy continues to favour progressive policies especially in relation to the treatment of young offenders and women in the penal system.[59] The interplay of historical change and continuity is evidently at work.

Penal reform groups

The penal reform organisations, especially the HLPR and its kindred bodies, are often assumed to be masculine pressure groups. Writing in the context of the mid-1950s, Helen Self has referred to the HLPR as 'male-dominated'.[60] While there may be some justification for such a description with regard to the evidence given to the Wolfenden Committee and of the period Self deals with, it is certainly not an appropriate adjective to use for the League more generally. In fact, 'female-dominated' would probably have been more apt during the first 30 or so years of the organisation's existence. However there is generally little indication of the extent of the role that women played in the League from historians and criminologists apart from a general acknowledgement of the pivotal role played by Margery Fry in its formation and development. Gordon Rose, a criminologist and HLPR executive member, whose 1961 publication *The Struggle for Penal Reform* is the most detailed account of the League's history, paid fulsome tributes to Margery Fry and acknowledged that 'in fact [she] did most of the work of the League' in the early 1920s.[61] He also praised the attributes of her successor Cicely Craven as Hon. Secretary: 'a reforming background, a good mind, ability to speak and write cogently . . . and sufficient family support to give her whole time to the work . . . entirely unpaid'.[62] (In fact she was paid an honorarium from time to time and for a few years took a job at Barnett Hall in Oxford. The 'family support' in a practical sense included her sister,

Millicent, with whom Cicely lived. One can only speculate about the sacrifices that the sisters made so that Cicely could carry on her work for the HLPR, which after her retirement became a salaried job done by a man.) Rose also made occasional references to the activities of other prominent women in the penal reform campaign, including Lady Astor MP, Mrs Wintringham (also, briefly, an MP), Eleanor Rathbone and Mrs Calvert (one of the first women barristers and the niece of Margaret Llewelyn Davies, the leader of the WCG), yet only once did he posit any connection between penal reform and the women's movement. Rose made the connection during his discussion of the establishment of the Committee on Sexual Offences against Young Persons and admitted his inability to account for the emergence of 'considerable disquiet' in the early 1920s regarding sexual abuse of children. Rather hesitantly he suggested that 'it was a result of freer discussion of sexual matters, combined with the increasing participation of women in the public sphere'.[63] The problem of the sexual abuse of children, and the legal response to it, was of course a long-standing concern of the women's movement, as Chapter 5 demonstrates. Moreover, it was by no means the only instance of the practical impact of the women's movement in influencing the criminal justice policy agenda.

The introductory chapter to this book explained that the suffrage struggle was the main causal factor in the establishment of the PRL, one of the two organisations (the other being the older Howard Association) that merged in 1921 to form the HLPR. Although the treatment of suffragettes in prison was neither the only, nor the dominant, theme in PRL propaganda, it was nevertheless an important concern. The treatment of conscientious objectors sent to the country's Victorian jails during the First World War fuelled further the unease among liberal and left wing intellectuals about the penal system. Margery Fry heard reports concerning poor prison conditions from her sisters, who as Quaker chaplains had visited conscientious objectors behind bars. These reports were a factor which (she later claimed) contributed greatly towards her adoption of the cause of penal reform.[64] (It is worth noting that Quakers and pacifists, as well as feminists, remained important elements of the penal reform network for decades to come.) Fry was a highly talented committee woman and campaign organiser and she soon set about the task of bringing the two, rather small, penal reform groups together and virtually simultaneously launching a new organisation, the MA, to represent JPs. Although she relinquished the post of HLPR secretary after a few years, Fry remained active in the organisation and was a dominant force until the early 1950s.

Throughout that time Margery Fry collaborated with many like-minded men and women. Fry had a charismatic personality and cultivated her personal, political and social network assiduously through correspondence and personal contact. The adjective 'formidable' was frequently applied to her, especially by men, indicating that she commanded their respect. But, arguably, her female network of co-workers, friends and political allies was of central importance. While her clever male collaborators, such as Hartley Shawcross, who was assistant HLPR secretary for a brief period, soon moved on to greater things,[65] highly educated and intelligent women were more likely to continue to work in a voluntary capacity, there being few career opportunities that were meaningfully open to them apart from what Fry herself dismissively termed 'eternal schoolmarming'.[66] As well as Clara Rackham, Theodora Calvert and Cicely Craven, Fry's female collaborators in the HLPR included the former PRL members Gertrude Eaton and Edith Bigland, former NUSEC activists Madeleine Robinson (neé Symons) and Winifred Elkin and the pioneer psychoanalyst, Dr Marjorie Franklin.[67] Most of these women had had the rare privilege of a higher education: Rackham, Robinson and Elkin all studied at Newnham College, Cambridge,[68] Craven at St Hilda's Oxford and Calvert at the college founded by her great aunt Emily Davies, Girton in Cambridge. Yet, apart from short periods in government service during the First World War, Elkin, Rackham, Robinson and Craven worked mostly in the voluntary sector, often without remuneration. Most of this group additionally performed voluntary service as JPs. Together they contributed expertise and dedication to the cause of improving the criminal justice system; individually they were experts in their chosen fields, serving on and/or presenting evidence to government inquiries, investigating a range of different issues and publishing their findings. Collectively they made an important contribution to British criminological research in the years before the latter became institutionalised in the universities, penning a significant number of articles for the *Howard Journal* and other publications between the 1920s and 1950s.

A separate, significant penal reform group is the foremost group campaigning for the abolition of capital punishment, the NCADP. This body originated in a conference held in 1923 of concerned groups ranging from the HLPR and the Society of Friends (Quakers) to the Theosophical Order of Service. Women's organisations were once again much in evidence: the Women's International League for Peace and Freedom sent the former suffragists Eva Gore-Booth and Esther Roper as its delegates to the inaugural conference and the WCG was also represented.[69]

Contacts with the WFL were established soon after. From 1925 the campaign was run by Roy Calvert, who gave up a civil service career to take on the work and became the acknowledged expert on capital punishment. Women activists played an important part in the NCADP, not least Calvert's wife Theodora who carried on with the campaign after his premature and sudden death in 1933 by editing and revising many of his publications. Noteworthy supporters of the NCADP also included many well-known feminists and peace activists, underlining the overlap that existed between supporters of radical causes such as women's rights, the reform of the penal system and pacifism. The first two women to sit in the House of Commons – Lady Astor and Mrs Wintringham JP – backed the campaign, as did Dr Ethel Bentham JP MP, who sat on the parliamentary select committee on the death penalty and Edith Picton-Turbivill. There were connections to several religious groups too: Louise Donaldson JP (who was the chairman of the campaign for three years in the 1930s) was the wife of the leading Christian Socialist Canon Donaldson; Maude Royden, suffragist, and campaigner for peace and for women in the Church was a supporter; and Quakers were also well-represented, for example the Barrow Cadburys, who donated money to the cause. Men who lent their names to the NCADP included many prominent male supporters of women's citizenship, including the journalist Henry Nevinson, Laurence Housman, Frederick Pethick Lawrence, Lord Buckmaster (the campaign's president) and George Lansbury.[70] As was the case with the MA and the HLPR, feminist women continued to be prominent in the campaign against capital punishment, at least until the 1940s.

The Magistrates' Association (MA)

Another project in which both Miss Fry and Mrs Rackham were centrally involved was the formation and development of the MA. Although open to both men and women, it nevertheless performed an important role in promoting and sustaining networks of women magistrates in the period 1921–39 and proved to be another outlet for feminist activity.

It was no coincidence that the first plans for a body bringing together JPs from all over England and Wales were laid at the same time as proposals for the introduction of women magistrates. The initiative for the MA came from the penal reform societies. In 1919 Cecil Leeson, secretary of the Howard Association, wrote to the Home Office seeking support for the formation of a 'committee' of magistrates to spread information on reforms such as probation. While the Home Office was able to offer guarded support for the scheme, progress was hampered since it was unable to provide Leeson with a list of justices.[71] However, there was no such problem with the first women JPs in 1920 as the names of those on the Lord Chancellor's list of appointments were published in the press.[72] Leeson and the new PRL secretary Margery Fry, who were by then working towards a merger of their societies, wrote jointly to all the new women JPs to introduce the latter to their groups.[73] Their initiative in contacting the first women magistrates probably partly accounts for the high proportion of females among MA members during the organisation's early years.

Once the Howard Association merger with the PRL was complete, Fry and Leeson turned again to their plans for a magistrates' association. At first the response from the majority of (male) magistrates was poor, but a conference sponsored by the Lord Mayor of London was held in October 1920 and a provisional committee was elected. Women were prominent in the association from its inception. According to *The Times* the first event attracted 'a large attendance, which included several women' and Miss Fry and Mrs Dowson of Nottingham were both elected to the committee (later joined by the former women's trade union leader, Gertrude Tuckwell). The meeting agreed that the objectives of the association would be the 'collection of information calculated to promote the efficiency of the work of magistrates and the diminution of crime, and the maintenance of a permanent office for collating and disseminating such information'.[74] At first Leeson worked half time for the HLPR and half for the MA, Margery Fry having arranged for his part-time salary to be doubled and paid for by the League.[75] The following autumn the inaugural conference took place, preceded in the morning by a special meeting of women magistrates, chaired by Tuckwell. This was the first of many MA-sponsored women's conferences in the interwar years, the timing of which may well have helped to ensure that a high proportion of women attended the organisation's annual meeting which customarily followed.

Not only were well-known feminist women prominent in the early leadership of the MA but women also made up a strikingly high proportion of the association's individual membership in its early years. Of 433 individual subscribers listed in the association's annual report for 1922, 146, approximately one-third, were women. Of course, it was also possible for whole benches of JPs to join collectively (although in the early years few did so), which would have greatly increased the amount of male members above those individually listed, but the proportion of women members is nevertheless remarkable, given how few women magistrates had been appointed in England and Wales at this stage. However, women were not so well represented in the hierarchy of the MA, holding only six out of the 21 council places in 1923 and only one place on the executive (held by Margery Fry). In 1923 women sat on the sub-committees dealing with poor person's defence, probation and juveniles, and the treatment of offenders but not on licensing or finance. This distribution seems to suggest a gendered pattern of responsibilities.[76] Nevertheless women continued to be fairly well represented in the organisation over the next decade. In 1936, by which time many more women magistrates had been appointed and many more JPs of both sexes had joined the MA, there were six women members on a 20-strong executive, giving women a quarter of executive places at a time when they numbered no more than one in ten of the lay magistracy.

Furthermore, the MA appears to have been broadly sympathetic to the agenda put forward by feminist women members. One of the first resolutions adopted by its council came from the 1921 women's con-ference concerning the abolition of sentences of death in cases of infanticide, a proposal also backed by the HLPR. A separate conference for women members took place annually (with the exception of 1923) until at least 1939. An attempt to discontinue the women's conference in 1923 on the grounds that it was 'inadvisable to make such provision as will in any way tend to distinguish between men and women mag-istrates' was fiercely resisted by women members who obviously valued the chance to meet with other women. It was therefore decided to leave the issue of whether there was a women's conference to the women magistrates themselves, and after many letters were received in favour, the event went ahead, 'the entire arrangements having been under-taken by the women members of the Council'.[77] Additionally, women JPs were given space in the MA journal *The Magistrate* (initially edited by J. St Loe Strachey) to raise the matters that especially concerned them, including assaults on women and children and the repeal of the solicitation laws, as well as on poor people's defence and penal reform generally. Most significantly, the MA, like the HLPR with which it remained associated, backed feminist-inspired campaigns for the manda-tory presence of women JPs in 'indecency' cases, for the employment of women police and for the appointment of a woman assistant prison commissioner.

Women JPs had a voice within the MA disproportionate to their numerical strength on the benches. However, until after the Second World War the MA remained a relatively small and unimportant organ-isation. Stipendiary magistrates, apart from a few maverick characters, would have nothing to do with it. Lay magistrates were sometimes put off by the cost of the individual subscription and the correspondence courses developed by the association to train magistrates were also said to be 'expensive'.[78] According to Winifred Elkin, who was highly critical of the majority of lay magistrates, in 1939, only a minority of JPs belonged to the MA, 'the majority remain cut off from any opportunity of hearing fresh ideas or comparing their methods with those of other courts'.[79] No doubt, that was the case for many women magistrates as well as a majority of men. In the post-1955 period the MA may have become more detached from the HLPR. Yet the enthusiasm among women for the MA continued to excite comment: in 1963 J. P. Eddy QC noted that women were still in a majority at its conferences, at a time when they made up about a quarter of active JPs.[80]

Local groups

Most women's organisations of the early and mid-twentieth century, including some of the most strongly feminist ones, operated local branch networks as well as national structures. This section will examine the work of women's citizens associations, some, but not all, of which were affiliated to national organisations, and local women's magistrates' groups. It should be borne in mind that there was a great deal of overlap of personnel in local women's groups as there was in national ones.

Women's citizens associations on the whole have been neglected so far by historians of the British women's movement in the twentieth century.[81] Most local WCA (and the National Association) came into existence at the time of the partial enfranchisement of women in 1918, although a pioneer WCA had been started in Liverpool by Eleanor Rathbone before the First World War.[82] Some of them (effectively the old NUWSS branches) affiliated to NUSEC, and a second group to a new body, the NWCA, while others (for example the Cambridge WCA) remained independent.

WCA activities were geared towards the education of women for their new role in national politics and the encouragement of more women to take an active role in local government. However, in 1920 WCA members quickly realised that a new opportunity for women to exercise their citizenship as JPs and jurors had arisen and WCA were among the first organisations to put forward the names of women for consideration for appointment as magistrates. Thereafter the work of magistrates was often discussed at WCA meetings and activists organised campaigns to urge the appointment of yet more women JPs. For example, in

Kent, members of the Maidstone WCA (formed in 1918 as a successor to the local NUWSS group) heard speakers on the criminal law and penal reform as well as on the need for women JPs and jurors in the early 1920s.[83] The role of local WCA was analogous to that of women's institutes and WCG branches in that their meetings' themes were very similar, and because their members were able to enjoy 'female cultural space'[84] in which to discuss them. However the rationale of local WCA was more firmly focused upon the politics of citizenship than that of the women's institutes, townswomen's guilds or WCG branches. In many ways the WCA was the principal inheritor of the non-militant suffrage tradition, in that it provided a local support network for women who became magistrates and/or local councillors, as well as a non-party, but nevertheless political, arena for social activism and debate.

Although some WCA were in decline by the 1930s (or merged with NUSEC branches) others survived at least until the 1940s,[85] and the NWCA carried on until the early 1970s. There may have been a tendency for the subject matter to become less obviously political as the years went by, as talks on gardening took the place of campaigns for women police, but the Cambridge WCA, for example, was still hosting talks on women and the magistracy in the 1950s as well as on topical subjects such as 'the modern approach to child psychology'.[86] But WCA were not merely 'talking shops': members were very active in their communities and in promoting the causes that they cared about. According to a survey conducted by the NWCA in 1956–7, 'judicial work' was seventh on the list of members' voluntary work behind local government, the care of the elderly, church work, hospital work and school governorship.[87] Even though (like the national feminist groups) WCA were suffering from declining support and an aging membership by the second half of the twentieth century, their members obviously continued to take active citizenship very seriously. For some women in the middle of the twentieth century a WCA could even be their entry-point into feminist politics, as it was for Constance Rover, who recalled hearing the inspirational oration of the barrister Helena Normanton at a WCA meeting.[88]

In some localities women JPs formed their own special clubs, enabling them to discuss matters of concern in a secure, all-female environment of mutual improvement and to plan their campaign strategies. Foremost among the local women magistrates' societies founded in the 1920s was the Gloucestershire Women Magistrates' Society (GWMS). Its founding chairman, Edith Sessions, had attended the NUSEC summer school in 1922 and together with Ethel Hartland she called an initial meeting of

Gloucestershire's women magistrates a few weeks later. The resultant society met quarterly to discuss their work on the bench and the difficulties they encountered.[89] Eight women attended the first meeting in September 1922, but later on, after more women in the county had been made magistrates, the attendance ranged between one and two dozen. Active members formed a representative sample of Gloucestershire's women justices, including Lillian Faithfull, the principal of Cheltenham Ladies' College; Rosa Pease, the founder of the Women Police Training School in Bristol; and Ada Prosser, a women's trade union activist of working-class origins. GWMS discussion subjects ranged from the more obvious topics of prison conditions, probation, licensing rules and adoption procedures to reporting restrictions and the sterilisation of mental 'defectives'. From 1924 the meetings took place in the convivial atmosphere of a Gloucester café, accompanied by lunch. GWMS meetings appear from the rather bland minutes to have been largely uncontroversial, with the exception of one occasion in 1930 when a member put forward a resolution in favour of the sterilisation of the 'mentally unfit'. But the GWMS was not merely a talking shop. Members also visited police cells and toured remand homes, approved schools and prisons. In the early years of the organisation they raised funds for a prison piano and to pay probation officers' expenses. Typically for women used to involvement in the voluntary sector, GWMS members were using their own resources to fill the gaps in statutory provision.

GWMS activities undoubtedly had a feminist orientation. The secretary, Miss Hartland, was an active participant of the PSMC and therefore part of the national network of feminist magistrates and penal reformers. Under her leadership the GWMS campaigned vigorously for women police, expressed publicly its condemnation of the practice of removing women from court in sex abuse cases and pressed for the appointment of more women magistrates and of women to local advisory committees and to the county's Standing Joint Committee of magistrates and councillors. Moreover, the timing of GWMS meetings (in the lunch interval on the days when the county's JPs gathered for the Quarter Sessions) ensured that there was a substantial presence of women magistrates when the membership of key local JPs' committees was decided. This mechanism may well have accounted for the fact that in Gloucestershire – unlike some other counties – there were women on most of the justices' committees.

GWMS activities had an impact outside their own area. In the 1930s the GWMS organised magistrates' training schools to which women JPs in neighbouring counties and boroughs were invited. The first 'school' took place in Bristol in 1933 and the second four years later in Birmingham. 'I do not know whether magistrates of the opposite sex have ever felt the need for such a school, but I rather gather this is the second to be held in the country – so presumably they haven't', commented a journalist from the *Birmingham Evening Dispatch*.[90] Women from Warwickshire, Worcestershire and Staffordshire attended the event along with those from Bristol and Birmingham and of course Gloucestershire, each wearing a name badge with a coloured ribbon to denote her bench.[91] Participants listened to talks on matrimonial jurisdiction, on women police and on the treatment of children committed to the courts, and visited some of Birmingham's judicial and penal institutions, including its juvenile courts. Geraldine Cadbury entertained them to tea. At least 80 women magistrates took part in this event,[92] which was important, not just in training terms, but also for the opportunity it provided for social interaction and networking amongst women JPs.

Gloucestershire women magistrates also became an example to JPs in other counties when their organisation was publicised by the NCW. In May 1930 Miss Hartland addressed the PSMC about the Gloucestershire organisation and copies of her talk were circulated, as was the custom, to all the committee's members, including some in Hampshire who were then inspired to form their own society, the Hampshire's Women Magistrates' Association (HWMA). Although the GWMS was not unique it was undoubtedly influential, and Miss Hartland was invited to speak at the inaugural meeting of the HWMA.[93] This organisation, which existed from 1931 to 1954, followed the pattern set by the GWMS, although it appears to have been somewhat less dynamic. The membership, no doubt reflecting the well-connected social milieu of the Hampshire bench where several members were titled ladies, lacked the social and political mix of the GWMS, a difference that may account for the Hampshire association's rather less energetic approach than its west-country counterpart.

The influence of the GWMS was not confined to women magistrates; increasingly they threw meetings with guest speakers open to men. Indeed, one of the sessions at the Birmingham women magistrates' school in 1937 was even opened to the general public.[94] In the previous year, the editor of *The Countryman* and Oxfordshire JP Robertson Scott visited the GWMS as a guest speaker. Subsequently he decided to establish the Quorum Club for magistrates in his own county[95] and recommended in a letter to *The Times* that every county should 'endeavour to have a magistrates' discussion society to be addressed informally by gaol governors, probation officers, psychologists etc.'[96] At a time when no official training was offered to JPs and the MA was still in its infancy, women magistrates such as those in Gloucester offered a template for professional development for lay justices. The GWMS became a model of good practice for JPs throughout the land by demonstrating that it was possible for magistrates to become better informed and more professional in their approach.

Of course it was not the case that only *women* magistrates were interested in education and training. In the MA and the HLPR they were able to work with sympathetic men. Male speakers were often invited to address meetings of women magistrates on the latest approaches to the administration of justice, suggesting a remarkable reliance upon the masculine 'expert', although male audience participation seems to have been less evident. Nevertheless, it is surely no coincidence that moves to educate JPs gained ground just at the time when women were first appointed to the country's benches, and the relatively higher attendance of women magistrates in conferences and training sessions continued to attract comment even in the post-war era. As late as the 1970s such events were still allegedly filled with women JPs. However, by then the portrayal of them could be extremely negative, as women 'with nothing else to do' who 'in places form almost a club of conference-going magistrates'[97] rather than worthy volunteers sacrificing their leisure to serve the community.

Women magistrates appeared to see less need for their own organisations in the second half of the twentieth century. The HWMA, for example, folded in 1954 after a dramatic fall in attendance at meetings. 'It is felt that the Association has perhaps outgrown its usefulness', the minutes recorded. One member expressed her feelings in a letter. She agreed that there was no longer any need for the HWMA but pointed out that it had been of great value to her when she was first made a magistrate. 'I feel I owe almost everything I know about magisterial work to the Association and would like to express my grateful thanks', she wrote.[98] In Gloucestershire, the GWMS was still a dynamic body in the 1940s and it appears to have survived the death of some of its founder members and the retirement of Miss Hartland reasonably well. The Society's end came finally in 1957 when it was disbanded and replaced by a branch of the MA. In the interwar years newly appointed women magistrates had been 'the new girls' on the bench, a ready made audience predisposed to soak up as much information about their new role as they possibly could. Although many of them were already mature in years and relatively well educated, citizenship was a novelty to them and they were prepared to practice it actively and to the full. Their organisations had developed ad hoc training programmes delivered in Summer Schools and at conferences where the latest, progressive criminal justice policies were debated 40 years before the official government JP training scheme was launched. In 1920 Leeson and Fry had expressed a hope that 'the appointment of women as magistrates . . . will mark the beginning of a new spirit in our criminal administration'.[99] It appears that they were not disappointed.

The impact of women's networks on criminal justice

Thanks to their extensive organisational and informal networks, partly inherited from the pre-1918 suffrage campaign, and partly created by post-1920 feminists and the early women JPs, the women's movement was able to exert perceptible influence on the criminal justice system in the early and mid-twentieth century as well as educating generations of women for active citizenship in the magistracy. The remainder of this book will focus in detail on some of the campaigns which illustrate the practical impact of feminist thought on criminal justice, including those regarding the treatment of women and child offenders, the place of victims in the justice system and the promotion of equal rights in the legal profession. This chapter has focused particularly on the feminist–criminal–justice reform network's structure and some of its personnel, the role of the new women JPs within it and the impact of conferences, summer schools and other forms of training organised by feminists for JPs, in conjunction with penal reformers and other allies, to prepare magistrates for their work. The networks was also mobilised to campaign for a series of causes that feminists held particularly dear, including changes to court procedures for juveniles, for legislation to improve the status of women under the criminal law, for the presence of women magistrates in 'indecency' cases, for the inclusion of women on juries and for the appointment of women police.

An important element of the campaigning network's tactics was contact with sympathetic parliamentarians. The involvement of several individuals in both the Commons and the Lords in supporting specific campaigns will be highlighted in subsequent chapters of this book. The MPs and lords who put down questions and promoted private member's bills were drawn from all political parties and from both sexes. Their action was facilitated by the pressure groups' employment of full-time secretaries and by the formation of all-party groups within parliament. The first and second women MPs to take their seats – Lady Astor and

Mrs Wintringham, respectively Conservative and Liberal – played an important part in advancing the agenda of women's and penal reform groups in the House of Commons: the former, despite no previous connection with the feminist movement, was advised by Ray Strachey and NUSEC and developed close connections with AMSH.[100] The all-party Parliamentary Penal Reform Group had its origins in 1923 when a group of MPs was organised to support the policies of the HLPR in the House.[101] The national pressure groups described in this chapter kept up their contacts with an ever-changing group of sympathetic MPs over the decades. Among the many parliamentarians of the 1920–70-period who could be relied upon to back at least some part of the feminist–criminal–justice reform agenda while on the back benches were Lady Astor, Holford Knight, James Lovat Fraser, Frederick Pethick Lawrence, Ellen Wilkinson, Irene Ward, Barbara Ayrton Gould, Barbara Castle and Joan Vickers, a group comprising members of all the main political parties. Later chapters in this book will outline in detail some of the parliamentary campaigns of the period and the role played by MPs acting in accordance with the advice of the pressure groups. Of course, criminal justice reform – and feminism – had to compete for the time and attention of even the most committed of MPs and it is worth highlighting the note of caution in the response of Pethick Lawrence to the suggestion that a group of MPs sympathetic to the campaign for reform of the solicitation laws be formed:

> Miss Rathbone is a very busy woman and of course she got into rather a muddle about this question last time. Lady Astor is too much absorbed I expect in other things though she would probably be on the right side. I do not know much about Lady Atholl's views on this question, and Ellen Wilkinson again is very much absorbed in other matters.[102]

Although the MPs undeniably were easily distracted – or even fickle – parliamentary tactics played a key role in the network's strategy. In many ways the tale of feminist-inspired reform of criminal justice in the twentieth century is just a part of the meta-narrative of political pluralism.

The following chapters will demonstrate that the years of patient, prudent campaigning by feminist groups on criminal justice matters was not unfruitful. Even in the years when feminism was supposed to be ideologically moribund significant successes were achieved both in the alteration of statutes and in the more diffuse process of incremental change. The feminist movement did experience some decline in the years after 1945, although probably not as much as was once supposed. For example, the NCW continued its traditional methods of dignified pressure. Attendance at meetings of the PSMC revived after the War, buoyed up by the increasing number of women appointed to the magistracy, and arguably the Committee's campaigning zeal underwent a revival in the early 1960s when its leaders – notably Charis Frankenberg – sought to confront the issue of gender inequality in jury selection.[103] However, exceptions such as Mrs Frankenberg notwithstanding, Pugh's view that 'it was during the 1950s that the failure of interwar feminism to recruit a large body of young leaders became apparent'[104] seems to be somewhat justified. Nevertheless, local NCW branches remained vibrant in the 1950s and 1960s and some WCAs also continued to function successfully. In any case, numbers appear to have been less significant than networks. The declining membership of national feminist societies was slow but undeniably painful: the WFL expired in the early 1960s and the SPG 20 years later but by that time even 'second wave feminism' was no longer a novelty. Unfortunately, because of their different generational and political perspectives, and with some notable exceptions, the young activists of the Women's Liberation Movement in the 1970s appear to have failed to fully recognise the significance of the older groups or their substantial achievements in improving the position of women in the face of an undeniably anti-feminist climate in the post-1945 period and thus may have contributed to the under-valuation of the latter's worth.

2
Juvenile Justice

> The Lord Chancellor is of the opinion that there is no
> class of case for which the new women justices . . .
> will be more suitable than cases arising under the
> Children's Act.[1]

Whenever interested parties discussed the need for women to be
involved in the administration of criminal justice it was almost invariably assumed (as in the above quotation) that women would be particularly adept at dealing with children who were brought before the
courts. Supporters of the appointment of women to the magistracy frequently argued that they were particularly well suited to appearing on
the bench in cases involving young people. Arthur Henderson MP
raised the need for women magistrates at an official level when he asked
witnesses during hearings of the 1910 Royal Commission on Justices of
the Peace whether a woman could be 'a suitable person to sit on suitable cases'. Neither Henderson nor his witnesses defined what they
regarded as a 'suitable' case, but it is highly likely that they had in mind
those matters dealt with by the special juvenile courts recently established under the 1908 Children Act.[2] The perception of a rising tide of
juvenile crime during the First World War provided further impetus to
demands for a dedicated system of youth justice, with special courts,
procedures and personnel. In 1919 participants at a National Council of
Women (NCW) conference argued forcefully that what the 'delinquent
boy and girl' needed was 'something more of maternal influence in
penalty and protection'.[3]

Throughout the period covered by this study, the special contribution
that women could make to juvenile courts continued to be the principal justification for their appointment as Justices of the Peace (JPs).

Once in post, many women magistrates made juvenile work the main focus of their activity as justices and derived great satisfaction from it. They assiduously attended lectures on methods for dealing with young offenders, visited institutions and read books on child psychology. Some, for example Geraldine Cadbury and Madeleine Robinson, were generally acknowledged as experts on the treatment of juvenile delinquency. Other women were voluntarily or professionally employed by the courts as probation officers working with children. This chapter will examine why the issue of the treatment of children in the courts and in the criminal justice system was such a major concern for feminists in the early twentieth century, questioning to what extent this interest was a product of 'maternal feminism' and widely held contemporary views on gender characteristics, or more simply a practical consequence of women's voluntary social work and expertise. The campaign for separate juvenile courts, and for women to work within them (which in the case of London required special legislation), will be examined as well as the promotion of 'penal welfarism' and 'liberal progressive' policies (such as the use of probation and the cessation of corporal punishment as a judicial penalty) by, and through, women's organisations. It will be argued, inter alia, that women made a significant contribution to the development of the juvenile courts both before and after the passage of legislation that entitled them to vote in parliamentary elections and sit as magistrates. Finally, the chapter will consider the controversy surrounding proposals to reintroduce corporal punishment for violent young offenders in the 1950s and consider to what extent a feminist perspective on this matter can be ascertained.

Juvenile courts: a feminist issue?

Why did women's organisations take such an interest in the work of the juvenile courts in the early and mid-twentieth century? The answer lies partly in the close relationships between the women's suffrage movement, the campaign for the introduction of women magistrates and the wider movement for reform of the criminal justice system, especially as it was applied to young people. Koven and Michel argue that women particularly focused on influencing state policy on maternal and child welfare[4] and special juvenile courts could be conceived as part of the same area of policy. Middle-class women had already established their right to participate in philanthropic social work, especially in a voluntary capacity, and had built up expertise in working with young people, for example by organising girls' clubs, taking a special interest in the education of workhouse children and working for bodies such as the Girls' Friendly Society. As Prochaska points out, philanthropic women played a major part in the growth of the reformatory and refuge movement in the Victorian era as well as in charitable bodies such as the Children's Aid Society and the 'Waifs and Strays'.[5] Work with delinquent children had been pioneered in the mid-nineteenth century by Mary Carpenter, whose particular example was mythologised and revered by twentieth-century-women activists. Pure voluntarism slowly gave way to professionalised practices (although not always accompanied by payment in full or in part) when in the last years of the nineteenth century and early part of the twentieth some young women chose to reside in the university settlements in order to conduct 'scientific' social work in the deprived areas of Britain's major cities. Thus, on a purely practical level, these well-educated, middle-class women could claim to have special skills in dealing with young children and older girls. Although there were some men with similar experience, for example the boys' club leader and juvenile court magistrate Basil Henriques,[6] the gendering of professional, middle-class occupations ensured that there were many more women than men with the appropriate career profile to substantiate such claims.

Many women social workers joined the women's suffrage movement in the early twentieth century, reinforcing the relationship between feminism and social activism.[7] Moreover, the promotion of social work as a profession was to remain close to the heart of the feminist project, particularly among the educated former residents of the university settlements, for example Elizabeth Macadam, companion of Eleanor Rathbone, and sometime editor of the *Woman's Leader*. Macadam was the author of several books on the subject of social work training and was a strong advocate of professionalisation.[8] However, feminist support for professionalism in social work should not be assumed to be the result of 'maternalism' or the 'maternal mystique': it did not necessarily entail acceptance of notions of women's superiority or even of fundamental gender difference. Macadam stressed that social work was a suitable occupation for men as well as women and simply ascribed the low take-up of posts and training opportunities by men to the poor pay offered, itself the result of the large number of women taking up the nascent social professions.[9] The strong links between the feminist movement and the supporters of the reform of juvenile justice became evident in the first two decades of the twentieth century and were consolidated further in the interwar period, as the following sections of this chapter demonstrate. Enthusiasm for the establishment of juvenile courts in England and Wales and for a role for women JPs within them was widely shared among the women's movement as a whole and was not the unique preserve of those who appeared most readily to endorse maternal or domestic ideology.

A strong connection between campaigns for separate treatment of juveniles in the justice system and the feminist movement was not confined to Britain, but was also a significant feature in the United States, although there it was arguably more clearly associated with 'maternalism'.[10] In the United States the 'child savers' intervened to remove endangered children from what they regarded as degrading home surroundings and pressed for the introduction of separate juvenile courts. In a classic study published in the 1960s Anthony M. Platt characterised female 'child savers' as women who were 'bored at home and unhappy with their participation in the "real world"', who turned to this form of work in order to fill a void in their own lives.

> The participation of the child savers in public affairs was justified as an extension of their housekeeping functions, so that they did not view themselves – nor were they regarded by others – as competitors for jobs usually performed by men.[11]

Platt was right to draw attention to the way this work conformed to conventional expectations of women's role, but he appears to have underestimated its potential for widening eventually what was regarded as women's proper sphere and for drawing individual women into the realms of public policy hitherto dominated by men. Moreover, it is not credible to ascribe female social activism simply to boredom. Philanthropic women on both sides of the Atlantic were inspired by the knowledge that their work was needed when the state played little part in social matters. Here was an opportunity for women to exercise at least some agency and influence policy.[12] Boredom would not have sustained them through the often exacting and time-consuming duties to which they were devoted. However dominant they were in class terms, middle-class women were nevertheless conscious of belonging to the subordinate sex and of a need to combat discrimination and negative images such as the one reflected by Platt. Mahood shows in her study of lady 'child savers' in Scotland that they had to fight for professional recognition, equal pay and the right to sit on decision-making bodies.[13] Similarly Linda Gordon has demonstrated the strength of feminist influence upon voluntary child saving as well as on the later professionalisation of social work in the USA when women workers sought to contest the 'demeaning

Victorian stereotype' of the 'Lady Bountiful' by emphasising the 'scientific' nature of their practices.[14] This again raises the possibility that 'maternalism' was more of a strategy than an ideology, developed to combat a range of negative images of women philanthropists and social workers that suggest that even seemingly uncontroversial, gendered claims to special talents and abilities could face outright male hostility.

New methods of dealing with young offenders were pioneered in the United States perhaps because that country's problems of rapid industrialisation and urbanisation were accompanied by mass immigration, resulting in an enormous increase in the urban population in the second half of the nineteenth century. Of greatest significance was the establishment of separate juvenile courts in Chicago, Illinois, at the end of the nineteenth century. Women took the lead in pressing for this development and Jane Addams' Hull House (itself inspired by the example of Britain's university settlements) supplied a volunteer probation officer to the court,[15] which soon became a showpiece for visitors from other countries. By 1917 all but three states in America had separate juvenile courts, some of which operated on the principle of guardianship rather than criminality. In some cases these courts were presided over by women judges or referees, most notably Dr Miriam Van Waters in Los Angeles.

These American developments soon became widely known to British feminists, penal reformers and social workers. No holiday, or even honeymoon, to North America was complete without a tour of courts and correctional institutions. Among the earliest English visitors to Chicago's Juvenile Court was Louisa Martindale, later a surgeon and Sussex JP, who went there in 1900 with her politically minded mother and sister, Hilda (later a factory inspector). While in the USA they also met Jane Addams and inspected a Roman Catholic reformatory for two thousand children in New York.[16] Later, after the First World War, Geraldine Cadbury (in 1922) was among several British visitors to Van Waters' Los Angeles court,[17] which had become particularly celebrated among British feminists, perhaps because some well-known suffragettes had settled on the Californian coast. It is evident that there were well-established connections between the leading figures on both sides of the Atlantic and similarities emerged in their ideas and strategies regarding young offenders. However, given the contrasting governmental and social contexts of the two countries, there were also many differences.

The campaign for juvenile courts, c. 1900–20

In England and Wales at the beginning of the twentieth century there was a perception that there was a worsening problem of juvenile delinquency in the towns and cities. This centred mainly on the 'boy labour problem', or what to do about young male school leavers who apparently had few prospects other than to take 'blind alley' jobs or merely hang around the streets making and/or getting into mischief.[18] New concepts of childhood and adolescence were emerging in response to the pressures of industrialisation and urban living in general. In particular, the growth of compulsory schooling towards the end of the nineteenth century and the concomitant diminution of child labour meant that young people were increasingly separated from older generations for significant periods of time and were thus perceived as a distinct group with their own needs and problems. In the early twentieth century a growing interest in psychology contributed further to the definition of adolescence as a potentially problematic life stage.[19] The notion gained ground that juvenile misdemeanours required specialist treatment from experienced individuals – such as youth leaders, probation officers, teachers or magistrates – many of whom were women.

The demand for separate treatment of juveniles in the judicial system became increasingly insistent towards the end of the nineteenth century and start of the twentieth. As adolescence became constructed as a distinct and problematic life stage, a time of 'storm and stress' as well as one in which impressions were made and the habits of a lifetime formed, so it became regarded as inappropriate for children and young people to be tried in the same courts as adults or incarcerated in adult prisons where they might become susceptible to contaminating influences. While the wholesome influence of the adults who led the burgeoning youth movements of the time was to be encouraged,[20] steps were taken to remove children from association with unacceptable, criminal role models by the formation of special courts to deal with children's cases held at different times and/or in separate places from the adult courts. This policy, which became law in the 1908 Children Act, was favoured by pressure groups such as the Howard Association and Penal Reform League and was promoted in the feminist press. For example, in 1913 the Women's Freedom League (WFL) expressed concern that the development of juvenile courts was being held back due to financial restrictions.[21]

As well as women's organisations, individuals with philanthropic and social work experience were at the forefront of discussion of the problem. Especially notable among the latter was Henrietta Adler, the secretary of the Wage-Earning Children's Committee (a pressure group established precisely to lobby on the boy labour problem). Adler, who became interested in this issue through voluntary work as a school manager (governor) in London, wrote a pamphlet advocating separate courts of justice for children published in 1908 by the Women's Industrial Council, an organisation that was more usually associated with investigations into women's work and supporting women's trade unionism than with youth justice.[22] A very well-connected Anglo-Jewish woman (as both daughter and granddaughter of former Chief Rabbis), Adler was an established lobbyist at the Home Office, supporting the introduction of probation as well as the establishment of juvenile courts and, later, the appointment of women magistrates. In her pamphlet Adler also argued for greater use of probation orders and when new probation rules were introduced in the same year she was consulted by the Home Office on suitable candidates for children's officer in London.[23] She was later to be among the first group of women appointed to the bench in London in 1920 and duly became a children's court magistrate when the capital's new juvenile courts were established in 1921.

Another important early supporter of juvenile courts in England was Geraldine Cadbury. The wife of Barrow, one of the directors of Cadbury Brothers, Geraldine, the eldest of nine children, had a Quaker upbringing. Her suffragist mother, who was among the first women to serve as poor law guardians in Birmingham, was also a pioneer of 'rational dressing'. After her education at Quaker schools ended and before her marriage, Geraldine helped her mother with philanthropic activities and managed her father's female employees. In 1905, as the mother of three children, she got involved in an experimental juvenile court in Birmingham as a volunteer probation officer. Geraldine and her colleague, fellow Quaker Mrs Priestman, sat as observers in the new children's court and followed up the case of every girl brought before the court. According to her biographer, Mrs Cadbury did not approach this work as an 'amateur' but set herself high standards of personal care of her 'clients'. She and Mrs Priestman were meticulous in their record keeping. They prepared advisory reports for magistrates and later worked alongside the court's appointed probation officers.[24]

As wife of one of the directors of Cadbury's, Geraldine was a wealthy woman with the time and resources to devote to voluntary philanthropy, but her motivation sprang from her deep religious faith and Quaker roots rather than from a mere need to relieve boredom. She could have dabbled in a great many causes yet she chose to devote herself to the 'delinquent' children of Birmingham, work which she was to continue in the 1920s and 1930s as a Birmingham magistrate and chairman of the juvenile court. Her personal brand of 'maternal' feminism was evident in the particular interest she took in girls who came before her in court. She recalled that

> For many years in Birmingham as a woman magistrate and a member of the Aftercare Committee, I have written at regular intervals to every girl who has been sent to an Approved School. When the girl leaves, she feels she has a friend and gladly visits me.[25]

Of course, Mrs Cadbury could afford to take this interest and had secretarial assistance with her work. She was careful to adopt a professional approach although she was merely a volunteer. Geraldine and Barrow also gave considerable amounts of money to support the development of youth justice in their home city, financing a remand home and England's first purpose-built juvenile court, among other projects. The Barrow Cadbury Trust, set up in 1920 by Geraldine and her husband, is still run by family members to fund social projects, including initiatives in the field of criminal justice.[26]

The 1908 Children Act extended the Birmingham experiment throughout England and Wales. Children under the age of 16 were to be tried by magistrates sitting at different times or in different places from the ordinary courts, children under 14 could not be sent to prison (nor those under 16 except in certain circumstances) and offenders brought before juvenile courts were further protected by the exclusion of the public from proceedings.[27] In addition to sentencing them to industrial schools, reformatories or corporal punishment, magistrates dealing with young people now had the option of placing offenders on probation or, in the case of older adolescents, recommending them for Borstal training. However, thus far there had been no attempt to specially select magistrates for work in juvenile courts. A magistrate was still regarded as a generalist, capable of performing all types of work, not as a specialist. This view was to change quite radically in the 1920s after the introduction of women to the magisterial bench even though the official line remained that appointments were not made for specific purposes.

While the role of the magistrate was usually seen as a judicial one, dispensing verdicts and punishment, the ethos of the new juvenile courts was centred on the need to get away from the overbearing formality of the police court and replace it with a domestic, homely atmosphere. Henrietta Adler claimed that 'the entire surroundings of Police Courts render them unfit places for children. The more nervous boys and girls face the ordeal with sobs of terror; the more hardened offenders consider themselves young heroes.'[28] Separate children's courts, she argued, would reassure the former group and disappoint the latter. Adler correctly pointed out that not all children brought to court and threatened by its contamination were accused of an offence: magistrates also routinely dealt with school attendance cases and applications for theatrical licences.[29] Within the more homely, domestic court promoted by reformers the magistrate's role was perceived as quasi-parental, so what could be more appropriate than having a 'motherly' woman on the bench?

By the time women were first appointed as JPs in 1920, juvenile delinquency had been defined and identified as a modern social problem and special, distinctive methods and processes were being established to deal with it. Increasingly, delinquency and youth crime were perceived as social diseases, symptoms of squalid living conditions and psychological ill health rather than innate wickedness or inherited weakness. While women (mainly working-class ones) were, as Jane Lewis suggests, regarded as culpable when their assumed neglect of their offspring was seen as the cause of the problem of delinquency,[30] women (this time, mainly middle-class ones) were also part of the solution. Their apparently natural talents as carers, nurturers and nurses could be used to good effect in providing the 'treatment' that juvenile offenders required. Therefore, as probation orders became more commonly used in the first decades of the twentieth century, women were employed as probation officers, both voluntary and professional. They handled cases involving women and children and either worked for nothing or for lower salaries than their male colleagues. Other women worked as volunteer visitors, educators and youth leaders, attempting to prevent delinquency and the conditions in which it flourished. Many of the early women magistrates had experience in these fields and, in a few cases – notably Miss Adler and Mrs Cadbury – they had already exerted some direct influence over developments nationally and locally.

Women's suitability for juvenile work

The assumption that working with delinquent children was especially 'suitable' for women was widely made during the early decades of the twentieth century when the modern youth justice system was under construction. Women's organisations engaged in campaigning for the appointment of women to the magistracy were naturally tempted to argue that women were especially needed for the juvenile courts. They seized upon official advice and circulars (which they had themselves often prompted) that recommended the presence of a woman in juvenile courts wherever practicable. Masculine opinion often concurred. In the Commons, Lieutenant Colonel Freemantle MP claimed that 'women, married or unmarried, have instinctively a feeling with the child'[31] and the Metropolitan magistrate Cecil Chapman used similar words when he said that women had a 'fuller, more instinctive understanding of childhood misdemeanours . . . than men'.[32] Even the steadfastly anti-feminist Lord Birkenhead, who although was no lover of the women's movement, was charged with introducing legislation to bring women into the work of London's juvenile courts, spoke fulsomely of ladies' 'sympathy, experience [and] maternal instincts' and their general suitability for juvenile work.[33] The linkage of women and children was assumed to be natural and the role of the woman magistrate in the juvenile court was perceived as a specifically maternal, caring one.

Clearly, as Olive Banks noted, there were striking similarities between the views of feminists and anti-feminists regarding the 'special' nature, qualities and role of women, which the former were successfully using to justify the incursion of women into male-dominated spheres such as the medical profession[34] – or in this case, the law courts. 'Nature' was of crucial importance: a woman did not actually have to be a mother to be an expert on children: all women were understood to possess maternal instincts and with them qualities of tenderness and intuition.[35] These and similar attributes, which it was hoped women would bring to the children's court as a corrective to masculine harshness and logic, were supposedly innate in all women, regardless of whether they were actually mothers. Banks asserted that, in accepting such notions of women's 'nature', 'social' feminists were succumbing to the 'maternal mystique', which was ultimately to entrap them. Furthermore, Banks argued that this acquiescence with maternalism was in direct opposition to 'the Enlightenment tradition of equal rights'.[36]

Undoubtedly there is abundant evidence that feminist campaigners for the involvement of women in the juvenile courts made frequent recourse to arguments concerning the suitability of women for handling children's cases. However, it is less certain whether their comments represented wholehearted commitment to the 'maternal mystique' or were merely the product of political expediency combined with practical experience. Campaigners argued strongly that equal citizenship implied that there should be no difference in practice between the roles of female and male JPs. They were also mindful of the inherent pitfall in the argument that women were most suited to dealing with children, that it could be a double-edged sword, used to restrict them to juvenile work. Bertha Mason of the NCW argued that the Public Service and Magistrates' Committee

(PSMC) should 'carefully watch that [women] were not only appointed to children's courts'.[37] The PSMC Secretary, Amelia Scott, expressed similar concerns in a newsletter.

> The value of women as magistrates in Children's Courts is so obvi-ous, and is so often quoted as an unassailable argument in favour of the appointment of women as justices that, as so often happens, there is a danger of public opinion being narrowed down to one point, namely, that women should be appointed as magistrates in children's courts only.[38]

It therefore seems probable that the emphasis placed by campaigners on the necessity of recruiting women for juvenile courts was primarily tac-tical, an interpretation supported by the fact that even so-called old or equalitarian feminists continued to make full use of the argument in the campaign for women JPs, particularly when making their case to audi-ences outside the feminist movement. Writing in *Reynold's News* under the predictable heading of 'Portia on the Bench: A Plea for Women Magistrates', Miss Underwood of the WFL claimed that 'women are much more used to dealing with children's delinquencies than men' and asked 'why, then should not a woman have equal power with a man . . . in deciding what is to be done with the young people who are brought into children's courts?'[39] Miss Underwood thus drew on both the equal rights and the 'special' qualities arguments, although it is noticeable that she based her claim for women's competency in coping with children on experience rather than on innate ability. Feminists were realists and were ready to use 'common sense' notions, but they steadfastly rejected the view that the only suitable role that women could play in court was in dealing with children. In 1926, after some years on the bench, Gertrude Tuckwell claimed that 'if any work can justly be called women's work that [in the juvenile court] surely is'. However, Tuckwell did not favour the restriction of women to this work alone: 'I am glad to say that the suggestion to limit us to cases where only women and children are involved has been dropped almost every-where', she added.[40]

It is worth considering whether claims for the suitability of women in dealing with children was based on assumptions about women's nature (or 'instinct') or on the practical experience of raising a family. Women had undoubtedly succeeded in moving into the public sphere in the late nineteenth and twentieth centuries by emphasising gender differences rather than similarities, as well as by harnessing notions of feminine propriety. But feminists (as in the above quote from Miss Underwood) by and large avoided making claims that women's suitability for working with children was instinctual, emphasising instead the depth of their experience in such matters. Such expertise was not confined to mothers since single women were also likely to have worked with children as teachers and club leaders, as well as in the many and varied social work roles which were often undertaken voluntarily by spinsters with private incomes. Of course, patriarchal constructions of gender difference, often vaguely described as 'women's nature and mission',[41] had shaped these career options in the first place, but nevertheless the depth of women's involvement in such activities enabled them to campaign for women's involvement in the juvenile courts from a position of responsibility and expertise – and, ultimately, of strength. Thus 'maternal mystique', in the circumstances of the early twentieth century was less of a trap and more of an opportunity. In the short term, at least, going with the grain of received opinions on gender roles reaped benefits, noticeably a much more significant involvement of women in the magistracy, in contrast to other public and legal roles. Nor was the commitment to equality necessarily undermined or opposed to quite the extent that Banks suggested: men who possessed the same 'special', empathetic qualities and relevant experience were also encouraged to take on the work of juvenile magistrates.

The women's movement and the composition of juvenile courts, 1920–55

Women's organisations continued to take a special interest in ensuring that women took part in the work of children's courts during the decades following the introduction of the first female magistrates. Activity centred around the succession of government enquiries and legislation, the main landmarks being the Juvenile Courts (Metropolis) Act of 1920, the Young Offenders Committee (which reported in 1927) and the 1933 Children and Young Persons Act.

The passage of the Juvenile Courts (Metropolis) Bill through parliament in 1920 was far less smooth than the legislation of the previous year which had introduced women magistrates, lawyers and jurors. This bill, which was necessary in order to enable women to play a part in the juvenile justice system in London, specified that the capital's children's courts should consist of one stipendiary (metropolitan) magistrate and two JPs, chosen from a panel nominated by the Home Secretary, of whom one would be a woman. The metropolitan magistrate would preside, having himself been deliberately selected by the Home Secretary, with regard to his 'previous experience and . . . special qualifications for dealing with the cases of juvenile offenders'. Thus the bill introduced an important new principle that, magistrates in juvenile courts should be specially selected for the job. It also provided that juvenile courts in London could in future be held in buildings other than those currently in use as adult courts.[42] Until the bill became law London-based women JPs were not able to take part in the work of juvenile courts since under the 1839 Metropolitan Police Court Act the stipendiary magistrates handled almost all criminal cases in the capital, leaving only administrative work to the lay justices.[43] When separate juvenile hearings began after the 1908 Children Act the police magistrates naturally presided. No woman was likely to become a stipendiary magistrate in the short term, as the requisite qualification was to be a barrister of at least seven years standing, and no woman was called to the Bar until 1922. In fact, the first woman metropolitan magistrate, Sybil Campbell, was only appointed in 1945 and even in the late 1960s only two out of 45 stipendiaries were women.[44] Therefore special legislation was required in 1920 to permit women in London to take up the work for which they were seen as best qualified, but in order for this to be accomplished the power of the metropolitan magistrates would be reduced, making some opposition inevitable.

Concern about the apparent rise in juvenile crime during the First World War was clearly one of the main inspirations behind the Juvenile Courts (Metropolis) Bill. In 1913 37,520 juveniles had been charged with an offence, rising to 51,323 in 1917. Although the figure had fallen back to just over 30,000 by 1923[45] and may be attributable to a greater willingness on the part of police to charge offenders in wartime, the rise was nevertheless a cause for concern. The reform proposals were backed by women's organisations, including the NCW, National Union of Societies for Equal Citizenship (NUSEC) and the Women's Local Government Society. The lone woman MP at this time, Lady Astor, spoke in the bill's favour in the House of Commons, claiming that 'all organised women's associations' backed the measure (eliciting the retort from Sir Frederick Banbury, 'that is a very good reason for voting against it').[46] The other main source of support was the two penal reform groups, the Howard Association and the Penal Reform League. In addition, groups interested in the welfare of children, particularly the State Children's Association, the National Society for the Prevention of Cruelty to Children (NSPCC) and the Wage-Earning Children's Committee, also played a part in lobbying for the bill.[47] This overlapping network of organisations (see Chapter 1) was to prove crucial in securing the changes to London's juvenile courts and demonstrated the continuing close co-operation between feminists and penal reformers.

Two key supporters of the bill were Sir William Clarke Hall, himself a metropolitan magistrate and an executive committee member of the Howard Association, and the women's trade union leader, Gertrude Tuckwell. The son of a clergyman, Clarke Hall was married to the daughter of the NSPCC's founder, Benjamin Waugh. As a barrister he often appeared as the NSPCC's advocate. After standing unsuccessfully as a Liberal in the1910 General Election, he was appointed as a metropolitan magistrate. According to his obituary he had 'a strong sense of the social side of his duties' but his progressive approach clearly did not go down well with his more conservative colleagues. As *The Times* candidly commented in his obituary 'his views on the merits of the law tended perhaps unduly to obtrude themselves in the form of observations from the Bench, speeches and articles rather more than is desirable in one holding magisterial office'.[48] Despite (or probably because of) this, Clarke Hall seems to have been very popular with women's organisations. He was a powerful advocate for probation especially for young offenders, and also strongly supported the appointment of women to juvenile courts. He was vehemently opposed to corporal punishment. Clarke Hall claimed that, in 12 months since October 1918, 139 juveniles had been placed on probation in his court, only 11 of whom had re-offended. The court employed two salaried probation officers assisted by no less than 70 volunteers. In contrast, Clarke Hall criticised 'provincial' courts for what he judged as over-reliance upon the birch, given that their recidivism rates were as high as 80 per cent.[49] However, it is likely some of his targets were closer to home: it is clear that by no means all of his London colleagues agreed with his methods. Significantly, Sir Chartres Biron, the chief metropolitan magistrate, was moved to describe Clarke Hall as 'the favourite of all the wild men and women'.[50]

Gertrude Tuckwell had followed her aunt, Lady Dilke, into leadership of the Women's Trade Union League, and evidently took a deep interest in the position of women in the law and in juvenile justice and probation. She was also an expert lobbyist, adept at working behind the scenes and applying pressure to government at just the right points. Tuckwell was London's first woman justice, taking the oath on 14 January 1920, and was a member of the Lord Chancellor's Women's Advisory Committee, which compiled a list of women suitable for appointment as JPs in the early months of 1920. Her interest in the campaign to allow women into the legal profession and magistracy is evident from the newspaper cuttings she kept. However she denied that she was a 'feminist', perhaps because she applied a rather narrow definition to the term and did not apply it to her own brand of women-focused politics. Tuckwell was later involved in the Magistrates' Association and served as chairman of the National Association of Probation Officers (NAPO), to which she was very devoted. In July 1920, when the parliamentary approval of the Juvenile Courts (Metropolis) Bill seemed far from secure, she organised the deputation of interested parties to the Home Office (see Chapter 1).

In essence, the objections of the metropolitan magistrates (with the exception of Clarke Hall) to the bill centred on the removal of children's cases from their sole discretion and professional competence to a committee-style situation, where they would have to consider their judgements together with two lay justices, one male and one female. But the suspicion that the legislation was prompted simply by the need to utilise the talents of the new women JPs prompted them to target their disgruntlement at the latter. The stipendiaries' opposition had some backing within the Home Office which argued that taking children's cases out of the hands of the professional, legally qualified, personnel might be seen as a retrograde step and instead proposed that women magistrates sit in an advisory capacity as assessors.[51] This suggestion also surfaced at a meeting of the metropolitan magistrates where opposition to the bill was evidently intense. While the stipendiaries apparently accepted arguments concerning the 'suitability' of women for children's cases, they were extremely reluctant to relinquish, or even share, their work with untrained amateurs, concluding that while a woman's 'point of view' would be welcomed, there should be no suggestion of equality with themselves. The 'assessor' proposal received little more enthusiasm, as it was unclear what role the woman JP would have in that case.[52] It was already evident that this highly trained body of men would resist any incursion into their professional territory to their utmost ability. The Lord Chancellor's Office also rejected the assessor plan, but on the grounds that women would not be satisfied with such a proposal and that it would make London an anomaly (which, of course, it already was). According to Schuster, his permanent secretary, the Lord Chancellor was hopeful that the professional judges would retain their power even with the addition of JPs in children's cases: he could not 'see why the competent stipendiary could not have sufficient influence over those who sit with him to control them in effect'.[53] Throughout the saga of this bill the Lord Chancellor's Office remained opposed to the assessor plan[54] despite the fact that there was clearly some support for it in the Home Office.

Further difficulties arose when the draft bill was published. Although the wording was vague, there was a suggestion that there might be as few as one central juvenile court, perhaps supported by three or four others in the outlying parts of the metropolitan area. The NSPCC, impressed by the example of Chicago, advanced this plan, envisaging the central court as a specialist facility, attuned to the needs of the young offender, staffed by probation officers, doctors and psychologists, all of whom would be experts in their field. The magistrates too would be specially selected and the stipendiary would be able to concentrate solely on children's cases. Reformers knew the man they wanted for the job: Sir William Clarke Hall.[55]

The hint that the other metropolitan magistrates would thereby lose their juvenile cases provoked even greater opposition from them and as rumours of the government's plans circulated they became more determined in their criticism. For example, the suggestion that one of the existing police courts would be transformed into the central juvenile court alarmed several stipendiaries who were fearful that it might be their court. The *Westminster and Pimlico News* reported as fact the rumour that 'the historic court of summary jurisdiction at Westminster' was to be converted 'into a sort of central bureau or headquarters for this latest feminist movement', a view that illustrates how conflated the position of penal reformers and women's organisations had become, at least in the minds of their critics. The newspaper quoted the Westminster magistrate, Cecil Chapman – 'a known and trusted friend of the cause of women' – as saying 'it is fallacious to suppose that women are specially fitted . . . to deal with children's cases',[56] a somewhat different view from the one he had apparently expressed in 1918. The article then claimed that 'lady probation officers' who were holding 'very comfortable and lucrative appointments from the Home Office, attend, watch and make suggestions . . . in children's cases' implying that the whole plan to introduce lay justices was quite unnecessary.

In May 1920 the debate filled columns in *The Times*. A leading article criticised the suggestion of a single juvenile court, claiming that 'Americans who have seen the experiment tried in their own country point out that its actual effect is emotional and sensational.' The existing system in London, the paper claimed, already made adequate concessions to the special needs of young people. The article criticised the suggestion that two untrained, lay justices should sit on equal terms with stipendiaries, and feared that, if both the lay justices were women, 'the possibility of their combining to overrule the decision of the stipendiary would be derogatory to the authority and dignity of his official position.'[57] (The bill actually stated that of the two JPs in the juvenile courts 'one shall be a woman' but officials tended to assume that the other would be a man, so the scenario proposed by *The Times* leader writer was unlikely. Anyway, the paper seems to have been more alarmed by the idea of women overruling a man, rather than lay people over-ruling a professional.) However *The Times* did back the assessor plan, which would make use of the women's 'motherly instincts'.[58] There followed an intense debate in the letter columns. Adler wrote to repeat her arguments for special children's courts and support the use of women JPs.[59] Her views were in turn contradicted by a London solicitor who insisted that 'the suggestion that the present courts stimulate a love of adventure does credit to Miss Adler's imagination, but has not the smallest foundation in fact' and by a barrister who described allegations of the police court atmosphere 'contaminating' children as 'simply rub-bish'.[60] It seems that the legal profession had been roused by the government's proposals to defend its status with all its might.

The next professional group to oppose the bill were the probation officers. A letter addressed to the Home Secretary from ten London women probation officers argued against any change in the present system.[61] Not only were the signatories of the letter (who were not named) opposed to the central court and the use of lay magistrates, but they also rejected the assessor plan. Tuckwell alleged that the probation officers had been encouraged to write anonymously by the metropolitan magistrates, as 'though [they were] opposed [to the bill they] would not dare to do this'.[62] Once again, the Home Office sided with the bill's opponents. '[The women probation officers] are genuinely afraid of interference in their work by inexperienced and faddy women magistrates', commented an official.[63]

Meanwhile, the 'London Beaks' continued to stir up trouble,[64] ensuring that the bill would receive a rough ride when debated in the House of Lords. Hay Halkett, one of the stipendiaries, wrote to *The Times*, claiming that, with the exception of Clarke Hall, the metropolitan magistrates opposed the proposals. He also repudiated Clarke Hall's views on corporal punishment and in direct contradiction actually argued its efficacy as a deterrent.[65] In the debate, Lord Salisbury expressed concern about the opposition from stipendiaries and said, 'we must not think too much of the interests of women.' He claimed that in any case, women could now ultimately qualify to become metropolitan magistrates themselves making the bill unnecessary, conveniently overlooking the fact that it would be many years before a woman barrister would accumulate the requisite experience and even then she might be overlooked for some other reason. Another participant in the debate, Lord Sheffield, criticised 'sentimental' talk about bringing a child into a police court while others resurrected the assessor plan. There were complaints about the lack of consultation and allegations that the changes were being made simply in order to give women something to do.[66] The Lord Chancellor played down the strength of the bill's opponents who he said could be 'counted on the fingers of one hand', claimed that the magistrates had been consulted at every stage and even alleged that Biron supported it. Rejecting the assessor plan, Lord Birkenhead said that such a subordinate role would not attract 'the voluntary services of the best type of woman'. He contended that adjudication in juvenile cases did not require specialist legal knowledge and that, being analogous to 'semi-administrative problems' it was work well suited to women.[67]

Behind-the-scenes lobbying ensured that Lord Birkenhead's position was supported in this debate by Lord Haldane, whose sister, Elizabeth, was on the Lord Chancellor's Women's Advisory Committee, and later on by Lord Crewe, London's Lord Lieutenant and the husband of Lady Crewe, the committee's chairman. The close family ties of supporters of women JPs to the political elite clearly worked in their favour. The Archbishop of Canterbury, who agreed to support the bill when it was made clear that the suggestion of a central court would be dropped, was an important convert.[68] Therefore, despite some difficulty, the bill was able to complete its stages in the Upper House, but only after the wording of the clause concerning the number of juvenile courts had been amended. It seems that the appointment of women JPs to the children's courts was the governments 'bottom line'; other parts of the bill were open to amendment but they would not give in on that point.[69]

As the bill moved on to the House of Commons, Schuster and Tuckwell continued to work together to counter the opposition. Tuckwell promised to get 'the Labour people' on side and to get a resolution in support of the bill at the Trades Union Congress: her influence may well have been responsible for the fact that the Labour Party was represented alongside the penal reform groups, the children's societies and women's organisations at the deputation to the Home Office in July. Tuckwell's position was a conciliatory one. She did not want to rule out the male JP 'who if he is the father of a family – & a sensible man – will supply a useful corrective to female enthusiasm'. Schuster offered her 'ten thousand thanks . . . for all that you have done', but added that he was afraid that 'if we do not do what we now have in prospect your enthusiastic sisters will hereafter storm the whole bench', indicating the strong support for the bill among feminist groups.[70] By the time the deputation took place, the names of three participants – Miss Adler, Miss Fry and the NCW representative, Mrs Ogilvie Gordon – had appeared on the list of about 30 new women JPs for the County of London produced by the Lord Chancellor's Advisory Committee.[71] The announcement of so many new women magistrates in London was a further signal that the government would persist with the Bill despite the opposition. As Schuster agued, the 'best' women in London would not want to come on to the bench 'unless there is really something for them to do'.[72]

The deputation seems to be something of a turning point in the controversy concerning London's juvenile courts. The stipendiary magistrates and their allies continued to grumble, but the bill passed through the Commons unchanged. Biron objected to the clause which stated that magistrates would be 'selected' for the work: 'to suggest that any metropolitan justice cannot try these cases satisfactorily is quite absurd', he complained.[73] In the Commons, familiar arguments were put about the inaccessibility of a central court (even though that idea had been dropped), the good job presently being done by the stipendiaries and the probation workers, and the assessor plan was again brought up. It was also suggested that the new courts would incur unnecessary expense and that the proposals were unpopular with the working class. The negative attitude of some MPs is revealed by their insistence that the bill was introduced 'for the convenience of women magistrates' or for 'ladies in high position in the West End, who are very anxious to come and sit on these magisterial benches'. Another view was that the bill was retrogressive in that it reversed the trend towards professionally qualified judges taking more of the work.[74] Nevertheless the Home Secretary claimed that the stipendiaries approved of the Bill[75] and it duly completed its passage through Parliament.

Far from expressing approval, the metropolitan magistrates continued to make public statements critical of the new act even as it was enforced. The Old Street magistrate, Mr Wilberforce, said that it was 'no secret that the Metropolitan magistrates as a body would have liked the continuance of the present system'[76] while Mr Bankes of the South Western Police Court warned the women JPs that they 'would find most of the methods . . . which they had been so earnestly advocating had already been tried and discussed by the old gang and that the problem of how to treat the children was by no means an easy one'. He suggested that a magistrate needed to be 'kind and sympathetic, but not sloppy and sentimental'[77] (the latter adjectives were often employed by opponents of women magistrates to convey negative images of a 'feminine' approach to judicial decisions). Neither did the chief metropolitan magistrate alter his views: in 1928 Biron clashed with Geraldine Cadbury when he appeared as a witness before a Home Office committee of which she was a member. He insisted that no special qualities were required for a children's magistrate or any particular knowledge of (working class) young people's schools. Furthermore, he doubted that JPs could cope without stipendiaries, thereby provoking Mrs Cadbury's retort – 'all through England it is done'.[78]

Nevertheless, the whole episode surrounding the Juvenile Courts (Metropolis) Act appears only to have strengthened the alliance between penal reformers and feminists. Far from undermining the quest for equality, placing emphasis on women's ability in dealing with children had actually secured power for women in London's juvenile courts even in the face of entrenched masculine professionalism. Most significantly, any suggestion that women should just play an advisory role in the courts had been swept aside in favour of equality, not only with other laymen, but also with trained and experienced barristers. Of course, women JPs could be outvoted by men, but the Lord Chancellor's expectation that the lawyers would keep control proved unfounded, while the fears of the stipendiaries were more or less confirmed. Although the idea of a central court like Chicago's had been abandoned, the government did push ahead with the consolidation of children's cases into nine special courts around London, reduced to eight in 1929, by which point none of them were held in police court premises. In 1929 only four metropolitan magistrates were chosen to preside in these special courts, taking two each, one of whom was Clarke Hall.[79] The Home Office also passed a critical eye over the work of the JPs, assessed their suitability and attempted to reduce the overall number so that the remaining (hopefully younger and more committed) magistrates would take more cases and improve their performance.[80] Seven years later the London JPs – including women – were even allowed to preside in juvenile hearings.

Elsewhere in England and Wales, special legislation was not required for women to work or to take the chair in youth courts. The pressure groups largely turned their attention to calling for women to be chosen for the bench in greater number and for juvenile panels of magistrates to be specially selected as the Home Office was also urging. These demands coalesced around the Report of Committee on the Treatment of Young Offenders in 1927 and the consequent legislation in 1932–3. With London now leading the way, the notion of 'specialist' magistrates for juvenile cases began to gain ground. Once again, women's organisations and penal reform groups were pressing a fairly receptive government for change, joined in the 1920s by the newly formed Magistrates' Association (MA) in which women JPs were playing an important part.

In April 1921 the Home Office issued a circular to magistrates' benches in England and Wales suggesting that they draw up a 'special' rota of men and women with 'special qualifications' for juvenile work, obviously in emulation of the Home Office's own rota for London. This advice evidently was not universally followed since in 1927 a further circular reiterated it.[81] Some benches simply ignored the government's policy, others, particularly in sparsely populated areas where juvenile crime was comparatively rare, did not regard it as applicable to their situation. In some cases entire benches elected themselves en bloc to the juvenile panel. It is highly likely that the more conservative minded country JPs were as resistant to the notion of specialist magistrates as the London stipendiaries had been.

Penal reformers and women's organisations again worked together to support and shape Home Office policy. The State Children's Association, for example, continued to lobby for special arrangements for young offenders. Its secretary, J. A. Lovat Fraser who, as an MP regularly tabled parliamentary questions about the number of women magistrates, contended that 'magistrates . . . in Children's Courts should be thoroughly in agreement and sympathy with the [reformed] system'. He felt they should be relatively young (a point the Home Office was obviously in sympathy with) and 'have experience and interest in educational and social work . . . in the Boy Scouts and the Girl Guides, in after-case committees, boarding out committees and child welfare work'. He argued that 'justices suitable for the juvenile courts should be appointed without regard to the political party to which the person belongs' and that more women should be chosen, adding, rather oddly, that 'in their case it is even more absurd than in the case of men that politics should be regarded as a guarantee of suitability'.[82]

The need for special rota of magistrates was discussed frequently by conferences of women magistrates and in the feminist press. By 1925 there was some dissatisfaction, not only at the slow speed at which women were joining the magistracy, but also at the failure of benches to form juvenile panels and to carry out other government recommendations, including the adoption of a probation system. Mrs Rackham recounted in the *Woman's Leader* the 'disappointing' results of a survey by the Home Office Children's Branch which revealed that over half of the respondent benches held juvenile hearings in the ordinary court and a third gave full details of proceedings to the press while 'in very few indeed are special magistrates designated to hear juvenile cases'.[83]

In 1925 the government appointed a committee to report on the treatment of young offenders. Members, including Geraldine Cadbury, heard evidence from 99 witnesses including Mrs Rackham (representing the MA), Margery Fry (for the Howard League for Penal Reform [HLPR]), Clarke Hall and Dr Ethel Bentham and Janet Courtney (for 'the London lady magistrates').[84] The report, issued two years later, claimed that 'there is an undoubted need for more Justices who are really suited for work in the juvenile court and are willing to give their time to it'. Although the report's authors were clearly referring to both sexes the mention of spare time as a factor might indicate they particularly had women in mind. The report recommended that the Lord Chancellor and Chancellor of the Duchy of Lancaster be requested to 'include a sufficient number of men and women who have special qualifications for dealing with children and young persons' when they appointed JPs, for example 'experience or interest in social work among the young as well as practical knowledge of the homes and conditions of life of the class of children who usually come before the juvenile court'. This approach may well have been designed to favour not only the type of middle class woman (and a few men) for whom 'social work' was a virtual vocation, but also working class men and women. The report concluded that 'it will obviously be necessary to secure the appointment of a sufficient number of women magistrates throughout the country' and echoed Lovat Fraser's views in insisting that 'the service of the juvenile court demands younger recruits' and warning that party political considerations should play no part in selection. The committee recommended that legislation should be introduced containing 'some general direction that Magistrates who sit in juvenile courts should have special qualifications' and that benches should select a small panel of up to 12 justices for the work, of whom no more than three should be present at one time.[85] Effectively the committee appears to have agreed with the views of the HLPR and the MA. The former argued that the presence of a woman magistrate was 'essential' in juvenile cases,[86] while the latter, championing the cause of the JP, was pushing for lay chairmen in London's youth courts by 1927.[87]

In January 1933 the Home Office convened yet another committee to draw up draft rules for juvenile courts under the new Children and Young Persons Act, which had decreed that a special panel of justices be formed for juvenile cases in each petty sessional division. Of the five members two were women: Geraldine Cadbury and Lady Cynthia Colville, a London JP recommended by Gertrude Tuckwell. The committee agreed to the wording that children's courts should be constituted of not more than three justices, to 'include one man and, so far as practicable, one woman'.[88] However, feminist organisations and women magistrates regarded this formula as unsatisfactory as it provided a potential loophole for benches who had appointed insufficient numbers of women justices. In October disapproval was expressed (notably by Eleanor Rathbone) of the wording at the conference of women JPs organised by the MA, and the following month a letter of protest was sent to the Lord Chancellor by the NCEC. Complaints were also received from individual benches, including Liverpool, although the Home Office felt that it was likely that Rathbone had engineered this reaction! Correspondents all objected to the fact that, in effect, a juvenile court could be made up of men only, but not of women only. As far as officials were concerned, the wording provided for sex equality in theory while remaining pragmatic in practice, but feminists regarded it as falling far short of their ideal of equal citizenship: in 1933 the Home Office received an entirely predictable resolution from the WFL urging that sufficient women be appointed for there to be at least one on every juvenile court.[89] There were further letters of protest but the wording remained unchanged, while the government merely expressed the hope that further appointments of women justices would eventually relieve the situation and silence the objectors.[90] However the problem of the courts' composition continued to rankle with women's organisations, particularly the NCW, who raised the matter with the Lord Chancellor yet again in 1948. It was also the subject of a conference resolution tabled by the National Union of Women Teachers in 1955.[91]

Women and the work of juvenile courts

Maternal ideology, had, by the middle of the twentieth century proved to be a useful weapon in the fight to carve out a role for women in the judicial system. Within 30 years of the appointment of the first women magistrates the notion of a woman presiding in court was completely normalised to the extent that a cinematic crime drama of 1948, *Good Time Girl*, featured a woman 'chairman of the juvenile court' played by Flora Robson. But the victory of women magistrates was also a triumph of amateurs over professionals. Suggestions that a woman barrister be specifically appointed to hear children's cases in London were swept aside by officials who were ready by 1936 to place the power in the hands of lay chairmen and women.[92] Although this use of volunteer labour was effective financially, it did not follow that it was legally inefficient. The 'amateurs' were professionals in that they went to a great deal of trouble to train and educate themselves for their role. In this process, women magistrates were the pioneers, making use of their existing network of organisations as well as helping create and mould new ones (such as the HLPR and the MA) to study and disseminate progressive approaches to youth justice.[93] The Home Office in the 1920s and 30s actually had a higher opinion of the women justices in London than of the men, a view reinforced by the Chief Clerk to the capital's juvenile courts who rated nine or ten of the women JPs as first class, as against eight or nine of the men.[94]

Among the many women to make their mark in the work of the juvenile courts in the first half of the twentieth century were (in London, where lay JPs were allowed to preside in 1936) Lily Montagu, Madeleine Robinson (neé Symons), Margery Fry, Cynthia Colville and Barbara Wootton. Elsewhere, Geraldine Cadbury was already renowned by the time she became chairman of the Birmingham court in 1923, while Miss Kelly took control in Portsmouth and Mrs Rackham carved out a strong reputation in Cambridge, notably receiving the approbation of the criminologist Hermann Mannheim.[95] In Gateshead, the WFL activist, Jeanette Tooke, achieved almost legendry status among the town's youth as an awe-inspiring adjudicator, although she was by her own account a 'progressive', favouring the use of probation and an 'ameliorative' rather than punitive approach to the problems of the young people who came before her.[96] Later in the century Charis Frankenburg, author of several books on child-care, rose to prominence, as did the social work education expert, Eileen Younghusband, who became a JP in 1933 following experience running youth clubs for the Bermondsey University Settlement. This brief roll-call of distinguished women who served as children's magistrates would be incomplete without mention of Lady Plowden, whose very name is still so strongly associated with the eponymous report which made several influential 'progressive' policy recommendations for primary education in 1967.

It is worth considering to what extent these women, many of whom were so strongly connected to the women's and penal reform movements, were able to influence the further development of juvenile courts in England and Wales and what their reform proposals were. As Miss Tooke succinctly summarised for readers of *The Vote*, there were three groups of cases that the juvenile courts dealt with, all of which required a different response: trivial misdemeanours that could be dealt with by 'a good talking-to', more serious cases that might require probation and lastly those that arose 'from mental disturbances or some lack of adjustment' for which more dramatic interventions were needed.[97]

As already mentioned, in addition to insisting that young people be dealt with by specially chosen, 'suitable' magistrates, reformers generally favoured the use of less formal premises and procedures. Adler had favoured the use of town halls as opposed to the police courts, a policy that was certainly followed in London. But while town hall premises may have been less threatening to young miscreants, they were not necessarily suited to judicial proceedings and were certainly not 'domestic'.[98] In East London the juvenile court was moved to the Toynbee Hall university settlement in 1929 at the express request of Clarke Hall and purpose built rooms were constructed there in 1938. Built to a smaller scale than a conventional court, and furnished less formally, the Toynbee court also had its own entrance to protect the children from the public gaze.[99] All these aspects were very much in keeping with the reform agenda: the 1933 Children and Young Persons Act restricted the reporting of proceedings in juvenile court and the identification of young participants. Liverpool was the first city to provide a separate building for its juvenile court, and in 1928 the specially built Birmingham court was given to the city by Barrow Cadbury and his wife. Within her own court Mrs Cadbury clearly favoured an informal approach, especially with the youngest children, one of whom she recalled would not speak a word to anyone until she asked him about the comic-book character 'Tiger Tim'. However, she felt that older children needed to know 'the gravity of the situation' they were in.[100] In essence, Mrs Cadbury believed strongly that the young people before her required 'a woman's touch', and that their needs were those of welfare and reform rather than punishment. This was the maternalist line she took in the many speeches she gave to magistrates across the country.

As Miss Tooke indicated, juvenile courts had several options open to them, depending on the circumstances of a child. Magistrates not only dealt with law-breakers, but with 'care and protection' cases. Punishments for those who had offended ranged from fines, through a probation or birching order to being sent to an approved school: the latter fate might also befall the 'care and protection' cases. The 1933 Act placed the responsibility on juvenile courts to act with regard to the welfare of the child. Although dispatching young offenders to approved school was an option open to magistrates, in general 'progressives' preferred not to remove children from their families unless the latter were regarded as either totally inadequate or dangerous. Geraldine Cadbury approved of Miriam Van Walters' maxim that no child should be permanently taken from his home unless it was impossible to make the environment there safe for him.[101] This bias in favour of not disrupting families was reinforced in the 1950s and 60s due to the pervasive popularity, even among many feminists, of the 'maternal deprivation' thesis. However, for teenagers, probation hostels and 'half-way houses' were firmly supported and in Birmingham the Cadbury family provided a girls' hostel as part of the juvenile court complex, with accommodation specially designed by Geraldine.[102]

Progressives strongly supported psychological interventions. Again Mrs Cadbury and Birmingham led the way with the introduction of psychological assessments in 1924,[103] swiftly followed by similar arrangements in other cities. In 1927 the Child Guidance Council was founded by another woman JP, Mrs St Loe Strachey, following a visit to the United States, where she had been impressed by William Healy's pioneering psychiatric techniques in child guidance. The council ran a clinic in London, initially supported by the Commonwealth Fund.[104] Margery Fry promoted the idea of observation centres following a visit to Moll in Belgium in the early 1920s. Boys were sent to Moll for a period of months during which they would be assessed psychologically and medically.[105] Fry publicised the Moll scheme through the journals of the HLPR and the MA and gave evidence on it to the young offenders' committee, but was disappointed to find that her plan for similar centres in England was not taken up by the Home Office or included in the 1933 Act. Instead, the newest psychiatric techniques continued to be funded by voluntary organisations, the very type of body philanthropic women were most familiar with, and to a lesser extent by local authorities, again on a voluntary basis until 1944. Fry also strongly supported her fellow HLPR executive member, Dr Margery Franklin of the Institute for the study and Treatment of Delinquency (ISTD), who developed the idea of 'planned environment therapy', first tried out in the so-called Q Camps established in the 1930s and 40s and later in a school ran by the Children's Social Adjustment Society.[106] Despite their general approbation for psychological approaches, the HLPR was initially concerned that the ISTD's efforts would overlap with their own campaigning when it was first founded in 1932. In the event, the bodies managed to co-operate rather than compete, perhaps due to the commitment to both bodies of Dr Franklin. Her HLPR Executive colleague, Madeleine Robinson, who presided over the Stamford House juvenile court in London, was another vocal enthusiast for the application of psychological research to the study of delinquency.

Above all, the feminist-criminal-justice reform network championed the use of probation orders and the abolition of corporal punishment as a judicial penalty. From the First World War onwards activists expressed their abhorrence of the latter. Naturally birching orders were never made in the 'model' courts, such as Birmingham's, and nationally there was a dramatic fall in their use after 1920 from 1380 orders in England and Wales in that year to less than 200 in every year from 1928 to 1934.[107] Reformers were especially incensed when courts ordered sentences of probation *and* corporal punishment, arguing that the reformative possibilities of the former were completely negated by the latter.[108] The corporal punishment debate came to a head in 1938 when the report of the Cadogan Committee, whose members unanimously recommended the cessation of judicial birching, arguing that the practice was 'surrounded with an atmosphere of importance which makes it unsuitable for use in minor offences'.[109] Their recommendation for abolition, which was embodied in the 1938 Criminal Justice Bill but was not enacted for another ten years because of the outbreak of war, sparked off a nationwide debate. This did not, however, prove to be the end of the subject as it was revisited once more in the 1950s.

Support for probation within the women's movement was possibly even more fervent than opposition to corporal punishment. Leading women magistrates, notably Tuckwell, Robinson and Fry, strongly supported the professionalisation of this branch of social work. Tuckwell served as president of the probation officers' association (NAPO) and Madeleine Symons was a key member of the Departmental Committee on the Social Services in Courts of Summary Jurisdiction, which reported in 1936, while Geraldine Cadbury had served on a previous committee in 1922. The increased use of probation orders was an early objective of the MA: in its journal Mrs Rackham urged magistrates to consider probation not only for first offences and children, but for a wider group of cases, and to take an active role in oversight through their local probation committees.[110] Once again the feminist press and women's organisations made a copious amount of statements extolling this 'progressive' policy, which was a popular discussion theme for meetings and was also widely supported by Labour Party women.[111]

Of course, further research is needed to ascertain the extent to which the reformers' policies were adopted across the country. Evidence from the Cadogan committee suggests that courts varied widely in their use of birching: in Ramsgate in 1935 only five per cent of juveniles found guilty of indictable offences received corporal punishment, in Windsor the proportion was 20 per cent[112] (and, of course, many courts did not use this penalty at all). The national figures indicate that many areas retained the birch in theory but seldom used it in practice. Child guidance clinics were only found in the largest towns and cities and in some rural areas the number of offences committed by juveniles was so small that elaborate arrangements for special courts and so on seemed to local JPs to be almost irrelevant. In these areas probation officers were few and far between, handled only small numbers of cases and sometimes held only 'honorary' status (that is, they were not paid). In the rural Welsh petty sessional division of Ystradgynlais the Probation Committee of JPs failed to meet at all between 1927 and 1944, by which time three of its four members had died.[113] Probation hostels, guidance clinics and observation centres were, even for the delinquents of the cities, either supplied by the voluntary sector or not at all and, in fact, these projects remained largely the subject of reformers' unfulfilled dreams, mainly due to the unwillingness of government to fund them. As Pamela Cox points out, the 'welfare' strategies for dealing with the perceived delinquency of the young promoted by reformers were anyway just as disciplinary as the more conventionally punitive approaches. [114]

However, the 'liberal progressive' agenda, which, notwithstanding its unachieved objectives, had so strongly influenced the policy of the Home Office's Children's Department, did not lack its critics. While in retrospect criticism has focused on the level of social control inherent in the twentieth-century reform agenda for youth justice, objections at the time concentrated on its alleged 'softness' and a concomitant belief that the juvenile courts had failed to stem the tide of young lawlessness. Much of the debate was centred round the question as to whether corporal punishment should be abolished, or whether, on the contrary, it should be revived and used more in cases where violence was involved. This debate, which took place in the late 1930s and again 20 years later, and the part played in it by women magistrates and their organisations, is the subject of the last section of this chapter.

The debate over corporal punishment, 1935–65

Women magistrates were by no means all of one opinion where the subject of corporal punishment was concerned. As *The Times* leader writer remarked in 1938 'the secretary of every debating society knows [that] corporal punishment is a subject that may be guaranteed to provoke adequate controversy'.[115] Some women JPs expressed support for the corporal punishment of juvenile offenders, although many were opposed to it. Typically, the NCW held a debate at which both sides of the argument were put and opinion was also divided among the Gloucester women magistrates.[116] Even within the generally 'progressive' MA there were contrasting views over birching: the division of opinion was so clear that the Association declined to give evidence to the Cadogan Committee.[117] One MA member, Mrs Titt of Manchester emotively asked delegates to a conference of Lancashire juvenile justices to 'visualise an underfed, half-starved, half-clothed child being beaten by a big, burly, well-fed and well-clothed policeman'. Ellinor Fisher, a JP from Hull, responded by rejecting the notion that such a child would receive corporal punishment. Moreover she argued that 'a few suitable cases dealt with birching would provide a great deterrent to others'.[118] Her views were hardly 'politically correct' in the late 1930s, but she obviously represented a strand of opinion among JPs. Feelings ran high on both sides of the debate: in the House of Commons Ellen Wilkinson MP questioned on one occasion whether 'it [is] time that the torture of children should be abolished?'[119]

However, despite the division of opinion in some quarters, penal reformers and the most avowedly feminist organisations were united in their abhorrence of corporal punishment. Mrs Titt, who is quoted above, was a staunch member of the WFL who before the First World War had performed social work alongside the suffrage group's leader, Mrs Despard, and sold *The Vote* in the streets.[120] The WFL was implacably opposed to corporal punishment in all its forms, even as a penalty for violent crime or sexual abuse.[121] The League's stance against physical punishment was consistently maintained in that it was also opposed to the death penalty. To an extent these views were related to the party political leanings of WFL members, many of whom were associated with Labour. In parliament the issue of the use of corporal punishment as a judicial penalty in England, Wales and Scotland was raised most often by Labour MPs.[122] However, both women's and penal reform pressure groups were capable of attracting cross-party support, ensuring that questions concerning the treatment of young offenders did not inevitably produce divisions of opinion along clear, party lines. Interestingly, Lady Elliot, the wife of Walter Elliot, the Conservative Scottish Office minister to whom Wilkinson's rhetorical outburst had been ostensibly addressed, was herself a strong opponent of corporal punishment.

While feminists tended to support 'modern' methods for tackling juvenile delinquency and oppose the use of birching, anti-feminists had the opposite inclinations. Regular publicity and the barrage of parliamentary questions in 1937 surrounding individual cases of birching prompted the Home Secretary, Sir John Simon, to instigate the Cadogan Committee's enquiry into the matter, with terms of reference covering not only the corporal punishment of juveniles but also the flogging of adult offenders, itself an increasingly rare occurrence. The debate where the younger age group was concerned became linked to the 'failure', perceived in some quarters, of the 1933 Act, the juvenile courts and the whole 'penal-welfare' strategy of the 'liberal progressives'. Importantly, this strategy, most clearly in the eyes of its critics, was itself associated with women magistrates, and therefore, by extension, with the feminist ideology of the women's organisations who had campaigned so forcefully for the modernisation of youth justice. Women were associated with modernity and progressivism since penal reformers and feminists appeared to be marching hand-in-hand on this issue. The following comment, received by the Lord Chancellor's Office illustrates the conflation of feminism and penal welfarism.

> This resolution [for gender equality in juvenile courts] is entirely in keeping with modern feminist ideas but completely disregards realities. The whole juvenile court legislation is a flagrant example of the intrusion into the working class home, under the guise of social welfare, of that obnoxious patronage so prevalent in the United States. Only the poor would tolerate it. But juvenile courts are now established facts, pushed through a House which did not take the trouble to realise that Law and Social Reform are two distinct spheres.[123]

Moreover, the progressives who opposed corporal punishment (described by a vicar in *The Times* as 'the little group of "advanced" theorists who lay down the rule for the working of the courts') were branded by traditionalists as 'cranks'.[124] Male supporters of corporal punishment argued that it had never done them any harm when inflicted on them in their schooldays and that the modern, homely (and by implication, feminised) 'courtrooms' failed to instil a sense of awe – or even of shame – in the young offenders. Instead of being punished, the miscreants allegedly felt they had been 'let off' when their court appearance resulted in a probation order.

Nevertheless, the 'progressives' won the day when the Cadogan Committee recommended unanimously that the judicial birching of juveniles should cease after hearing evidence from a range of organisations and individual experts including juvenile court magistrates.[125] The committee's consideration of the evidence it received and opinions it heard was so thorough that even 20 years later it was not thought necessary to hold a completely new inquiry. Instead, the Home Secretary in 1960 (R. A. Butler) merely asked the government's Advisory Committee on the Treatment of Offenders (ACTO) to 'review' the Cadogan Report's conclusions.

In the intervening period interest in the problem of juvenile delinquency and the work of the children's courts ebbed and flowed. The

Cadogan recommendation was incorporated into the Criminal Justice Bill, but the bill failed to complete its parliamentary passage before the outbreak of war in 1939. As early as June 1940 there were claims that the war had led to increased juvenile delinquency yet the Home Office's policy remained steady. A circular to courts the following year urged the appointment of younger men and women to the juvenile panels and reminded justices of the Cadogan Committee's view that corporal punishment was neither a 'suitable or effective remedy for young offenders'. Courts were instead enjoined to consider the use of probation.[126] Progressives anyway played down the increase in recorded juvenile offences. For example, Joan Thompson JP, in a lecture to the National Council for Civil Liberties, alleged that press reports were sensational and 'wantonly exaggerated', that many young people were brought to court for their own protection and that the police were bringing forward charges on trivial matters, 'bits of mischief which in the old days would have caused little fuss'.[127] Of course, when the statistics showed a drop in recorded crime progressives displayed far less scepticism about their veracity. After the war ended a fall in recorded juvenile crime in the immediate post-war years, coupled with optimism about the prospects for a 'New Jerusalem', merely confirmed their views that their 'modern', penal-welfare methods were preferable to out-dated forms of punishment, and that emphasis should shift towards the prevention of delinquency through improved 'schools, clubs, clinics and playing fields'.[128] Nevertheless, the abolition of corporal punishment as a judicial penalty remained an important item of unfinished business for penal reformers until the Criminal Justice Act was passed in 1948. Even then there was a price to be paid: the Labour Home Secretary, Chuter Ede, announced the introduction of detention centres for young offenders where they would receive a 'short, sharp shock', a proposal that was explicitly designed to meet calls for a punitive, short-term measure to replace birching.

The new Act was barely in operation when the next wave of moral panic about the behaviour of young people began. While *The Times* accepted in 1950 that there was 'no conclusive evidence that boys of today are more vicious than boys of twenty or a hundred years ago' it was nevertheless concerned that there had been a growth of hooliganism among boys' gangs, such as the 'Diamond Gang of Islington'.[129] As Geoffrey Pearson has shown, the 1950s witnessed an increasingly gloomy public mood about the younger generation and the methods of the modern juvenile court were once again questioned. Far from having cured social evils, the Welfare State was now accused of weakening the traditional family while affluence was assumed to have 'undermined the nation's moral fibre'.[130] This mood was reflected in parliament where a number of Conservative MPs continued to make the case for a reintroduction of the birch. Even the MA was affected by the malaise when its members voted in 1953 in favour of corporal punishment for crimes of violence, even though the Association's annual meeting – at which female and London-based JPs were probably over-represented – had consistently refused to support such resolutions. This decision was clearly unwelcome to the MA Executive (which appears to have been more progressive than the membership) since they took no action as a result of the referendum.[131]

After experiencing some discomfort on the 'law and order' issue at successive Conservative Party Conferences in the late 1950s (see Chapter 5), Home Secretary Butler decided to refer the question of the reintroduction of judicial corporal punishment to ACTO. Although the Committee's official task was to review the Cadogan conclusions, they did invite organisations to give evidence and, controversially, also requested the opinions of the general public. In contrast to the earlier investigation (when witnesses included representatives of the Women's Co-operative Guild and the Standing Joint Committee of Industrial Women's Organisations as well as many individual women JPs), the opinions of women's groups were conspicuously absent in the 'evidence' gathered by ACTO. As Chapter 5 demonstrates, there was some division in the women's movement during the late 1950s over the best response towards violent crime even though, despite their concerns for 'the victim', the leading women's organisations defeated resolutions in support of flogging. It is, however, important to note that their debates centred, in fairly vague terms, on the punishment of violent offences, not necessarily committed by juveniles. However, the division of opinion was probably the main reason why organisations such as the NCW held back from giving evidence to either of the enquiries on corporal punishment, although declining support for the women's movement by the 1950s may also have had an effect, coupled with the likelihood that the women's groups had other campaign priorities.

The letters from members of the public in response to the ACTO invitation for comments on the issue of corporal punishment, perhaps predictably, were overwhelmingly in favour, with majorities in support among women and even among teachers and youth workers. Magistrates were more cautious – half were in favour of corporal punishment and half against – perhaps because they would have the responsibility of passing the sentences. Of course, the sample of letter writers was self-selected and could not be regarded as a 'scientific' survey of opinion.

An Oxford undergraduate wrote in to complain about the Home Office's 'research'.

> It is monstrous and absurd that the 'views' of a half-educated or wholly educated public should be of the slightest relevance . . . Have we become so indoctrinated with the ideas of democracy that the views of Tom, Dick or Harry can carry any weight at all on such a thing as the treatment of criminals and offenders?[132]

This student should not have worried: ACTO was not going to take the advice of the 'public'. As the Home Office report on the 'vox pop' exercise demonstrated, few of the correspondents had any grasp of the complexity of the issue and some had even managed to confuse the issue with that of capital punishment![133] ACTO members duly produced the result that Butler had desired when they agreed unanimously to recommend no change in the law and the progressive agenda continued to shape government policy on youth justice throughout the 1960s.

Conclusion

For at least 50 years after the introduction of women JPs, their role continued to be identified most strongly with the work of juvenile courts. Here women were not only in their 'proper sphere' – dealing with the problems of the younger generation – but were also able to draw on their experience as mothers and/or teachers and social workers, develop their expertise in the work and exercise 'professionally' their power and autonomy, for example by presiding in court and becoming acknowledged experts on 'juvenile delinquency'. Both individual women magistrates and the organisations to which they belonged helped to construct the 'liberal progressive', 'penal-welfare' project of youth justice as it was conceived during the early and mid-twentieth century. Feminists welcomed these developments, and while some women may have personally dissented from certain aspects of 'progressivism', the association of feminism with the welfare-orientated practices of the juvenile court was ultimately beneficial in enhancing the citizenship and status of the (mainly middle-class) women who took up this work. Whether progressive penalty was as beneficent for the children who were its subjects is a completely different debate, and one which has been taking place among historians and criminologists for some years. Although the new penal strategies were in their own way as controlling as the less subtle punishments they replaced, it should not be forgotten that the penal-welfare complex was seen by its supporters as an important advance in civilization, underpinned by humanitarian discourses and the fruits of scientific research into the human mind and behaviour. The enfranchisement of women could be seen therefore to have not only brought greater freedom and rights to women but also to have added momentum to wide-ranging reform in the youth justice system.

3
Women in the Criminal Courts

'You gentlemen are totally incapable of administering justice with decency and fairness without the help of women'.[1] These words of the suffragist, Nina Boyle, in 1913 encapsulate the frustration felt by feminists in the face of the overwhelmingly masculine courts of law and the male domination of penal administration. By then personal experience had brought home to a number of (mostly middle-class) women the reality of Britain's system of justice as they faced trial in the courts and incarceration in the jail. Although their numbers were relatively small, the suffragette prisoners were anxious to share their experiences with the wider public in periodicals and prison memoirs. The courts were recollected as an alien environment devoid of feminine influence, where elderly magistrates dealt perfunctorily with 'ordinary' women, even if they took a little longer to decide on the fate of ladies.[2] Suffragette accounts of police cells and prisons revealed unimagined levels of dirt, inadequate clothing and poor food and, significantly, an absence of women in authority. Although prisons housing women invariably had female warders (the same could not be said about police cells) there were no women governors or even medical officers.

As suffragette prisoners began hunger-striking and the authorities responded with forced feeding, attention became even more firmly focused on the failings of the criminal justice system. Feminists were increasingly suspicious that justice was not blind where sex was concerned, that men and women received unequal treatment before the law. In 1912 the Women's Freedom League (WFL) 'earnestly invited' any of its branch members who had some legal knowledge to observe court proceedings. This scheme was borne out of the conviction that their observations would reveal evidence of comparatively heavy sentences for women and light ones for men. The court-watching activities of

Boyle and other WFL members and the National Union of Women Workers' (NUWW's) court rotas (see Chapter 5) were prompted both by concern for female and child victims as well as for the women in the dock. More than 50 years before the first stirrings of 'second wave' feminist criminology suffragists were documenting and analysing the sexual double standard in the legal system and articulating their suspicion that women received harsher treatment in the courts because they were women.

Before 1920 women's presence in the courts of law can best be described as marginal. As Nina Boyle's statement, quoted at the start of this chapter, indicates, the lack of feminine involvement in the legal process had created a lack of faith in the system among feminists. Although the suspicion generated focused mainly on the treatment of young and/or female victims, there were also concerns about injustice meted out to women in the dock: for example in 1913 the WFL criticised the different attitudes evinced towards men and women accused of alcohol-related offences at the Bow Street court in London. While the men appearing were 'let off' with paltry fines and no rebuke, 'women were addressed with the utmost contempt and insolence'.[3] The inference of this article (probably also the work of Nina Boyle) was that, far from being the beneficiaries of chivalric attitudes on the part of magistrates, women were subjected to greater criticism than men who had committed similar offences. As an argument this contention bears a strong resemblance to the 'second wave' feminist criminological discourse concerning 'double deviance'.[4] Alcoholic women were seemingly punished not just for their breaches of the criminal law, but also for offending against gendered behavioural norms.

As Boyle's words suggest, feminists of the early twentieth century had also reached a conclusion as to how the balance of justice could be redressed, not only through the acquisition of the parliamentary vote but also by the invasion of women into the masculine space of the court room. Across the feminist movement, demands were made for the appointment of women as magistrates and police: in addition women needed access to the jury box and the legal profession in order to safeguard the rights of female defendants and victims. Suspicion of the justice system remained strong even after partial women's suffrage had been achieved. In 1919 the Sex Disqualification (Removal) Act opened the way for women to train and practice as lawyers and to sit on the magistrates' bench and in the jury box, but still there were no women prison governors and the number of women police – already small – was being reduced in response to demands for economies in public spending.

Sustained campaigning and continued monitoring of the courts was clearly needed to keep up the pressure.

This chapter and the following one examine the work of the feminist–criminal–justice reform network in critiquing the treatment of women in the criminal justice system of the early and mid-twentieth century, seeking to redress the perceived gender bias of the courts, provide advocacy for women and improve the treatment of women and girls in the penal system. The first part of this chapter is concerned with the campaign to allow women to become legal professionals, with particular reference to barristers. The second section of this chapter will focus on campaigns for changes in the regulations regarding jury service, which despite notional equality after 1919, continued to discriminate against women until the 1970s. The final section deals with the treatment of women charged with 'street offences' in court and examines the campaigns for changes in the law regarding prostitution. Similar tactics were used to promote these seemingly disparate causes, namely the maintenance of contacts with sympathetic parliamentarians, the presentation of evidence to official enquiries and the promotion of private members' bills. The next chapter analyses the continuing engagement of the women's movement with the treatment of female offenders and the reform of women's prisons.

Advocacy for women

The 1919 Sex Disqualification (Removal) Act not only paved the way for women magistrates, it also allowed women to become jurors and lawyers for the first time. The opening of the legal profession had been an important demand of the women's movement since at least the late nineteenth century, but whereas a few enterprising women and their feminist backers had forced open the doors of the medical profession in the 1860s and 70s, the legal professional bodies (the Law Society and the Inns of Court) remained implacably closed until after the First World War.[5] Albisetti claims that the women's movement devoted only a 'comparatively low level of attention' to the opening of the legal profession.[6] However, while there were clearly more pressing priorities for feminists in the early twentieth century – most obviously the suffrage cause before 1918 – it was by no means the case that entry into such an important sphere of activity as the law was neglected by campaigners. As this section will show, aspirant women lawyers were not left to act alone, but could count on solid support from women's organisations and from the usual backers of women's rights in parliament.

Obviously the acquisition of a legal education was an important first step, although it should be noted that the legal profession resisted large-scale graduate entry until the 1950s.[7] Nevertheless the higher education of women had been an early demand of the feminist movement, so aspirant women lawyers naturally sought to equip themselves with an education in law. A notable early example was Eliza Orme, who began her studies in law and political economy at University College, London in 1871. Five years later she was awarded the Hume scholarship in jurisprudence and a first prize in Roman law. Despite serving an apprenticeship at Lincoln's Inn, Orme was refused admittance to professional bodies, but she anyway ran an apparently successful 'legal' practice from an office in Chancery Lane 'devilling' (i.e., working on commission) for a number of male solicitors, at times in partnership with other women.[8] Orme was obviously not alone in receiving an education in law, although numbers were small: only 23 women studied law at Oxford and Cambridge Universities before the First World War.[9] Overall, universities proved to be only a minor obstacle in the way of women's entry to the legal profession, certainly in comparison with the professional bodies that rejected their applications and the judges who ruled that women should not be allowed to become lawyers.

Perhaps unsurprisingly, Orme was a committed suffragist and she was by no means the only women's movement activist to be interested in a legal career or education. Most notably, Christabel Pankhurst, who was the daughter of a barrister (interestingly a significant proportion of women who sought a legal education were the children of lawyers), was persuaded to study the subject at the Victoria University in Manchester by the city's leading NUWSS stalwarts, Eva Gore-Booth and Esther Roper.[10] In 1904 Christabel applied unsuccessfully to join Lincoln's Inn, following in the recent footsteps of both Bertha Cave (who had been accidentally admitted to – and subsequently excluded from – Gray's Inn in 1903) and Ivy Williams. Christabel ran a 'Committee to secure the Admission of Women to the Legal Profession' for a while and, along with Williams, publicly debated the admission of women to the legal profession, although she was never to became a lawyer herself, perhaps because of the way in which her involvement in the militant suffrage struggle subsequently dominated her political life. Significantly, Christabel emphasised the way in which women barristers would be able to plead for other women in court while emphasising that her aim was the achievement of equal rights and opportunities for women with men.[11] However, similar support for advocacy for women, by women was less pronounced in the arguments advanced by other aspirant women lawyers, who tended to concentrate more on matters of equal rights and counteracting their opponents' allegations concerning women's (lack of) professional competence.

Support for women's entry into the legal profession was firm in the wider women's movement, especially in the sections of it that took a strong interest in the treatment of women in the criminal justice system. Not unnaturally the WFL was at the forefront, *The Vote* reporting in 1913 on the progress of the legal action brought by Gwyneth Bebb following the refusal of the Law Society to admit her to membership. The attempts by sympathetic, legally qualified parliamentarians such as Lord Buckmaster (Bebb's original attorney) and Lord Robert Cecil (her representative on appeal) to introduce legislation to open the legal profession to women were also closely followed by the feminist press and women's organisations generally. The WFL was particularly inclined to ground its arguments for the admission of women to the law in its wider critique of gender bias in the legal system. Commenting on Bebb's suit, *The Vote* argued that justice for women could only be achieved if women were permitted to practice law, since a woman would be able to understand another woman's point of view.[12] The WFL understood well that the courts were masculine space and would remain so until the male monopoly of the legal profession was ended. However, the issue was by no means neglected in other parts of the women's movement. The National Union of Women's Suffrage Societies (NUWSS) made the securing of women's entry to the legal profession, their appointment as Justices of the Peace (JPs), and their right to sit on juries their main objectives alongside equal franchise in 1918. The National Union of Women Workers (NUWW) (National Council of Women [NCW] from 1918) was also most supportive, voting unanimously at its 1913 Annual Conference for a resolution in favour of the opening of the legal profession to women.[13] Nor was support for this cause confined to suffragists: a 1917 deputation to the Lord Chancellor in favour of women solicitors included two leading anti-suffrage women, Mrs Humphry Ward and Violet Markham (both of whom later accepted nomination as JPs), alongside the more predictable presence of Millicent Fawcett, Lord Robert Cecil and the trade unionist, Mary Macarthur.[14] Newspaper cuttings from 1915 onwards retained by Macarthur's colleague, Gertrude Tuckwell, suggest that she too kept a close watch on the progress of this particular campaign.[15]

Despite Buckmaster's abortive parliamentary bills of 1917–19, which addressed entry to the legal profession alone, by 1919 the question had become firmly attached to the issue of a more general removal of women's legal disabilities, in particular those preventing women from sitting on juries and as JPs. Thus the Labour opposition's Women's Emancipation Bill of 1919 – and the government's Sex Disqualification (Removal) Act that replaced it – was designed to enable women to hold any civil or judicial office. Helena Normanton, a WFL activist who nursed a powerful, personal ambition to become a barrister, appreciated that the campaign should be broad-based. Having been refused admission by the Middle Temple in early 1918 (despite – or because of – the backing of the WFL and the NCW), Normanton threw her energies into campaigns in support of the emancipation legislation, speaking publicly in favour of women JPs and jurors on a number of occasions over the following two years.[16] On Christmas Eve 1919, the day after the Sex Disqualification (Removal) Act received its Royal Assent, Normanton re-presented herself at the Middle Temple and was entered as a student for the Bar.

Other early women barristers with strong connections to the women's movement included Normanton's fellow WFL member Florence Earengey (who was the sister of one of the League's leaders, Edith How Martin, and wife of a judge), and Theodora Llewelyn Davies, great niece of Emily Davies (who had done so much to open both higher education and the medical profession to women) and niece of the WCG leader Margaret Llewelyn Davies. Theodora, who was born in 1897 and had studied law at Girton, the college established near Cambridge by her great aunt, was the first applicant to the Inner Temple in January 1920. According to her daughter, Theodora's first dinner in the Inner Temple hall was quite an ordeal for the young woman, due to a certain amount of masculine 'prejudice and hostility'.

> She told how her elder sister came with her as far as the gate for moral support. The head waiter took charge of her, showing her to a place at the end of a bench where she would not have to climb into her seat.[17]

Theodora was also disappointed – but not surprised – to find a lack of washroom facilities for women, being obliged to use a cloakroom for 'lady visitors'.[18] Despite the strong backing of her family and of Theo Matthew, whose chambers she joined as a pupil, it is clear that even a woman as well-educated and well-versed in the cause of the women's movement as Theodora still entered the masculine world of the legal profession with some trepidation.

In the 1920s *The Vote* continued to celebrate the successes of women in the legal profession, printing the examination results of the early women candidates for bar examinations and celebrating a range of other legal 'firsts' for women.[19] But it was soon apparent that women were not going to take the legal profession by storm. Ivy Williams, who due to receiving exemption from some of the examinations was the first to complete her training, did not practice as a barrister, but preferred to teach law instead. Other women who had been called to the bar found it hard to make an adequate living from the work of barrister: Helena Normanton persisted, but her fee book suggests that she was unable to earn a great deal from her practice.[20] Theodora Llewelyn Davies was determined to practice at the criminal bar rather than take divorce or family law cases and she joined the South-eastern circuit, but she made little money from what she perceived to be a badly organised profession. Dissatisfied with the state of the criminal law, she contacted Margery Fry and thereafter became involved in the Howard League for Penal Reform (HLPR).[21] By 1929, when she married her fellow Howard League activist, Roy Calvert, Theodora had given up the bar, although she later acted as a 'poor man's lawyer'.

By 1927 there was clear dissatisfaction in the women's movement about the results of the opening of the legal profession to women. The *Woman's Leader* reported that a reader,

> who happens to be a member of the legal profession, has criticised our tendency to rejoice unduly over the entry of women examinees to her profession (which, she points out, is really a very easy achievement for persons of average intelligence), while at the same time devoting insufficient attention to the prospects that await them after entry has been secured.

The article laid the blame for the situation on male solicitors for failing to brief women barristers and 'the professional etiquette which precludes women from pushing one another'.[22] However, these factors represented only a small part of the difficulties women faced in the clubbable, homosocial world of the law. As Corcos points out, a crucial aspect of life at the bar was membership of the circuit and session messes which, according to an American lawyer who observed them before the First World War, had 'interesting traditions of midnight carousels [sic] and records of fines of bottles of port inflicted upon members for various delinquencies'.[23] Mess membership was important, not only for the socialising and bonding benefits it bestowed on the circuit lawyers, but also because members would be able to take advantage of specially negotiated rates in hotels in the towns where the Assizes were held. Crucially, membership was controlled by the barristers themselves. While the South-eastern circuit's bar mess voted to allow Miss Llewelyn Davies and Miss Bright Ashford to join in 1923, the Midland circuit was excluding women from all mess activities until 40 years later.[24]

While the feminist movement had campaigned vigorously for the initial entry of women into the two branches of the legal profession, it does not seem to have applied much pressure to improve women's prospects within them over the following decades. This is in stark contrast both to the continuing exertions aimed at ensuring the appointment of more women magistrates[25] and to the energetic – if spasmodic – attempts at improving women's representation on juries (see section, 'Women on juries'). The reason for this neglect may lie in the attitude of women lawyers themselves, some of whom seem to have deliberately distanced themselves from the support network offered by women's groups, preferring instead to 'go it alone'. As was the case with women politicians, it may have been a good career move not to be associated in any way with feminism or the women's movement. Even Helena Normanton, who appears in the main to have retained her feminist instincts, heavily criticised the direction taken by much of the women's movement in the 1930s, and declared that she would not give money to NUSEC because they were doing 'an insufficient amount of work for pure feminism'.[26] In the 1950s Hazel Hunkins Hallinan persistently attempted to recruit the leading QC, Rose Heilbron, to contribute a section on 'women in the legal profession' to a Six Point Group (SPG) pamphlet Hallinan was preparing. Despite the latter's application of a little flattery and emotional blackmail – 'if we are deserted by the women who have done the most to prove that equality of opportunity produces just as magnificent women as it does men, then we are deprived of our strongest and most dramatic argument' – Heilbron resolutely refused the request, pleading the pressure of work, domestic responsibilities, and even a bout of the flu![27] It is hard to assess how genuine her regret at not being able to help Hallinan was, or whether she had strong professional or political reasons for avoiding public association with an overtly feminist organisation like the SPG.

Whether it was due to the inaction of the women's movement and the lack of interest or involvement in it among women lawyers, or to the cultural practices and effective resistance of a male-dominated professional oligarchy to the incursions of women, or even to sexism in society generally, it is undeniable that the legal profession remained overwhelmingly masculine for many decades after it was formally opened to women in 1920. Among solicitors, the proportion of women increased only slowly, from 1.7 per cent of admissions to the profession in the 1920s to 9.9 per cent 50 years later.[28] The number of women barristers remained pitifully small for an even longer period: in 1990 women represented only 18 per cent of active barristers and only 4 per cent of 'silks' (Queen's Counsel).[29] It is therefore questionable as to what extent such a small group of women could provide effective advocacy for women as some feminists had hoped. It was only in the voluntary part of the justice system – the magistracy, where lay-men and women predominated – that women were to able to make a significant impact in terms of sheer numbers before the 1970s, and perhaps to at least partially realise the feminist objective of reducing masculine bias in the justice system. As early as the late 1940s more than a fifth of JPs in England and Wales were women, although this average proportion disguises much variation between different areas, women being better represented on the whole in urban areas and locations with a well-organised feminist lobby.[30] However, there is no unequivocal evidence that the presence of women on the bench had any tangible effect upon the treatment of female defendants, either towards greater leniency or in the opposite direction. There were frequent claims that women were actually harder on their own sex, but little proof that this was actually the case. Nevertheless, apart from the welcome opportunity for wealthy women to consult female solicitors or barristers about their divorce cases, the feminist aspiration of advocacy for women remained largely unrealised.

Women on juries

The initial reaction from the women's movement to the inclusion of women on juries under the Sex Disqualification (Removal) Act was understandably largely positive, reflecting feminist optimism that another male bastion had been breached and that female victims and offenders could hope to receive justice at last. *The Vote* quoted Holford Knight, a barrister and keen supporter of women's rights who had campaigned for women's admission to the Bar in 1913: '[t]he opening of jury service to woman is a symbol of her comradeship with man in building a new and better order'.[31] Early attempts to organise 'schools' for women jurors also suggest a good deal of enthusiasm for women's new rights and duties on the part of women's organisations, while readers of *The Vote* were naturally informed when the first women jurors appeared at the Old Bailey in London.[32]

However, enthusiasm was tempered by the realisation that few women would actually qualify for jury service. The feminist press set out for readers the somewhat archaic rules for jury qualification:

1 Householders assessed to the Poor Rate, or the Inhabited House Duty, at not less than £30 in the County of London and Middlesex, or in other counties at £20; or 'joint occupiers' with men; or
2 Residents in the district from which the jury is drawn, with £10 a year in real estate or rent charge, or £20 in lease-hold for not less than twenty-one years; or
3 Burgesses in certain boroughs.[33]

Although the rules appeared complicated, the implications at least were clear: as Edith Bethune-Baker JP concluded for readers of the *Woman's Leader*, 'the vast majority of married women living with their husbands are disqualified'.[34] Women's organisations swiftly drew the conclusion that the law was unsatisfactory and that changes in the rules for jury service would be needed, before female defendants really could be tried by their peers and victims would receive the justice they deserved.

Moreover, feminists soon detected the indications of a backlash against the improvement of women's rights from the legal profession and, in some cases, the criminal classes. Lilian Barker sensed that objections to women on juries were 'the beginning of an attempt to get the Sex Disqualification (Removal) Act rescinded, and incidentally to jeopardise the position of women in public life'.[35] One drawback, evident from the early 1920s, was the defendant's right of peremptory challenge, which some defence barristers were obviously using in order to remove empanelled women from the jury. A further – and more immediately recognised – source of dissatisfaction was the proviso in the Act that allowed a judge the discretion to exempt women from jury service on account of the 'nature' of the evidence.[36] Thanks to this proviso, for which detailed arrangements were announced in the Rules of the Supreme Court (Women Jurors) in 1920, a judge in effect was entitled to order a single-sex jury if he wished. Of course, this power was most likely to be used in the very cases in which feminists thought that a woman's perspective was most needed. However, it was apparently granted at the specific request of the Lord Chief Justice.[37] The failure of MPs to remove the proviso from the Bill was a major source of disappointment to the women's organisations which began a campaign to change it immediately.

It is pretty clear that the assessment of Schuster that the judges were unhappy with the Act[38] was largely accurate. Some judicial quibbles were relatively minor, for example one judge objected to having to use the phrase 'members of the jury' rather than 'gentlemen of the jury'.[39] Others were more serious. Judges were not only making use of their discretionary powers, they also appeared to be attempting to bully women into withdrawing from jury service. *The Vote* quoted a sample peroration:

> A woman's place is in the home and not in court, unless she is compelled to come here as a witness or otherwise. If you want to hear the mysteries formerly heard by men only, then it is your privilege to stay; but it is my advice that you do not listen to the filth involved in the cases that will be brought before you.[40]

Former suffragists sensed that the same anachronistic, faux-chivalric sentiments that had been expressed so regularly by anti-suffragists before the First World War were being deployed once more in order to maintain masculine control of justice. Potential (often middle-class) jurywomen were advised to avoid hearing about 'unpleasant' matters (probably meaning charges of sexual assault and rape) which might offend their 'delicacy' and any women who held her ground ran the risk of appearing rather more interested in the salacious details than was 'proper'. In 1921 there was an attempt to amend the Sex Disqualification (Removal) Act to allow women who did not wish to serve on a jury to have a right to simply withdraw without a specific reason, something which no man would be allowed to do. Supporters of this measure argued that women should not be compelled to attend cases where their presence was not 'desirable' and even claimed that this proposed alteration in the law would ease the acceptance of women on juries. According to *The Times*, letters it received opposed to this measure came from 'those women who have been the strongest advocates of the present political rights of women', that is, feminists. Against them were the 'men of practical experience of the Courts',[41] i.e., lawyers. As one anonymous correspondent – a barrister – put it,

> I should shudder even at the thought of having to discuss such [sexually explicit] evidence with my wife, who is now, however, by law liable to be called upon at any moment to consider 'filth' in all its details, and, worse still, discuss it in a public Court with men and women who are comparative strangers to her.[42]

Thus under the cloak of chivalric propriety and 'decency', attempts were being made by the legal profession to reassert the courtroom as masculine space.

Feminists responded by springing to the defence of women's rights to sit on juries, however onerous and unpleasant the duty might be. *The Vote* criticised the 'patronizing interference' of judges while Bethune-Baker reiterated the feminist conviction that it was exactly those 'unpleasant' cases in which women jurors, lawyers and magistrates were most essential.[43] Millicent Fawcett was even blunter, pointing out that the evidence in such cases was often of harm done to women and children and arguing that to exclude women from the jury in such circumstances would be both absurd and unfair. She was one of many commentators to emphasise that women had a duty to undertake jury service as well as a right.[44]

The attempt in 1921 to change the law on juries came to nothing. Nevertheless judges continued their efforts to persuade women to withdraw and lawyers habitually encouraged their clients to use their right of peremptory challenge against female jurors. The debate, and the continued judicial machinations designed to minimise the 1919 Act's impact placed feminists firmly on what they saw as the moral high ground of openness and modernity in the legal system and against the 'Victorian' prudery displayed by the judiciary in particular. As *The Vote* commented, '[i]t is high time evil was exposed to the light of day'.[45] Moreover, the inadequacy of the law on juries had been made clear, especially with regard to the property qualification which made most women ineligible for service. Thereafter the women's movement and its parliamentary allies made periodic attempts to reform the rules on jury service in favour of the inclusion of more women, attempts which proved unsuccessful until the law was finally changed in 1972.

Legislative proposals varied in their details, but they all attacked the three main obstacles to gender equality in jury service: the property qualification, the exclusion of eligible women through the use (or abuse) of peremptory challenge and the residual power of judges to rule in favour of an all-male jury. While there was agreement across the women's movement over the necessity for the removal of judges' discretion, there was no unanimity over the best way to tackle the more fundamental obstacle to full equality – the property qualification. As early as 1921 the WFL expressed support for the most radical, democratic measure for tackling this problem by suggesting that the property qualification should be abolished altogether and eligibility linked to the register of electors. The NCW took a more moderate stance: its bill in 1933 proposed to make the spouse of any qualified juror also eligible.[46] These two options continued to frame the terms of the debate during the ensuing decades. Nearly 30 years later there was a similar division of opinion between the SPG and National Unions of Townswomen's Guilds (NUTG), with the former arguing in 1962 for the electoral register to be made the basis of qualification while the latter merely supported the inclusion of householders' spouses.[47] However, by the early 1960s the distinction between these two positions was less significant since inflation had eroded the value of the property qualification to the extent that 87 per cent of householders were potentially liable for jury service.[48]

There was greater unanimity across the women's movement surrounding peremptory challenge. All organisations agreed with the provision in the NCW bill that any female jurors who were successfully challenged should be replaced by other women. A series of high-profile cases in the late 1950s and early 1960s in which potential women jurors were challenged and then removed (including the trial in 1961 of a man for the rape of an 11-year-old girl guide) seems to have reignited the smouldering embers of the women's movement discontent over this practice, which they suspected was motivated by a desire to obtain all-male juries. Consequently the whole jury issue moved up the agenda. The Public Service and Magistrates' Committee (PSMC), led by Charis Frankenberg, began to put pressure on the government and wrote first to the Home Secretary, R. A. Butler, about the issue and later to all the women MPs. In the 1950s and early 1960s NUTG, NCW and the SPG all passed resolutions on the subject, which was also taken up by the Status of Women committee. In March 1962 the Labour MP Judith Hart introduced a Ten Minute Rule Bill on jury qualification. Hart's bill followed the SPG proposals by intending to make the electoral register the basis for eligibility for jury service. But her feminist motives were made clear in her speech to the Commons in which she made specific reference to the 1919 Act, claiming that its 'intentions' had been 'thwarted'.[49] The bill was supported by a cross-party group of MPs, in which well-known penal reformers and pro-feminist politicians featured prominently, but was nevertheless narrowly defeated in the division. The following autumn, in reply to a parliamentary question from the Conservative Dame Irene Ward and following an NCW deputation, Butler's successor, Henry Brooke, announced the establishment of an enquiry into jury service, to include the question of the representation of women on juries.[50] This instance of success on the part of both legal reformers and the women's movement, which, through concerted, cross-party action, had succeeded in placing the issue of women's rights and duties in court once more on the political agenda, suggests that the feminist–criminal–justice reform network was far from moribund in the early 1960s.

Nevertheless the law remained unchanged for another decade, despite favourable recommendations from the enquiry headed by Lord Morris of Borth-y-Gest (see below). Newspaper reports of criminal trials in the 1960s routinely described the juries of 'ten men and two women', or 'nine men and three women' as in the case of the trial in 1966 of Ronald 'Buster' Edwards, one of the Great Train robbers, at Nottingham Assizes.[51] The use of peremptory challenge remained a key problem. Most notoriously, and to the outrage of many feminists, the trial of the 'Moors Murderers', Ian Brady and Myra Hindley, was held before an all-male jury after defence counsel had objected to the four women who had originally been sworn in.[52] Hazel Hunkins Hallinan of the SPG characteristically blamed the male-dominated legal profession: 'It seems to be the last defiant act of legal men to preserve for themselves the right to pass judgement; the preserve legal men maintain for their own sex' she commented, continuing somewhat despairingly, 'it is sadder that women tolerate it'.[53]

Reform also necessitated the removal of judges' discretionary power to order all-male juries. Although this power seems to have been used less than the right of peremptory challenge to exclude women from hearing cases, it was still invoked on some occasions. Significantly, the reasons given, even in the 1960s, were almost exactly the same as the ones in the 1920s. In 1967 an all-male jury was ordered to hear charges under the 1959 Obscene Publications Act of the novel, *Last Exit to Brooklyn*. The judge, having read the book himself, ordered that there should be no women on the jury in case they were embarrassed by having to read a work allegedly about homosexuality, prostitution, sadism, drugs and 'sexual perversion'. He told the all-male jury that they would be 'shocked' by the book. 'You will probably be disgusted by parts of it. You may have physical nausea by parts of it, but . . . keep well in mind the issues which you have to determine. Your task is to determine whether the book is obscene. Read it with an open mind with no prudish feelings, use your common sense and good judgement.'[54] Clearly Judge Graham Rogers felt that this was a task far beyond the capability of women even in the supposedly 'liberated' and televised 1960s. Even the less overtly feminist women's organisations disagreed with him. As *The Townswoman* plainly stated in a rather one-sided 'discussion' of the jury issue, 'women [now] share with men the unpleasant aspects of life [as] presented by the press and the BBC'.[55] Nevertheless some members of the judiciary appeared to still be living in Edwardian – if not Victorian – times, believing that certain subjects were unfit for mixed company and remaining content to maintain masculine hegemony in the higher courts.

The women's movement, did, however, have some important allies in its campaign for reform of the law relating to jury service. A number of factors were contributing to a shortage of jurors by the 1960s, to the evident frustration of judges, not all of whom were reactionary opponents of equal citizenship. These factors included the use (or abuse) of peremptory challenge, as well as the regulations which exempted many people from jury service and the (often successful) efforts of those actually called to be excused. Judges seem to have been especially keen on mixed juries where the defendants were women. In 1965 the judge at Leeds Assizes complained that there were only two women among a panel of 60 jurors. As a result, the trial of a woman accused of abortion was heard by 12 men.[56] The following year the deputy chairman of Middlesex Sessions objected to the efforts of a defence lawyer to secure an all-male jury for his client, a woman on drink-drive charges. It is possible that the defence attorney in the case believed that women would be harder on the defendant than men, a view which was frequently expressed without any real justification. In the end, a jury of ten men and two women did indeed find her guilty.[57]

As indicated above, attempts to seek exemption from jury service were common and demonstrated that the need for reform was pressing. On one occasion in1966 *The Times* reported that 42 potential jurors (male and female) had asked to be exempted at the Central Criminal Court.[58] Although the property qualification – which dated back to an Act of 1825 – had lost much of its value it was clearly in need of revision after 140 years. An Act that had, according to the Morris Committee, 'greatly enhanced' the political reputation of Sir Robert Peel might be a little outdated by the 1960s.[59] Meanwhile, the list of exempted groups (including, among others, peers, MPs, the clergy, lawyers, armed forces officers, the police and vets) had grown substantially since the Juries Act of 1870 introduced the principle of exemption.[60] The result of the rules on qualification, coupled with the exemptions, was that the pool from which jurors were drawn was estimated in 1964 to be only 22.5 per cent of the names on the electoral register. Of this group, only 11 per cent were women.[61] In a period when there was much public concern about rising crime and in which more and more cases were being brought forward for jury trial this situation was not sustainable.

In an echo of the suffrage struggle half a century earlier, the issue of women's equal citizenship in the courts of law could undoubtedly still provoke a high proportion of organised women into action. The Morris Committee received written and/or oral evidence from an extensive list of women's organisations, including the NCW (represented by

Mrs Frankenberg and two colleagues), the SPG (represented by Hunkins Hallinan, Mary Stocks and Joan Vickers MP), NUTG, the NFWI, the NWCA, the St Joan's Alliance, the Society of Women Writers and Journalists, the Women's Liberal Federation, the Status of Women Committee, the Conservative Party's Women's Advisory Committee and the Suffragette Fellowship. This all-encompassing feminist lobby group achieved some notable success. The report accepted the point, 'put to us very forcefully by several women's organisations' that the existing law on jury qualification was unsatisfactory and acknowledged that 'a system which has the effect of arbitrarily restricting the number of women jurors is indefensible'.[62]

However, lobbyists failed to convince the committee of the merits of the NCW and SPG proposal that women jurors who were removed as a result of peremptory challenge should be replaced by others of their own sex. Committee members were in any case unsure as to whether this issue was covered by their terms of reference, but nevertheless decided to comment. The report cited statistics drawn from the Central Criminal Court and the London Sessions in early 1964. At the Old Bailey between January 7th and March 16th, 1693 jurors were empanelled of whom 167 were women. Women jurors were challenged in seven cases, and in five of these there was a strong suspicion that the intention was to obtain an all-male jury. In the London Sessions 648 jurors had been empanelled of whom 66 were women. Women were challenged in six cases, and in two – which concerned charges of driving while unfit due to drink and drugs, and receiving stolen jewellery – there was a likelihood that an all-male jury was the object. The committee had also examined evidence from other courts and reached the conclusion that, overall, few jurors were challenged, but that challenges were disproportionately aimed at women.[63] While the report was sympathetic to the case put forward by the NCW, it nevertheless concluded that if the supply of women jurors was increased as a result of its proposal to make the electoral register the basis of eligibility, then the impact of peremptory challenge – even if it was used deliberately as a result of prejudice against women – would be considerably lessened, and it would become far harder to obtain a single-sex jury.

Despite the Morris Report's rejection of their proposal on peremptory challenge, women's organisations reacted very favourably to the committee's recommendations. Hunkins Hallinan of the SPG called the report 'excellent' and was prepared to wait and see if the proposed changes ended discrimination before pressing for further safeguards to maintain women's presence on juries.[64] Predictably the NCW also welcomed the report's central recommendation of the abolition of the householder qualification: like the SPG it seemed unconcerned that its plan for the replacement of challenged female jurors with other women had not been supported.[65] Outside the women's organisations the reaction was slightly more mixed. *The Times* called the Morris Committee's recommendation 'persuasive', although a letter published in its columns raised the spectre of female-dominated juries – given that 53 per cent of registered electors were women.[66]

Surprisingly, almost another decade had passed before the Morris Report's seemingly logical and 'modern' suggestion that jury qualification should simply become a matter of citizenship was brought into practice. The Labour government promised that it would introduce legislation that would have the effect, 'among others', of greatly increasing the number of women eligible for jury service, yet it had failed to do so by the time it left office in 1970.[67] The new Conservative administration was then repeatedly questioned by MPs in the 1970–1 parliamentary session as to when it would act on the Morris report. Again legislation was promised, as soon as pressure on parliamentary time permitted.[68] In the event it was 1972 before the measure was enacted and March 1974 before the new rules for jury qualification, based on the electoral register, came into force. Perhaps it is ironic that such a delay in equality legislation took place during the years when the Women's Liberation Movement was revivifying the supposedly long-deceased corpse of feminism. It is hard to ascertain the reason for delay: the proposed measure on jury qualification was not especially controversial (except perhaps in the still socially conservative and male-dominated legal profession) and although the women's organisations did not rally in the way that they had in the early 1960s, MPs from all parties were still keeping up the pressure for reform. It is possible that the standard ministerial excuse of a lack of 'parliamentary time' may have been more truthful than cynics might assume and that, where feminists were concerned, campaigns surrounding other equality issues took precedence in the late 1960s and early 1970s. This was, after all, the era of the landmark Equal Pay Act and of the campaign that resulted in the successful passage of the Sex Discrimination Act of 1975.[69]

Despite the delay, the eventual democratisation and modernisation of jury service qualification can be seen as a success for the feminist movement, even if it was a long overdue one. Moreover, in the early 1960s this issue had provided a rallying point for women's organisations whose well-organised lobbying of government and of the Morris committee demonstrated that the issue of women's engagement in the criminal justice system was as significant a concern for them as it had been for their predecessors in the early decades of the twentieth century. In the mid-1960s newspapers were declaring – not for the first or the last time – that feminism was out of date and even Hunkins Hallinan feared that 'the great crusading spirit of equality which was so strong at the turn of the century has petered out'.[70] Yet by 1982 she had changed her mind and she was able to recognise that a new generation of feminists had taken over from hers, just as they in their turn had taken over from the suffragists.[71] However, Hallinan's generation had had to play a long game, not least in seeking the reform of Britain's archaic and undemocratic jury system. When success came at last, it was sadly but inevitably overshadowed by the noticeably different campaign tactics of the younger generation of the so-called second wave feminist activists.

Prostitution and the treatment of 'street offences'

Any campaigner concerned with the position of women in the criminal justice system sooner or later has to confront one of its most long-standing and seemingly intractable problems: the treatment under the law of women found accused of offences related to prostitution. Such offences made up a significant proportion of court convictions of women in large towns and cities in the Victorian era, although exact numbers are uncertain and may have been exaggerated. Zedner points out that in the second half of the nineteenth century, convictions of prostitutes under the Vagrancy Act fell by half, but it is quite possible that charges of drunkenness or indecent behaviour were brought to bear on women in the streets instead,[72] especially in view of the fact that it was not uncommon for them to have alcohol and other problems. The 'New Police' of the nineteenth century had the maintenance of order, often interpreted as the cleansing of urban streets of 'undesirable' characters and habits, as their central mission[73] and officers probably did not analyse which charges were most appropriate for each arrested individual too closely. While prostitution was not in itself illegal, a range of statutes, such as provisions of the Vagrancy Acts, could be used to target female suspects if they were thought to be causing an 'annoyance' to passers-by, that is, men. If they were found guilty, they would be labelled a 'common prostitute'.[74]

For feminists throughout the late nineteenth and early twentieth centuries there were several specific and longstanding problems with the law. Leaving aside the related issues of trafficking, sexual abuse and measures to control sexually transmitted diseases, the main concerns regarding solicitation were as follows. Firstly, the women's movement objected to the description of women as 'common prostitutes', a term with strong connotations of frequency and vulgarity[75] and a tendency to label them and place them into a category from which it was very hard to escape.[76] Secondly, there was a great deal of suspicion of the police and of the courts in the way they dealt with the women. Doubts were especially strong concerning the nature of police evidence, the frequent absence of corroboration and the readiness of male magistrates to believe police testimony. These suspicions naturally fed demands for the appointment of women police and matrons. The WFL also saw this problem as a powerful argument in favour of women magistrates, since soliciting charges were generally brought before the petty sessional courts, known as 'police courts'. However there is little hard evidence to suggest that the early women JPs, with the exception of the most avowedly feminist, were any more sceptical of police evidence than their male colleagues. Furthermore, in London (where the majority of charges were laid) the offences were mainly dealt with by the professional, stipendiary magistrates, all of whom were male until the 1940s. It should be also noted that most of the women pleaded guilty and that justice in these courts could be very swift: a former NCW president, Lady Nunburnholme, who gave evidence to the Wolfenden Committee in the 1950s, claimed she had seen 23 cases dealt with at Bow Street Magistrates Court in 19 minutes.[77] The third main feminist objection to the law was that it bore heavily on women who sold sex but left untouched the men who purchased it. Thus a class of women was stigmatised and subjected to gender-specific penalties under the law. No man who annoyed a woman in the street would be treated in the same way.

Much has been written about the attitude of British 'first wave' feminists towards the law on prostitution, particularly with regard to the Victorian campaign against the Contagious Diseases (CD) Acts, and it is not my intention to cover this topic here.[78] In the early twentieth century, feminists, who continued to be inspired by the memory of the charismatic leader of the Ladies' National Association (LNA) Josephine Butler, railed against any attempt by the State to regulate prostitution or to treat any woman unequally before the law simply because she chose to sell sex. However, not all feminists were in agreement concerning the best response to legislation in this field. For example, as Lucy Bland points out, some activists supported parliamentary efforts to combat the so-called white slave trade while others, notably the former WSPU and WFL member, Teresa Billington-Greig, suspected that the scare stories about women who were drugged and abducted were somewhat exaggerated and that they could be harmfully interpreted and used by anti-feminists as 'evidence' of feminine weakness.[79] More generally, there was a long-established division between the more repressively inclined advocates of 'social purity' who dominated the National Vigilance Association and similar groups and those who doubted, in the words of Josephine Butler, that it was possible to 'oblige people to be moral by force'.[80]

From 1915 the Association for Moral and Social Hygiene (AMSH) was the leading feminist-inspired (and libertarian) pressure group concerned principally with the law of prostitution.[81] As a direct descendent of Mrs Butler's LNA (it was eventually renamed the Josephine Butler Society), the AMSH remained true to its founder's creed and opposed all legislation that sought to regulate the 'sex trade' (including various wartime measures imposed in the name of public health) and agitated against the perpetuation of the 'sexual double standard' (i.e., gender inequality) in the law. Its long-serving secretary, Alison Neilans, was a former WFL organiser and executive member, who had served at least three prison sentences for suffrage-related offences and had undergone a hunger strike and forced feeding in Holloway.[82] Neilans and her organisation were well-integrated into the women's movement: she was also an executive member of the Open Door Council and on the board of the International Woman Suffrage Alliance, while the AMSH itself was affiliated to the NCW. Co-operation with the HLPR was also strong in the 1920s and 30s, since the two pressure groups appear to have regularly supported each other's resolutions at annual meetings of the NCW, and the *Howard Journal* published articles by both Neilans and the AMSH Assistant Secretary E. M. Turner (who was a biographer of Josephine Butler).[83] The Howard League broadly concurred with the AMSH's approach to the series of general statutes, local acts and by-laws that the latter organisation collectively labelled the 'solicitation laws'.[84] The *Howard Journal's* comment in 1927 (probably penned by the secretary Cicely Craven), that '[t]here seems to be an injustice in selecting the professional prostitute for capricious severity, while others of both sexes, equally immoral, escape from censure',[85] hinted at the essence of the liberal feminist critique of the law on prostitution, that it was grounded in gender discrimination and offended fundamental principles of human rights.

During the First World War feminists concentrated their anger on government attempts under the Defence of the Realm Act (DORA) to arrest the spread of venereal disease through imposing controls which applied solely to women. Although merely one of several repressive measures taken by government, military and local authorities to control women, DORA Regulation 40D, which prohibited any woman suffering from a communicable disease from having sexual intercourse with a member of the armed forces,[86] was especially resented by women's and purity organisations because it was seen as effectively a reimposition of the CD Acts, in that it presumably sought to ensure a supply of 'clean' prostitutes for soldiers through the detention and examination of women suspected of being 'unclean'. A mass protest meeting against 40D was organised at Westminster with support from the Free Church League for Women's Suffrage, the Independent WSPU,[87] the Women's Labour League, the WFL and several other organisations, and was addressed by a range of speakers including the pacifist Labour MP George Lansbury and suffragist Esther Roper.[88] Despite continuing differences of emphasis between the groups represented, any perceived 'double standards', which targeted the (im)morality of women (but not of men) would continue to be a rallying point for feminists.

After the First World War and the partial enfranchisement of women the attainment of an 'equal moral standard' remained a key objective of both NUSEC and the WFL. In 1924 NUSEC surveyed parliamentary candidates on the question of the abolition of the solicitation laws and obtained assurances of support from 119 MPs.[89] NUSEC was effectively canvassing support for the 'Public Places (Order) Bill' that the AMSH had drafted in order to tackle what they regarded as the key problems: the repeated use in statutes and by-laws of the term 'common prostitute' which was applicable only to women, and the way in which most women were mainly convicted of soliciting merely on the uncorroborated testimony of a policeman.[90] The feminist-criminal-justice reform network continued to build support for the AMSH strategy in the mid-1920s. In 1924 a conference of about a hundred women members of the Magistrates' Association (after hearing speeches from Neilans and Clarke Hall) resolved that the existing solicitation laws were 'unsatisfactory',[91] and two years later Lady Astor introduced the AMSH bill into the Commons and Lord Burleigh brought it before the House of Lords. After a second reading was obtained the government responded to pressure and promised to set up an enquiry.[92] It seems that in the mid-1920s feminist-inspired campaigns on this issue were not lacking in political purchase, perhaps because politicians were still wary of the women voter and unsure about the extent of the influence of women's organisations over the female electorate.

Nevertheless, the government dragged its metaphorical feet somewhat, opting for a departmental investigation instead of a select committee, and waiting until October 1927 to announce the enquiry's membership. When the committee finally convened, Neilans appeared before it to give evidence for NUSEC, the WFL and the St Joan's Social and Political Alliance as well as the AMSH, while representations were also received from Florence Keynes JP on behalf of the NCW and from Lady Astor. In the event, despite the Savidge case in 1928 (which put the whole issue of the police force's unequal treatment where public 'decency' was concerned of young working women and 'respectable' – and in this case, eminent – older gentlemen once more into the media spotlight[93]), the momentum was lost and no reform resulted. This was partly because the Street Offences Committee members, who included Margery Fry; Miss Kelly JP; the Chief Metropolitan Magistrate Sir Chartres Biron; an inspector of constabulary, Sir Leonard Dunning; a reactionary bishop; and (rather surprisingly) Lady Joynson Hicks, wife of the Home Secretary, were unable to agree completely on their recommendations. The incompatibility of this group can be ascertained from Fry's initial suspicion that most of her fellow committee members were 'hard-faced reactionaries', although she was later relieved to find that Lady 'Jix' (whose appointment the *Howard Journal* had called 'incomprehensible')[94] was 'very stupid but not too wicked'.[95] The result of the selection of such an ill-assorted group, most of whose proper place, was, according to the *Howard Journal*, 'at the witness table',[96] was that there were no less than six memoranda of reservations appended to the report's recommendations signed by (in total) eight of the committee's members.[97] Another reason for the lack of any concrete result was the rejection by the AMSH of much of the report, despite the fact that it had recommended the abolition of special laws against 'common prostitutes' and proposed that evidence from aggrieved persons would be needed in order to prove a charge of solicitation. The problem for the AMSH was that the suggested new, gender-neutral law would allow prosecution of individuals found to have importuned members of the opposite sex for immoral purposes. Thus, the AMSH leadership argued, the law would make the *purpose* of an act illegal, although the act itself was not.[98] As Self points out, in retrospect, it seems that the AMSH lost a significant opportunity for reform of the solicitation laws in the late 1920s.[99]

Despite this setback, the AMSH and its allies continued to campaign for change in the law throughout the 1930s and 40s. The NCW in particular regularly supported AMSH resolutions for repeal of existing statutes dealing with solicitation and their replacement with measures that would treat men and women equally with regard to 'administration, evidence and penalties'.[100] The AMSH itself meanwhile continued unsuccessfully to promote its cause in parliament through contacts with pro-feminist MPs such as Pethick-Lawrence.[101] Nevertheless the whole question of the treatment of women under these laws continued to be a thorny one and there were many disagreements between, and even within, organisations. Feminist supporters, including Mrs Keynes (convenor of the NCW's Public Service and Magistrates' Committee) and Elizabeth Abbott of the WFL, remained suspicious of any measures to tackle prostitution that could be construed as repressive or aimed solely at women. As an AMSH pamphlet asked rhetorically, '[d]o you think that because a woman – often a young girl – is immoral she has no right to justice?'[102] Thus the AMSH condemned even those measures proposed in the name of 'social hygiene' or 'progressive penology' which may have commanded some support elsewhere in the women's or purity movements, on grounds of civil liberties and equal rights. For example, during the passage of the Criminal Justice Bill in 1939 Neilans became concerned that the term 'medical' examination was being inserted instead of 'mental' examination. While she supported the 'progressive' view that offenders might require psychological assessment, she clearly feared that the use of the word 'medical' might open the door to forced examinations of women charged with soliciting for signs of venereal disease. However, Neilans' suspicions were not shared by the MP she wrote to on the matter, Irene Ward.[103]

The AMSH's connections with the HLPR and its secretary, Cicely Craven, which were notable in the 1930s, seem to have been less strong after Neilans' death in 1942: surprisingly the League was not listed among the large group of societies that attended a conference on the solicitation laws held in 1948.[104] However, contacts with individual HLPR Executive members, especially Margery Fry and Gerald Gardiner KC, clearly were maintained into the 1950s, as was League's commitment to gender equality before the law.

Margery Fry took a great interest in all aspects of criminal justice reform but her membership of the Street Offences Committee had no doubt given her a special insight into the specific problems of the solicitation laws. She remained personally supportive of AMSH objectives and deeply critical of any discriminatory laws and practices. In 1943 Fry commented on the treatment of prostitutes in the USA following an investigative visit there. She was disturbed to find that the US federal laws permitted 'very one-sided' handling of prostitutes as opposed to their clients, especially around military camps, and that the former were also often subjected to compulsory examination and detention (if they were found to be diseased) under state laws.[105] In 1950 Fry was called upon to offer the AMSH secretary advice on the wording of the organisation's draft Public Places Order Bill which exposed a disagreement between her and her HLPR Executive colleague, Chief Inspector Hewitt. Hewitt was also a member of the AMSH legislation subcommittee, but he and Dorothy Peto (former head of the Metropolitan Women Police Division) felt that if the relevant clause in the bill explicitly excluded a police officer from being the 'aggrieved person' who could testify in support of an allegation of importuning, then it would effectively cast a slur on the integrity of the police. Fry clearly took a different view and seems to have considered that the problem of convicting women on the basis of police evidence alone was sufficiently serious to warrant the suggested proviso.[106]

The HLPR as a body remained broadly supportive of the feminist standpoint on prostitution. When, in the mid-1950s, the first major official investigation of the solicitation laws since 1928 took place under the remit of the Wolfenden Committee (see below), the HLPR reiterated its stance that the term 'common prostitute' should be dropped from the statute books and Fry once again argued that no one class of persons should be 'singled out and submitted to a special law'.[107] However, in common with the Wolfenden Committee itself, the League's sub-committee was far more exercised about issues relating to the law on homosexuality than those concerning prostitution. After the Wolfenden report's publication the HLPR did comment critically on the recommendations, expressing fears that the proposal to raise penalties for solicitation would encourage a call-girl system that 'could lead to the emergence of large-scale professional vice racketeers'.[108] MPs associated with the HLPR were vocal opponents of the 1959 Street Offences Act, which enacted the Wolfenden proposals, and the League continued to support in essence the stance of the Josephine Butler Society (JBS) throughout the 1960s and 70s.[109]

The story of the Wolfenden report and its aftermath, dealt with below, tends to indicate that the 1950s and 60s were not a period in which feminist campaigns on prostitution made much impact. However, the 1950s were not completely devoid of feminist-inspired legislation concerning prostitution. 1951 saw the passage into law of a small, but significant, legislative change that had been promoted by the AMSH. This new Criminal Law Amendment Act (CLAA) extended protection from procuration under the similarly named 1885 Act to categories of women who had previously been denied it, namely 'common prostitutes' and girls 'of known immoral character'. As the promoter, Barbara Castle MP, explained when she introduced her ten-minute rule bill to the House of

Commons in December 1950, '[i]f we want to curb [the procurer's] power, we must strike where his exploitation is most effective, and that is among the prostitutes and the semi-professionals'. Furthermore, she also argued an important point of principle, 'that it is wrong to withhold the protection of the law from any citizen on the grounds of his or her moral character'.[110] When the bill returned to the Commons for its third reading (the first introduced under the ten-minute rule to do so), Castle firmly reiterated her point that the bill was all about securing equality before the law.[111] Therefore this seemingly minor reform was in fact a significant achievement for the principle of gender equality for which liberal feminists had fought so long, although the prejudice that crimes committed against prostitutes were less serious than those in which an 'innocent' girls were victimised was not yet overcome, as some of the reaction to the so-called Yorkshire Ripper murders in the 1970s showed.[112] Whereas, as Self claims, Wolfenden and his colleagues were largely ignorant both of the history of Josephine Butler and her 'crusade' and of the deliberations of the League of Nations and the United Nations (UN) on the subject of human trafficking,[113] Castle was clearly well-versed in both subjects. She referred to the work of Butler and the repeal of the CD Acts in her Commons speech and had evidently recently discussed the trafficking issue with the American delegate Mrs Roosevelt at a meeting of the UN social committee.[114]

This CLAA was not, of course, the only legislative improvement in women's rights brought into parliament by Mrs Castle, despite her frequent denials in the period up to the late 1970s that she was a feminist.[115] In her early years in parliament as a backbench MP, Castle was a generalist, asking questions and conducting campaigns on a variety of political issues as well as matters concerning her constituents in Blackburn: she did not show any particular interest in the criminal justice system. Arguably during the first two decades of her parliamentary career 'feminist' was not a useful label for an ambitious woman in the male-dominated world of politics to acquire and Castle was clearly anxious to avoid the 'typecasting' which over-identification with 'women's issues' in parliament could bring.[116] Nevertheless, in 1954 she joined women MPs of all parties in a 'photo opportunity' for equal pay and 40 years later included the evidence of it in her published memoirs.[117] It is also significant that she aided and approved of the political careers of other Labour women, such as Jo Richardson, who in her own time as an MP was unafraid of identification with women's issues and feminist politics.[118] Castle always refused to be tied down to what she called 'single issue politics' however important the issue was, but that does not mean that her sympathies did not lie broadly with feminism as well as social-ism. Her official biographer comments that 'her political motivation was always to improve life for the underdog; gender was relevant only because more underdogs were women than men'.[119] It can be added in the context of her CLAA that prostitutes were the most 'underdog' of all women.

In her book *Prostitution, Women and Misuse of the Law* Helen Self elo-quently analyses what she argues was the marginalisation of the women's movement in general and AMSH in particular during the discussions of the Wolfenden Committee. This new enquiry into the solicitation laws was prompted less by the feminist agitation and concerns about police behaviour that had occasioned the appointment of its predecessor in 1927, and more because of a mass-media panic about the visibility of streetwalkers in London, which especially concerned the Home Secretary, Maxwell Fyfe in the lead-up to the 1953 Coronation of Queen Elizabeth II, when it was expected that the eyes of the world would be on the British capital. Self demonstrates that any feminist perspective on the legal treatment of prostitution was suppressed in the first instance by the narrow way in which the committee's terms of reference were drawn in relation to prostitution, and subsequently by decisions taken by Wolfenden and his civil service advisor regarding the conditions under which evidence would be heard (in private) and over who they would actually invite to be witnesses, and crucially, who would be left out. She quotes many examples of their contemptuous, even misogynistic, atti-tudes towards women's groups: Wolfenden apparently referred to the AMSH as 'the Old Women's Society'.[120] Moreover, committee members, but not witnesses, were privy to a report on the handling of prostitution in American cities which claimed that it was unusual to see open solici-tation on the streets there as a result of harsh sentences for streetwalkers on the one hand and the police turning a 'blind eye' to the use of 'call houses' on the other.[121] Thus the problem of ensuring the protection of innocent passers-by from being offended by the flagrant display of dis-reputable women appeared to have been solved in the USA, although clearly the problem of prostitution per se was not. The recommendation of this strategy, which made the women on the streets (rather than their clients or any social conditions they faced) the issue and which was likely to make them even more vulnerable to violent exploitation, would have attracted severe criticism from British women's organisa-tions had they been able to see this report.[122] The adoption of similar proposals to the American approach in Wolfenden's recommendations and in the subsequent Act therefore undermined the traditional feminist perspective on prostitution by privileging the right of 'respectable' citizens to be protected from offence over the rights of prostitutes to obtain natural justice.[123]

The enactment of the Wolfenden proposals in 1959 was a significant defeat for campaigners. Self explains that the AMSH/JBS secretary Chave Collisson was exhausted by the organisation's unsuccessful opposition to the Street Offences Act and gave up her post in 1960.[124] In the 1970s the JBS also ran into difficulties due to financial problems and infighting and it even seems to have undergone some uncertainty about its core philosophy.[125] Nevertheless, the adverse effects of the new legislation – driving prostitution out of public space and into more commercial settings, while further stigmatising and endangering those left on the streets and increasing the number sent to prison – did not go unnoticed or uncriticised in the media and in parliament. The JBS continued to work with sympathetic MPs and peers, male and female, to introduce amendments to the law. Of the handful of women in the Commons at this time, two, Eirene White (Labour) and Joan Vickers (Conservative), served as JBS vice-presidents.[126] Feminist campaigners may have been down, but they were by no means out.

Meanwhile, practically minded penal reformers and social workers concentrated their efforts on helping the women who found their way into prisons as a result of prostitution, despite the fact that they were often thought to be disruptive and unsuitable for 'treatment' in the penal system. It is noteworthy that in 1963 nearly half the women in Holloway Prison on account of non-indictable (i.e., relatively minor) offences were there for 'offences related to prostitution'. A further, smaller group of inmates had been found guilty of the indictable offence of brothel-keeping. In addition, according to the prison's governor, Joanna Kelley, many larcenists were prostitutes, and vice versa.[127] She tried to 'rehabilitate' them through the operation of small counselling groups which could, in some ways, be seen as similar to the interventions of 'rescue' workers and 'lady visitors' in the nineteenth century in that they sought to show the women the error of their ways. The difference was that Holloway in the 1960s dealt with the supposedly 'hardened' cases who had been apprehended repeatedly and/or failed to pay fines, whereas the rescue work of the previous century tended to concentrate on younger, more compliant and 'reclaimable' women.[128]

Feminists in the 1950s and 60s found it hard to fight the dominant perception, fostered by some criminologists, politicians and commentators that sex work was a form of social deviance chosen by women with a specific personality type who had been seduced by glamour and easy money, and the associated denial that there could be any economic imperative for women to sell their bodies in an age of prosperity, an argument used to justify the harsher penalties for solicitation imposed under the 1959 Act. Kelley certainly seems to have supported the view that the imprisoned sex workers were suffering from psychological abnormalities, claiming that '[t]he prostitute lives in a world of illusion' and even suggesting that the most 'disturbed' prostitutes had 'a deep seated conflict with their feminine role' and preferred to seek 'their emotional outlet in lesbian relationships'.[129] As these views suggest, Kelley was probably not a feminist in the political sense, although she was a powerful woman with a successful career who was dedicated to improving the penal treatment of women, both in her time as governor and subsequently in a senior role in the prison department. Of course, as a public servant it would anyway have been inappropriate for her to question the law which had resulted in the imprisonment of the women in her care. The NCW's Public Service and Magistrates' Committee, to whom Kelley spoke in 1971, had more freedom to express their opinions: they continued to maintain their historic opposition to the inherently discriminatory term 'common prostitute'.[130] Nevertheless, members probably shared at least some of the popular preconceptions about prostitution.

Attitudes began to alter again in the late 1970s when 'second wave' feminists, long-term campaigners such as Joan Vickers (by then a life peer) and the newly formed English Collective of Prostitutes (ECP) joined forces to once more try to reform the law. After attending, apparently almost by accident, a public meeting on the subject chaired by Vickers, Maureen Colquhoun MP introduced a ten-minute rule bill in 1979 to abolish prison sentences for soliciting,[131] create a single, gender-neutral offence covering all street nuisances that required evidence from the annoyed person to replace the old laws, abolish the term 'common prostitute' and alter the legal definition of a brothel. Once again this attempt to change the law was unsuccessful. However, the bill did receive a second reading (allegedly because of, rather than despite, the outspoken opposition to it of the Reverend Ian Paisley) and fell simply because parliament was suddenly dissolved for a General Election in which Colquhoun herself was to lose her seat.[132] As a private members bill that lacked government backing, it probably would not have reached the statute book in any case. Nevertheless the story of this bill illustrates the point that the assumption that 'first wave' feminism was dead long before the emergence of the 'second wave' is thoroughly unfounded. In the 1970s this campaign united feminists of different generations, class backgrounds and political leanings. It is hard, for example, to think of a more 'establishment' figure than the indomitable septuagenarian Lady Vickers, who was renowned for her 'Tory' blue-rinse hair and whose early life had been spent riding side-saddle and attending parties as a debutante,[133] working in collaboration with members of the ECP.

In the early 1980s, this time against a background of economic recession, it was once again argued strongly that the lack of financial power and resources of some women, coupled now with their reliance on uncertain and reducing welfare benefits, was a crucial imperative in their decision to resort to prostitution.[134] Thus the relevance of poverty was once more recognised. 'Second wave' feminists also claimed that prostitutes were 'victims of sexually repressive legislation and male exploitation and control',[135] an analysis which in no way would have surprised Josephine Butler or her early twentieth-century-successors in the feminist–criminal–justice reform network. At the same time there was a re-emergence of concerns over the sexual abuse of young people and reports of the recruitment of vulnerable children by gangs of pimps.[136] In the twenty-first century there has been more evidence of the continuation of human trafficking and of the violence endured by women in prostitution. The almost unchanging nature of this problem, which remains rooted in social, economic, racial and – crucially – gender inequalities, is plain to see. It is unsurprising that there is as much historical continuity in the feminist analysis of this issue as there is in the criminal law, which still punishes and stigmatises women for a technically legal activity while leaving the men involved largely unaffected, in much the same way as it has for the last two centuries.[137]

Conclusion

The three campaigns featured in this chapter may seem to have little to do with one another, but they all demonstrate ways in which liberal feminists in the twentieth century have sought to redress the gender bias in British courts with varying degrees of success. Activity in these campaigns ebbed and flowed, but the effort to reform the rules governing jury selection stands out as an interesting example of an ultimately successful crusade launched at a time when (it is often assumed) the women's movement was at its lowest ebb. However, the extent to which juries are capable of reaching just and gender-neutral decisions in difficult cases is still a matter of debate. In contrast with their efforts for jurors and JPs, there seems to have been little active support among women's organisations for measures to improve women's access to the legal profession after the initial legislation to open it was passed in 1919. I have suggested that this may have been because women who wanted to succeed in the legal profession may themselves have preferred not to be seen to require the backing of the feminist movement. Moreover, the achievement of greater equality in the legal profession was to a large extent contingent on substantial change in gender relations, something which is far harder to achieve through traditional pressure group activity than a new parliamentary statute. The persistence of gender discrimination at the bar is exemplified by evidence quoted in the 2004 Fawcett Society report, which found that women still made up only eight per cent of Queen's Counsel. The commission's recommendations included that the Law Society and the Bar Council undertake research, require their members to carry out equal pay reviews and 'continue their efforts to ensure [they] take diversity into account during recruitment and promotion processes'.[138]

Understandably, campaigners during the 1920–70-period concentrated on obtaining achievable legislative changes that marked gradual improvements in the status of women. Their tactics rarely involved the type of activity that would attract the attention of the press. Although their objectives appear to have been limited, they were at least focused in their approach. Campaigns usually involved close liaison with sympathetic parliamentarians, briefing them for parliamentary questions and presenting them with draft bills. As with all pressure group activity, the levels of success varied considerably. The laws governing jury selection were changed, and although it is noticeable that they were extremely archaic by the time of reform, pressure from the women's movement undoubtedly played some part in this development. However, the laws surrounding prostitution have altered only in detail over the decades, suggesting that this was one of the most intractable problems confronted by the feminist–criminal–justice network.

4
Women in the Penal System

'It is not always realised that the prison system was made by the people of this country, and that, if anything is amiss with it, we citizens and voters are accountable, not those who bear the burden of putting our laws into operation.'[1] These words of a former Lady Inspector of Prisons published in 1922 reminded readers that the country's penal system was a proper matter of concern for electors, including recently enfranchised women. As Elizabeth Crawford has recently noted, one long-term consequence of the imprisonment of suffragettes during their struggle for the vote was the development of a campaign for improvements in prison conditions.[2] Of course, the concern and interest of middle-class women reformers in the penal system had other, deeper roots, extending at least as far back as the era of Elizabeth Fry and her 'lady' colleagues, who visited women in prison almost a century before the suffrage struggle reached its height. Many late nineteenth- and early twentieth-century-women, not just feminists, regarded social welfare issues – especially those such as the treatment of female prisoners that had strong moral overtones – as quintessentially the province of educated women: notions of what constituted 'womanly work' were shared by suffragists and anti-suffragists alike.[3] For example, the Duchess of Bedford, president of the Lady Visitors' Association from 1900 to 1920, committed herself to social work with the women in Aylesbury Convict Prison, yet she was less than sympathetic towards the hunger-striking suffragettes.[4] Moreover, even among feminists there were many differences of opinion regarding specific questions of penal policy and justice.

Nevertheless, there were cogent reasons why feminist-inclined women were strongly represented in penal reform campaigns. Estelle Freedman points out that nineteenth-century-female prison reformers in the USA disproportionately belonged to religious sects such as the Quakers and

Unitarians, and that many of them also actively supported other liberal causes, such as feminism and the abolition of slavery.[5] In Britain too, it is possible to identify such tendencies among activists, although in political terms twentieth-century-penal reformers might support any of the three main parties or none. Brian Harrison has located a network of moral reform activists in nineteenth-century-England who exhibited shared attitudes, personality traits and campaigning styles while supporting a range of causes ranging from the protection of animals to the repeal of the CD Acts.[6] Similar networks can be identified throughout the twentieth century. The eyes of feminists (and, to an extent, the general middle-class public) may have been opened further with regard to the state of prisons by the reports of suffragettes, but they were to be constantly reopened by further revelations from politically engaged middle-class prisoners, including conscientious objectors in both World Wars and nuclear disarmament activists in the 1960s. The overlapping personnel and close connections between some feminist groups, the peace movement and penal reform bodies suggest that their activists held similar views and values. Although religious belief declined among some – but not all – reformers in the twentieth century, there remained a strong sense of moral purpose and of social obligation in their attitudes. Above all, they believed in the efficacy of political campaigning to right the wrongs of society while through the suffrage battle they had gained awareness of more matters of social justice including the treatment of prisoners.

This chapter focuses on the four main areas of penal reform for women that feminists were most interested in during the twentieth century. The first concerns the persistent demands for the employment of women in leadership roles in the prison service and Prison Commission and the extent to which the voluntary work of committed female reformers filled the void left by the shortage of professional staff. The second area is the seemingly interminable debate about improvements to the day-to-day treatment of the women and girls held in the country's jails and borstals. The section on this theme concentrates (largely as a result of the metropolitan bias of the evidence) mainly on Holloway Prison in London, where the largest concentration of England's female prisoners were kept,[7] and on the girls' borstals, also in the south-east. The next part of the chapter deals with broader questions about the philosophy of punishment in relation to women, including discussions about after-care and alternatives to prison. Finally, the last section considers the relevance of gender to the campaign against the death penalty, focusing particularly on infanticide legislation and the aftermath of the execution of Edith Thompson for murder in 1923.

The employment of women professionals in prisons

It is a striking fact that the employment of women in a professional capacity in the prison system seems to have become established practice in the United States many decades before it became so in Britain, despite the inspiration, common to both countries, of Elizabeth Fry. The female section of Sing Sing Prison in New York was headed by a woman as early as 1844 and Massachusetts' Framingham Reformatory, which was opened in 1877, was thereafter run by a succession of determined and powerful women.[8] In England and Wales, the first woman to hold a professional position in the penal administration was Dr Mary Gordon, who was appointed as 'Lady Inspector' of women's prisons in 1908. Gordon's appointment, which was suspected by the top civil servant in the Home Office merely to have been a 'sop to feminism',[9] was not swiftly followed by others and Gordon appears to have struggled for acceptance among her male colleagues and peers. The chairman of the Prison Commission, Sir Evelyn Ruggles-Brise apparently preferred to rely upon the labours of volunteers such as the Duchess of Bedford to bring a 'feminine' touch to the penal system.[10] Male officials were clearly giving strong signals that professional women were neither welcome nor (in their opinion) necessary within the prison service.

Naturally, therefore, the appointment of women to positions of responsibility, particularly in institutions catering for women and girls, became a key objective for the women's movement in the early twentieth century. The WFL demanded the appointment of a woman commissioner of prisons as one of its main objectives in 1918. This demand, which was also supported by National Union of Societies for Equal Citizenship (NUSEC), the National Council of Women (NCW) and the Howard League for Penal Reform (HLPR), was reiterated repeatedly during the 1920s and early 1930s but was only met in 1935 when Lilian Barker became a commissioner and inspector of prisons.[11] WFL resolutions also called for women to be in charge of all women's prisons as both governors and deputies. While that aspiration was by no means met in the short term, there were some precedents. Selina Fox, a doctor who had practiced in India, was made 'Lady Superintendent' (effectively matron, under a male governor) of the four penal establishments at Aylesbury in 1914, and was succeeded first by Margaret Arbuthnot and later by Lilian Barker as governor of the girls' borstal there.[12] Mary Size, who entered the prison service in 1906 aged 23, served as Barker's second-in-command and eventually became the deputy governor at Holloway Prison.[13] But the latter institution – England's main women's jail – did not come under female leadership until 1945 when another doctor, Charity Taylor, became the first woman governor. A few years earlier Cicely McCall, a former Holloway employee, had criticised the habit of appointing a medical man, often from outside the service, 'because of his sex, over the head of a woman with many years' experience and considerable administrative experience'.[14] At the time of McCall's writing there were just three women deputies and one female governor in the service.[15]

It seems therefore that world wars hastened the appointment of women in senior prison posts as they did in analogous roles in the civil service and the police. Feminist pressure may not have played much part, although arguably the decisions of individual men in positions of power who were sympathetic to aspects of the feminist penal reform project were surely significant in advancing women. Herbert Morrison, for example, who was Home Secretary at the time of Dr Taylor's appointment, was remarkable for his patronage of women in politics and administration during the 1930s and 40s.[16] Earlier in the century Lilian Barker (who had been the Welfare Supervisor of women munitions workers at Woolwich Arsenal during World War One) was recruited personally by the borstal reformer, Alexander Paterson, as a result of his search for someone to introduce more 'progressive' policies at Aylesbury.[17] Barker apart, there seems to have been a bias in favour of candidates with medical qualifications, especially in the case of Holloway, which may suggest something about officialdom's perceptions of its inmates.[18] But, as women's organisations would have no doubt pointed out, there were plenty of female doctors by the 1930s. It seems therefore that the main reason for the delay in appointing women to the top jobs was the masculine bureaucracy's resistance to putting women in charge, exemplified earlier in the century by the poor treatment of Dr Gordon. McCall's allegation of gender discrimination appears therefore to have been justified.

Of course, in the mean time there was plenty of scope for women to undertake voluntary work within the prisons – in both the men's and the women's jails – some of which was performed in a most professional manner.[19] The lady visitors have already been mentioned, but the interwar period saw the opening of important – and responsible – new opportunities for women volunteers. One of these was connected with the opening of the magistracy to women in 1919. When the country's local prisons were taken over by the Prison Commission in 1877 the local magistrates who had previously run the jails retained the right to appoint official 'visiting justices' from among themselves. These were a group of JPs who undertook to inspect the penal establishment concerned regularly and listen to any complaints from inmates.

At first women were usually only appointed as visiting justices if female prisoners were incarcerated in the jail concerned; hence the appointment in 1920 of extra women magistrates in London, Durham and Birmingham.[20] Mrs Bramwell Booth (of the Salvation Army) was the first visiting justice at Holloway in 1921, followed six months later by Margery Fry.[21] In 1930 Mrs Jean Dewar Robinson, a WFL member, became Chairman (sic) of the Holloway Visiting Justices Committee, which by then consisted of ten men and ten women.[22] She was later succeeded by a barrister, Florence Earengey, who had also been in the WFL. Earengey, who continued her association with Holloway for 20 years, earned the approbation of Mary Size, who recalled the former's 'meticulous care' and generosity in offering her legal expertise to help the prisoners.[23]

Feminist women magistrates in the 1920s appear to have approached the task of prison visiting in a manner highly reminiscent of women philanthropists of the late nineteenth century approached their charitable work in public institutions.[24] The words of Margery Fry at the NUSEC Summer School in 1922 echoed the exhortations of the nineteenth-century-founder of the Workhouse Visiting Society, Louisa Twining, to women workhouse visitors and poor law guardians. Women visiting magistrates should be 'thorough' and 'see everything' including punishment cells and padded cells. They should 'inspect and taste the food, enquire what use is made of handcuffs and give prisoners the chance to make complaints'.[25] This approach was evidently grounded in the tradition of women's philanthropy in that it conflated the role of official inspector with that of voluntary social worker and was based on gendered notions of where women's expertise lay – in the kitchen, in the small domestic details of life and in the ability to listen to complaints as a mother listens to her child. But, crucially, Fry was also concerned that visiting justices should obtain a realistic notion of the prison's environment and not be fobbed off by the management and staff. Her own involvement with Holloway Prison as a visiting justice was certainly close and sustained when she lived in nearby Dalmeny Avenue during the early 1920s.[26]

In addition to undertaking official inspections, women magistrates also conducted unofficial visits to prisons in order to familiarise themselves with the conditions in institutions to which they habitually sent offenders. The women magistrates' societies in Gloucestershire and Hampshire organised group visits for educational purposes years before such trips became a mandatory part of training for JPs. Their observations led in many cases to their creation of voluntary schemes aimed at the amelioration of some of the harsher aspects of prison life. For example, one of the earliest activities of the Gloucestershire Women Magistrates' Society (GWMS) was to raise money for a piano for the Gloucester Prison, and one of the members Lillian Faithfull (the head of Cheltenham Ladies' College) also undertook to supply bedding plants for the garden at the governor's request.[27] Margery Fry recommended in 1922 that women justices should provide books for the prison library and organise concerts, although she admitted that these initiatives were 'just palliatives'.[28] Public money was not available for these 'extras' at this time: evidently the State relied not only on the unpaid work of middle-class women as magistrates and visitors, but also upon their wealth and generosity.

Women magistrates and visitors did not restrict their involvement to women's prisons, although their right to affect or even comment on the running of penal institutions for men was far harder to establish. Louisa Martindale was one of the first women to be appointed as visiting justice at Lewes Prison, probably not until the late 1930s or 40s. She appears to have followed Fry's instructions, listening to prisoners' complaints, which 'they loved to pour out', tasting the food and inspecting the library. Martindale, however, was obviously not disposed to be too critical, she found the food 'quite excellent' and 'plentiful . . . the bread made by the cook was the best I ever tasted, especially during the war' while the library was 'surprisingly adequate'.[29] One wonders how searching her inquiries were. Mrs Helena Dowson, a former suffragist who was appointed as visiting magistrate in Nottingham in 1921, was less easily satisfied with her monthly excursions to the city's prison. 'I began to feel after a time that these visits were rather perfunctory and that I should like to get in closer touch with both the warders and the prisoners', she recalled.[30] Her knowledge of a 'mutual welfare league' set up in an American prison by the renowned reformer Thomas Mott Osborne[31] prompted her to launch a similar experiment in Nottingham. Fourteen men with no previous convictions were chosen by the governor and chaplain to take part in the scheme, which became known as the 'league of honour'. The men elected the officers and set the rules and chose the name of the organisation. Details of the activities are vague, but it seems that members played games such as chess and dominoes and were sometimes joined by 'decent people' – presumably volunteers from outside the prison – but not by the governor or his staff. Eventually the prison had two leagues with a total of 226 members. Mrs Dowson claimed that the organisation gave the men 'a public opinion and in addition to mental health, something to look forward to and a reasonable interest in the corporate life of the prison' and that she had learned that prisoners did not want to be preached to or patronised, 'just treated as human beings'.[32] Her initiative in establishing the league was generously covered by the feminist press and penal reform journals.[33] This scheme could be interpreted as yet another form, albeit subtle, of surveillance and control over prisoners, but its establishment by Mrs Dowson is also indicative of the way in which feminist women readily undertook schemes for reforming penal treatment, even that of adult males.

Work with younger men, who were potentially susceptible to 'motherly' influences, was more readily regarded as 'women's work'. In another initiative, 30 women were recruited to visit young offenders in Wormwood Scrubs under the direction of a salaried social worker, Mrs Le Mesurier. Her charitably funded and professionally organised work also received extensive coverage from the feminist press and was strongly supported by Margery Fry and Alexander Paterson.[34]

Despite the public perception that criminals were increasingly being 'pampered' in the country's penal establishments, budgets remained very tight even after the Second World War and voluntary efforts continued to provide many 'extras' such as educational facilities. Margery Fry herself had served as Holloway's first 'honorary' education advisor in the 1920s. In 1945 Xenia Field, a London JP and former Labour councillor, organised the first 'Field Lecture' in Holloway, which appropriately enough, consisted of an address by Cicely Hamilton on 'Votes for Women'. Hamilton had, of course, been imprisoned there as a suffragette. Field interestingly recalled that Hamilton's 'story of her struggle for social justice appealed strongly to her audience'.[35] The initiative must have been something of a success as the so-called Field Lectures were later extended to the men's jails in London and were joined by concerts and entertainments, all organised by Field herself, who also took an interest in the prison libraries and publicly appealed for book donations.[36] At this time government funding for educational and cultural activities in prison was still very limited: in 1947 the Home Office revealed in a written parliamentary answer that only £37, 10 shillings and 5d had been spent on garden tools, entertainment, materials for needlework classes and radio licences and equipment for Holloway in the previous year.[37]

In 1952 the principle of female leadership in penal institutions for women was enshrined in legislation: the Prison Act of that year effectively provided that there should be 'positive discrimination'. The same year Joanna Kelley, a Cambridge economics graduate, replaced the retiring Mary Size in charge of the new Askham Grange Open Prison for Women near York and seven years later she took the helm at Holloway. Lady Taylor then moved up to become an assistant prison commissioner.[38] It seems therefore that the demands made by the WFL in the interwar years had at last been met. WFL members were firm believers in equal opportunities and fair treatment rather than favours for women. They nevertheless consistently argued that women should be in charge of women. However, for equal rights feminists this was not necessarily a matter of ensuring 'maternal justice' in the way of the nineteenth-century-American reformers discussed by Freedman, but rather a more pragmatic and twentieth-century-response to the existing situation in Britain by effectively calling for a form of 'affirmative action'. Fundamentally feminists were interested in establishing a woman's right to leadership roles and to professional employment and status. But British women did not merely wait for the appointments to be made: they meanwhile continued to 'fill the gaps' and provide through voluntary effort many imaginative schemes aimed at making improvements – however small – in the lives of the country's prisoners.[39]

In the event the era of female-only leadership in England's women's prisons was fairly brief. Shortly after the commencement of the Sex Discrimination Act in 1976 (which repealed the clause of the 1952 Prisons Act referred to above) the *Daly Mail* carried an interview with the newly-appointed, male deputy governor of Holloway, who was erroneously described as 'the first *man*' to hold the post.[40] This was, of course, very far from the case, but it indicates perhaps how 'normal' the situation of a woman in charge had become by the 1970s as well as suggesting a great deal of historical amnesia and poor journalistic research.

The treatment of women in prison

All the activity surrounding prison-visiting naturally brought volunteer women a greater understanding of the conditions under which inmates were living and helped to prompt campaigns for improvements in penal treatment. Yet there was often a marked divergence between what the authorities said about changing penal conditions and the views expressed by the (usually middle-class) authors of exposés of life 'inside'. Prison visitors and penal reformers seem to have occupied almost any position on the continuum between the two extremes. The HLPR has been portrayed as an 'insider' pressure group, which cultivated close relationships with the Prison Commission and the Home Office to the extent that it may have been 'subject to bureaucratic colonisation'.[41] While it was certainly the case that Margery Fry and other leading League members enjoyed excellent social and political connections, their closeness to government did not preclude the adoption of a critical attitude and some healthy scepticism concerning the achievements of the prison reform programme. In the early decades of its publication the *Howard Journal* ran an occasional series entitled 'Prisoners' Forum' in which former convicts gave their own analyses of the progress – and limits – of change in the penal system.[42] The journal also included reviews of many of the prisoners' published memoirs. Moreover, the first-hand experiences of the suffragettes and conscientious objectors – which had given early impetus to the Prison Reform League and the Labour Research Department's 1922 Prison System Enquiry Report – were not swiftly forgotten either by the individuals involved or by their friends.

Feminist penal reformers therefore cannot have been unaware of the criticisms made periodically of the treatment of women in England's prisons. Sometimes the critique came from an unexpected quarter: those who had been in positions of authority in the penal system. A prime example came in Dr Gordon's *Penal Discipline*, an outspoken indictment of the existing system.[43] Gordon had been a secret supporter of the WSPU in the period immediately before the First World War, until the discovery of her letters to Emmeline Pethick Lawrence during a police raid on the suffragette group's headquarters precipitated a damaging conflict with her employers in the Prison Commission and the Home Office.[44] But although Gordon was highly critical of the penal regime in general and the girls' borstal in particular, she had little time for reformers who were simply interested in ameliorating prison conditions. Nor was she particularly concerned about the smaller details of prison life. Unlike her friend, Emmeline Pethick Lawrence, who later recalled the harsh conditions she had endured in Holloway, Mary Gordon thought the 'coarse food and clothing' was a good enough for most inmates and represented a punishment only for the 'refined and well-brought-up prisoner'.[45] Despite her undoubted feminist sympathies (which came over clearly in her discussion of the solicitation laws) Gordon was contemptuous of 'every shade of crank and amateur [who] took me on in turns' and of the misguided philanthropists who wanted to send cakes to prisoners or who asked her to intercede with the Home Secretary on behalf of 'some poor dear'.[46] Gordon's critique of the system, which was much more profound than a focus on mere material conditions or on individual miscarriages of justice, will be returned to later in this chapter.

They Always Come Back by Cicely McCall, published in 1938, also recorded the observations of a former prison service employee, albeit one in a less exalted position than Dr Gordon. McCall, a psychiatric social worker, first experienced Holloway as a visitor and then later as an officer. Like Gordon's, her book occupies the significant terrain between the general complacency of prison memoirs from figures of authority, such as governors, and the more subjective but penetrating accounts of former inmates.[47] Significantly, McCall's book contained a foreword by the popular novelist, E. M. Delafield. Renowned for her witty insights into the life of the eponymous 'Provincial Lady' diarist serialised in *Time and Tide*, Delafield (her real name was Elizabeth Dashwood) was also a JP in Devon. She was a close friend and holiday companion of McCall's, but there is no reason to doubt Delafield's sincerity when she confessed in the foreword that she would never again be able to use the 'comfortable phrase, "the whole [penal] system is so much better than it used to be"'.[48] McCall first briefly described her initial visit to the women's prison, when the officer who showed her round used the memorable phrase that McCall took as her book title. Thereafter she catalogued a series of complaints, many of which were reprised in prisoners' 'memoirs' of Holloway during the next 25 years: the superficial medical examinations, poor clothing, dirt and petty rules.

More significantly, McCall made the serious allegation that attempts by the authorities in the preceding decade to improve the lot of the prisoner had had little impact in Holloway, but instead were applied almost entirely within men's institutions.[49] For example, the scheme for prisoner earnings, so strongly supported by the HLPR, was only introduced into Holloway in 1938, around a decade after it was pioneered in Nottingham and Wakefield jails. This delay can hardly be ascribed to trade union opposition (which was sometimes an obstacle where men's work was concerned)[50] or necessarily to the Victorian infrastructure of Holloway, since the earnings scheme was successfully introduced in the even older Maidstone prison in the early 1930s.[51] McCall also criticised the lack of cultural activities in Holloway (she was writing some years before Xenia Field's initiative began). In effect, her contention was that female prisoners were neglected in a system that was tailored to men, a remarkably similar argument to some 'second wave' feminists' views about the 'invisibility' of women offenders.[52] McCall gave the example of the prisoners' newspaper, introduced in the 1930s and printed at Maidstone prison where a Paterson-recruited reformer was governor. To McCall, this was a perfect example of 'one of those . . . reforms so excellent in theory and worth so little in practice', at least to the women of

Holloway, since around a quarter of the space was devoted to football results! She claimed that she had sent cuttings herself to the editor of the newssheet for inclusion, but that only two of them – about the zoo – had been printed.[53] Although a trivial example, McCall evidently felt this was indicative of the neglect of women in the penal system which resulted in them not receiving equivalent treatment to men's.

Of course, as Alyson Brown has recently demonstrated in the case of Dartmoor Prison, the reforms of the interwar period did not impact equally on all the men's establishments either.[54] Nevertheless, Holloway and its inmates were at a distinct disadvantage in the interwar years, as they arguably continued to be afterwards. Because the women's prison population was so much smaller than men's, and was falling in this period, the jail catered for women from far and wide.[55] Effectively, it was the 'local' prison for the south of England, as well as a 'convict' prison for women convicted of penal servitude (until its abolition in 1948). In addition Holloway housed from time to time remand prisoners, borstal 'recalls', 'preventive detainees', 'corrective trainees' and all the other categories of prisoners invented periodically by government. Such 'classification' as there was of these disparate groups took place in the one institution, whereas men were often separated into completely different facilities. Furthermore, Holloway's large 'catchment' area was also a source of inequality with men, since female prisoners were even more likely to be kept geographically remote from their families. Women prisoners were also more prone to be 'inside' for short spells occasioned by minor offences or inability to pay fines and thus lacked any access to the rehabilitative schemes and earned 'privileges' aimed at long-term inmates, such as participation in evening classes.[56] Such gender inequality in penal treatment was over and above the more obvious distinctions made between men and women that related to biological differences and the latter's culturally determined domestic role. Feminist penal reformers in the interwar period were well aware of all the criticism (which it must be reiterated, is not dissimilar to the critiques of the 1970s and beyond) and problems related to the women's prison regimes were widely discussed at gatherings of women JPs and feminist and penal reform pressure groups in the late 1930s. Attention often focused on the unsuitable nature of the accommodation for remand prisoners, but reformers were also supportive of plans afoot shortly before the outbreak of war to close London's women's prison and replace it with a 'cottage style' institution in the country,[57] presumably on the lines of the much-admired Clinton Farms and Bedford Hills reformatories in the United States.

These plans, however, were to come to nought and the onset of war in 1939 provoked further controversy over conditions in Holloway, prompted once more by the imprisonment of articulate, educated, middle-class political 'offenders', this time as a result of their conscientious objection to registration for war work. On this occasion the assault, led by a Quaker scientist, Dr Kathleen Lonsdale and a new pressure group, the Prison Medical Reform Council (PMRC), called into question the stance both of the HLPR and of the NCW, and highlighted the continuing synergies between the supporters of pacifism, feminism and penal reform.

By the 1940s, Lonsdale, a crystallographer, had established a distinguished career in research chemistry in addition to becoming the mother of three children.[58] Looking back on her life in 1970 she claimed to have enjoyed three lives, one as a 'housewife', mother and grandmother; a second as a Quaker, 'old lag' and borstal Visitor; and a third as a scientist and teacher of science.[59] Superficially, Lonsdale can be seen as a pioneer for the 'having it all' generation of high-achieving women that was to emerge in the second half of the twentieth century, especially in view of the fact that her self-described status as an 'old lag' had failed to prevent her election to the Royal Society as one of the first two women 'fellows' and her appointment as a Dame of the British Empire in 1956. But, however brief her spell at His Majesty's Pleasure as a result of her principled refusal to register for civil defence was,[60] her weeks in Holloway undoubtedly had a profound effect upon Lonsdale. Her pamphlet for the PMRC, written shortly after her release, detailed the unsanitary state of her cell at Holloway (in which she found dried bread crusts and faeces), the lack of hair combs, handkerchiefs, soap and toilet paper, shortage of sanitary towels and dirty clothing.[61] In short, she had found the jail to be an affront to civilisation, deficient in basic hygiene. Obviously her scientific expertise as well as her lucidity made this critique especially powerful. Interestingly, many of the specific points she made – such as the cursory nature of the 'medical' on admission to the jail – were similar to those in McCall's book, as well as later accounts, although the official response at the time was that conditions had temporarily worsened at the start of the War[62] (Lonsdale was imprisoned early in 1942).

In addition to Lonsdale's broadside against the treatment of prisoners in Holloway, the PMRC pamphlet contained contributions from four other women who had been 'inside' for similar reasons, including Sybil Morrison, a pacifist former WSPU member and lover of Dorothy Evans (one of the leading feminists of her generation).[63] Morrison and Evans were listed on the pamphlet as sponsors of the PMRC along with 25 other names, more or less comprising the 'usual suspects', including Maude Royden, Vera Brittain, E. M. Delafield and Fenner Brockway. The PMRC revelations created quite a stir in feminist and penal reform circles. The matter divided members of the NCW's Public Service and Magistrates' Committee, some of whom, such as Florence Earengey (Chairman of the Holloway Visiting Justices) thought the claims 'exaggerated', while others were more inclined to believe the testimony of as respected a scientist and credible a witness as Lonsdale. However, NCW members were mindful of the fact that by the time the crisis over Lonsdale's allegations occurred Dr Taylor had taken over as governor, and they were anxious not to do anything that might undermine confidence in the first woman to be placed in charge of Holloway.[64] Solidarity with pioneer women criminal justice professionals was clearly a major factor to the committee members, most of whom were magistrates.

Similarly the HLPR faced a crisis over the emergence of the PMRC as a rival, and seemingly more radical, pressure group. Yet with hindsight there seems to have been little cause for serious concern on the part of League members. The HLPR was certainly not inactive in response to Lonsdale revelations: in 1943 Eleanor Rathbone was briefed for parliamentary questions by the League's secretary, Cicely Craven, and the latter joined a deputation of Margery Fry and the NCW magistrates' convenor, Mrs Holman, to the Prison Commission.[65] Moreover, despite its impressive list of sponsors, the PMRC probably had very few members (most were conscientious objectors whose main political commitment was to pacifism) and a shoestring budget – nothing like the resources of all kinds that the HLPR had at its disposal. Nevertheless there is evidence that League activists felt rather threatened by the new group, especially when the latter put up some of its members for election to the Howard League executive.[66] The HLPR chairman, George Benson MP, was certainly dismissive of the PMRC whose propaganda he regarded as 'too emotional'[67] and there is clear justification for Mick Ryan's view that Benson was not prepared to risk the excellent access he had to the Home Office as a member of the government's Advisory Council on the Treatment of Offenders by courting any association with as radical a group as the PMRC.[68] However, it is not the case that HLPR executive members were completely unsympathetic: the League's objections to the PMRC can be interpreted as mainly tactical and a few of its executive members even joined the new association and tacitly supported the suggestion of a merger between the groups when it was proposed in 1945.[69] More importantly, the whole episode ensured that the treatment of women prisoners again became a high priority for the Howard League, a pressure group that is often assumed to have been dominated by men and men's issues. In 1945 Cicely Craven, Margery Fry and Theodora Calvert drew up a 16-point plan on behalf of the HLPR for the improvement of conditions in Holloway and for the remainder of the 1940s the League women kept a close eye on developments in the prison and liaised with sympathetic MPs (notably the ex-suffragette Barbara Ayrton Gould, and Florence Paton, wife of another MP and HLPR executive member, John Paton) in order to bring the problems of women prisoners to light through parliamentary activity.[70]

The Prison Reform Council (which had dropped 'medical' from its title) undoubtedly helped to refocus attention on some of the problems faced by women prisoners.[71] It also seems to have reinvigorated the campaigning zeal of some key women members of the HLPR in circumstances not dissimilar to those that had originally prompted the formation of the Penal Reform League during the suffrage era. Notwithstanding the fears of Benson and the faintly contemptuous attitude towards the radicals evinced by the League's first historian Gordon Rose in his 1961 account,[72] it was probably stimulating for the HLPR to reconnect with some of its roots in feminism, pacifism and Quakerism. Meanwhile, Sybil Morrison (whose account of her sentence, 'Holloway in the Blitz', was published in the *Howard Journal* before the formation of the PMRC)[73] and Kathleen Lonsdale both became Howard League members – Morrison being elected to the Executive.

Lonsdale, an eminent scientist and hard-working woman in her prime was a valuable recruit to the cause and remained interested in penal reform for the rest of her life. In 1949 she was appointed (probably at the League's suggestion) to the Board of Visitors at Aylesbury Girls' Borstal and in 1962 took on the same role at a new institution at Bullwood Hall in Essex.[74] Although she seems not to have belonged to any women's organisations (with the not insignificant exception of the Women's International League for Peace and Freedom [WILPF] of which she was for a while the British president) Lonsdale was undoubtedly a feminist according to the definition laid out in this book's introduction.[75] However, despite the overwhelming impact of her (relatively short) stay in Holloway, and her undoubted interest in the borstal 'girls', Lonsdale does not appear to have identified particularly strongly with them, separated as they were from her by age, class and education. Nevertheless she was an assiduous attendee at the Bullwood Hall board meetings and the Magistrates Association-organised conferences for Visitors, fitting her voluntary activities into a busy work schedule as an academic and mother.[76]

Notwithstanding the changes introduced in Holloway by Dr Taylor during the 1950s the HLPR kept up the pressure for further improvements to the regime. The publication in 1952 of Joan Henry's damning indictment of conditions in Holloway – which she contrasted with a more positive depiction of the 'open' system at Askham Grange – and the subsequent release of the film adaptation of her book (*The Weak and the Wicked* starring Glynis Johns and Diana Dors) put women's prisons back in the headlines. Once again Benson appeared to side with the Prison Commission and was quoted in the press making negative comments about the book. Mrs Allen, a member of the HLPR and the Magistrates' Association, objected to his stance. The League's executive therefore agreed on a carefully worded press statement 'regretting the inaccuracies and exaggerations in the book' but agreeing with the author 'that the regime in Holloway requires revision' including, in the short term, better sanitation, fresh fruit and vegetables for expectant and nursing mothers, more work and educational facilities.[77] It is worth noting that, once again, women activists took charge of HLPR policy where Holloway was concerned, refusing to allow Benson to control the pressure group's strategy. This incident suggests too that intra-League politics was not quite as consensual or as dominated by a male, metropolitan elite as is sometimes suggested.[78]

Borstals

In the 1950s the women of the HLPR Executive also turned their attention to the problems of the young women serving their sentences in borstal institutions. As already mentioned, the initial regime of the girls' borstal in Aylesbury had been condemned by Mary Gordon in 1922. The borstal had been opened alongside the inebriate reformatory (itself a failing institution) and the women's convict prison in 1909. The concept of borstal training, based around military-style discipline, physical activity and the possibility of advancement through grades was originally developed by Sir Evelyn Ruggles-Brise entirely with young men in mind. Gordon argued that this regime, in its adapted, feminised form was counterproductive and untenable. She described the girls' work as 'dull' and 'at a very low level', the staff as too busy to show inmates an example and the rewards offered for good behaviour as so insubstantial as to offer no real incentive for reform.[79] The result, Gordon stated, was either the cultivation of passivity in the girls or outbursts of hysteria and violence. Shockingly, she claimed that while just one out of 226 borstal 'lads' were put in irons the figure for Aylesbury girls was one in eight. Indeed, the

Prison Commission report for 1921–2 recorded 111 cases of violence in that year at the girls' borstal of which 33 resulted in the use of physical restraint by handcuffs and straitjackets.[80] Furthermore, Gordon argued that there was no necessary correlation between doing well in the borstal system and truly being reformed since the regime provided no scope for inmates to demonstrate any real improvement or trustworthiness.[81]

In 1923 Gordon's damning account of the application of the borstal system to girls was reported by the *Woman's Leader*[82] and throughout the 1920s the feminist–penal–reform network kept a close eye on subsequent developments at Aylesbury as the regime was changed by Lillian Barker. Barker was already well known to the women's movement through her work at Woolwich Arsenal during the war and her role as Executive Officer for the Central Committee on Women's Training and Employment from 1920 to 1923, although according to her niece, she was not herself a feminist, despite 'applaud[ing] the aims of the suffrage movement'.[83] Barker was personally selected by Alexander Paterson, an Oxford-educated social reformer, who on his appointment as Prison Commissioner in 1922 set about changing the ethos of the borstals by aiming to replace penal discipline with self-discipline.[84] Paterson famously remarked that '[i]f the institution is to train lads for freedom, it cannot train them in an atmosphere of captivity and repression'.[85] Barker endorsed his aims and claimed that under her tutelage the girls too would learn 'how to use [their] freedom' through a 'system of self-government'.[86] In common with her counterparts in the 'lad's' borstals, she organised day trips for trusted 'trainees' and in 1924 *The Vote* reported approvingly of her 'experiment' in taking 19 'girls' on a seaside holiday.[87] Although the Paterson/Barker approach may seem to be simply a more subtle form of social control than the overt discipline of the Ruggles-Brise era, or could even be described as naïve,[88] it was undoubtedly less punitive than the old system that Gordon had criticised and it was heartily endorsed by feminist penal reformers. Barker was invited to address women's organisations while groups of inquisitive women magistrates were welcomed to Aylesbury by the new governor to see the changed uniforms, the educational classes and meals taken 'in association'.

Despite the reforms, the regime at the borstal remained a cause for concern. Visitors, impressed by the transformation of cells into 'bedrooms', the organised games and the swimming pool were of course unlikely to see the 'smashing up' episodes, which, as Barker acknowledged, still occurred during her reign.[89] Although the recidivism statistics for borstal 'graduates' in the 1930s suggested that Paterson's approach was producing encouraging results, even Barker's legendary charisma could not ensure complete success: McCall's text includes an apocryphal quotation from a Holloway inmate ruefully remarking, 'I don't know wot [sic] Miss Barker'd say to me', and some years later Joan Henry described borstal as 'a preparatory school for Holloway'.[90] Women's organisations were not unaware of the problems and continued to take a keen interest in the borstal in the 1940s. According to Barker's successor at Aylesbury, in a speech to Hampshire's women JPs, the onset of war had 'complicated the training' and made the girls 'excited and unbalanced'[91] (like her predecessor, she clearly regarded 'the girls' as 'over-sexed'[92]). Even in wartime there were problems finding the inmates work after their release on licence and apparently even the Land Army had refused to take them.[93] The problems continued after the war: by the late 1940s girls awaiting allocation either to Aylesbury or to the new 'open' institution at Sutton Park in Kent, as well as borstal 'recalls' (those who had broken the terms of their licence), were sent to Holloway, a place which penal reformers were convinced was most unsuitable, especially for younger women.

After the war, women activists in the HLPR also became concerned over the mental health of women in borstals. However the evidence suggests that they did not necessarily accept some of the prevailing discourses concerning deviant women's supposed innate 'abnormality',[94] instead arguing that the conditions of captivity were in themselves destructive of mental health. Although the medically qualified Mary Gordon had argued in 1922 that *some* prisoners required psychiatric treatment, she by no means advocated a wholesale medicalisation of female deviance, rather she argued that the circumstances of captivity themselves and poor penal methods bred the neurotic, emotional states that precipitated 'smashing up' and the consequent use of punishment and restraint.[95] As already stated, the new penal strategies of the inter-war period had not solved the problem and the system still had adverse and probably unintended consequences for mental health. At Aylesbury 'smashing up' continued to be a problem and in 1949 the HLPR raised concerns over restraining techniques and close confinement via a parliamentary question and a deputation to Lionel Fox, the Chairman of the Prison Commission.[96]

The issue was brought to the HLPR executive by Mrs Strand, a Visitor at Aylesbury. She was not satisfied that the Home Office statistics on punishments, given in the parliamentary answer, were accurate and she subsequently resigned from the Board of Visitors. Moreover she claimed to know of borstal girls who had been mentally certified simply for having illegitimate children. Another HLPR executive member, Madeleine Robinson, also took up the question of mental health: she was concerned about some girls who had been sent to Broadmoor Hospital from the borstal, at least one of whom had allegedly only been brought before the courts as in need of 'care and protection' and not for a criminal offence.[97] In 1954 Robinson, Margery Fry and Violet Creech Jones[98] became agitated about the borstal girls sent to Holloway for psychiatric treatment, apparently because no psychiatrist was employed – even part-time – at Aylesbury.[99] Once again, it seemed that female prisoners were disadvantaged in comparison with their male counterparts as the borstals for 'lads' had more psychiatrically trained staff. Using their tried and tested tactics, the HLPR women organised parliamentary questions to elicit information about the situation, this time through Peggy Herbison, a Labour MP. A HLPR deputation consisting of Fry (now aged 80), Dr Marjorie Franklin, a psychoanalyst and pioneer of environmental therapy[100] and Mrs Brophy visited Aylesbury but found the governor there hostile to the idea of psychiatric treatment.[101] The HLPR women continued to champion its use and openly question why such facilities as therapeutic communities were available in men's institutions, but not in women's.

Although feminists and penal reformers during the period 1922–55 generally welcomed official attempts to make the borstal system an effective method of rehabilitation and reform of 'difficult' young people, they were not without their criticisms of the system even in the era when the penal–welfare ideology of Paterson predominated. They should not, therefore be seen as cat's-paws for the government or the Prison Commission even though, as practically minded pressure group activists, they were ever conscious of what R. A. Butler called, 'the art of the possible'. Nor can they be stereotyped as uninformed, sentimental do-gooders, always on 'the side' of the prisoners and lacking any concept of justice. Women like Margery Fry, Madeleine Robinson and Marjorie Franklin were intelligent and creative women who were well acquainted with the problems and paradoxes of the penal system and never felt able to offer any easy solutions to them. Perhaps that was the reason why they seemed to concentrate so much on the amelioration of seemingly small details of prison life on the understanding that for people who had to endure the 'unpleasant sensation when the iron door was slammed and the key turned'[102] the little things mattered. But the feminist penal reformers did not ignore the bigger picture either, as the next section of this chapter shows.

Aftercare and alternatives

By and large the feminist–criminal–justice reform network took an active interest in arrangements for the aftercare of prisoners, both male and female. Women JPs, especially, were apt to bring their experience of practical social work to bear in adopting a 'casework' approach and following the later careers of the offenders who had appeared before them. Lady Reading JP (founder of the Women's Voluntary Service) defined aftercare as 'the applied endeavour to prevent a man returning to crime':[103] as such it was envisaged by its advocates in the twentieth century as part of the wider rehabilitative project of penal welfarism. The effectiveness of penalties could only be evaluated through following the subsequent careers of offenders and in the absence of any systematic study women magistrates often undertook this work themselves. Feminist penal reformers were vociferous enthusiasts for the commissioning of 'scientific' study and university-based research aimed at following up ex-offenders, both young and old, and calculating rates of recidivism.[104] In the meantime their anecdotal impressions gathered in the course of their work as JPs caused many of the campaigners seriously to doubt the rehabilitative qualities of prison sentences, particularly, but not exclusively, in the case of women offenders.[105]

Aftercare for adult offenders was mainly a matter for the voluntary sector until the 1960s. Only former borstal trainees, who were catered for by the Borstal Association from 1908, corrective trainees and preventive trainees had any statutory provision.[106] The voluntary discharged prisoners' aid societies (DPAS) originated from the activities of prison visitors during the nineteenth century, for example those of the working-class philanthropist, Sarah Martin who used money from Elizabeth Fry's British Ladies' Society to set up a fund for discharged prisoners in Yarmouth during the 1830s.[107] Prochaska has argued that the Prison Commission's success in restricting the access of women visitors to prisons after the Commission took full charge in 1877 prompted philanthropists to turn their attention to DPAS.[108] However, as with assisting former workhouse inmates, there were inherent problems in this type of philanthropic project. Activists not only had to contend with the bureaucratic attitudes of officials in charge of the state-run institutions, they could also face indifference from the public who often viewed ex-prisoners as undeserving of their financial assistance. Whereas the earliest efforts tended to concentrate on giving immediate charitable aid if requested, DPAS also initiated schemes for hostels and 'halfway houses', institutions which were seen as especially relevant to the need of women ex-offenders.

It is surely no coincidence that Holloway's DPAS was set up in 1922, shortly after the appointment of the first women Visiting Magistrates. It originally raised money from the 13 counties for which the London jail was the 'local' women's prison, it later raised to 16. The society supported a hostel near to the prison, in Dalmeny Avenue,[109] the same road that Margery Fry lived in. Visiting justices played an important part in the organisation. In 1939 Florence Earengey became the chairman of the Holloway DPAS and, according to Mary Size, who clearly had great admiration for her, '[w]ith almost super-human effort . . . kept the [DPAS] branch in existence all through the war years when several other branches failed to function'.[110] Later, when Holloway's management was under the leadership of Joanna Kelley, the governor herself took a lead in the organisation of welfare work with prisoners both before and after release, spearheading in the early 1960s the transformation of the prison's DPAS into the Griffins Society in response to the development of statutory aftercare led by the probation service.[111]

Despite these continuing voluntary efforts, feminist reformers were by no means convinced that the imprisonment of women was capable of achieving rehabilitative objectives in view of the well-known rates of recidivism. Mary Gordon was blunt about the system she had inspected:

> During my service I found nothing in the prison system to interest me, except as a gigantic irrelevance – a social curiosity. If the system had a good effect on any prisoner, I failed to mark it. I have no shadow of doubt of its power to demoralise, or of its cruelty. It appears to me not to belong to this time or to civilisation at all.[112]

As well as criticising the borstal at Aylesbury, Gordon was scathing about the local prisons claiming that they failed to deter, reform or even annoy their clients: 'as a vindication of the law, [they are] merely a bad joke', she concluded.[113] The thoroughness of her critique of her subject – 'penal discipline' – should not be underestimated. She viewed the convict prisons and inebriate reformatory as every bit as conducive to the passivity of inmates as the borstal regime. 'As long as we give [the prisoner] no outlet, but foster in him [sic] those emotional states which lead to unreality and fresh crime, he will remain our manufactured article', she wrote.[114] Moreover, her solution to the problem was potentially as far-reaching and her attitude as dismissive of piecemeal improvements in penal routines as that of the 'Alternatives to Holloway' campaign led by the Radical Alternatives to Prison (RAP) group 50 years after her book appeared.[115]

> We talk endlessly about proceeding step by step, and manage, withal, to cling to the bad elements of our old system, while adding small 'reforms' and ameliorations as a salve to our consciences. The piano, the concert, educational lecture . . . – all these things and more, we bestow on our captive to enable her to bear our discipline better . . . But the prisoner will tell you that if you really want to lighten her sentence, the way to do so is to let her out of prison.[116]

While she gave few precise details of her alternative penal policy, Gordon compared the treatment in England's jails unfavourably with the regimes in France, and argued for measures that would assist offenders to manage their lives outside prison, for example by deferring the execution of sentences.

Gordon's critique of the penal system was picked up and endorsed by the feminist–criminal–justice reform network. A reviewer in the *Woman's Leader* concluded that on the basis of Gordon's evidence '[t]he prison system appears . . . not so much cruel as costly and useless'.[117] The pointlessness of short sentences, on which so many women were incarcerated in the local prisons, was widely discussed and understood by women JPs, and the enthusiasm penal reformers showed for the palliatives mentioned by Gordon should not be taken to infer that they were unaware of any deeper problems with the system. Probation was undoubtedly a favoured alternative, especially for younger women offenders, and in the interwar period there was much optimism about its efficacy. In 1930 Jean Dewar Robertson JP told *The Vote* that 'the best way to keep young people out of prison is not to send them there' and attributed the falling numbers in Holloway to magistrates' use of probation orders.[118]

The feminist critique concerned not only the short-term imprisonment of fine defaulters, alcoholics and prostitutes, none of whom in their view were suitable for penal treatment, but also encompassed the specific problems of mothers in prison. In 1930 Miss Kelly JP wrote to the *Magistrate* to propose that pregnant prisoners should be transferred to outside hospitals for their confinements, a recommendation that had been endorsed by the Magistrates' Association by 1938.[119] Although this recommendation was made mainly in the interests of the child rather than the mother, it is nevertheless interesting in view of the fact that hospital confinements were becoming more common among the general population at this time. Feminist magistrates do not seem to have dissented from the view that motherhood was of central importance in women's lives but were generally hopeful that women sent to prison for child cruelty could be educated out of their ways. Perhaps in anticipation of the post-war vogue for domesticity the plan drawn up by HLPR women activists for Holloway in 1945 included the provision of training schemes with an emphasis on 'house craft and mother craft'.[120] But Margery Fry retained a critical attitude towards definitions of 'cruelty' by mothers (which she translated as 'in every case *neglect*') and quoted Dr Charity Taylor's research on women sent to Holloway for the offence which found them to suffer from 'bad health, bad husbands, bad luck, bad surroundings & anaemia, "the occupational disease of the housewife"'. Furthermore, ever the supporter of gender equality, Fry added that 'a similar report on men imprisoned for this dangerous offence is needed', and referred to a scheme in Sweden where parental rights were withdrawn from abusers.[121]

Importantly, feminist penal reformers were also concerned about the admission into prison of women with young children. The theories concerning 'maternal deprivation' associated with John Bowlby are of particular significance in this context. In 1953 Margery Fry edited and abridged an edition of Bowlby's report 'Maternal Care and Mental Health' which was originally written for the World Health Organisation.[122] Her royalties were donated to the Howard League's research into cruelty to children. Fry was an enthusiast for what she saw as the progressive nature of Bowlby's work, but her support for attachment theory did not entail a thoroughgoing acceptance of the belief that married women should be confined to home, since she openly expressed admiration for working mothers.[123] Meanwhile, her HLPR colleague, Madeleine Robinson, who by 1953 was chairman of the Holloway Visiting Justices, made use of the maternal deprivation thesis specifically to argue *against* the practice of imprisoning the mothers of young children for child neglect.[124] A Gloucestershire JP, Clare Spurgin, made a similar point when she appealed to her fellow magistrates not to send neglectful mothers to jail: 'by sending her to prison you break the family link, a link which it is vital to preserve', she told them.[125]

Thus, a decade or more before the genesis of the 'second wave' critique of women's imprisonment, the feminist penal reformers of the 'first wave' had developed their own critical analysis of Britain's penal policy as it applied to women. Plans for alternatives to short sentences were widely discussed. However, it would be misleading to suggest that every campaigner was of the same view. For example, Barbara Wootton, who was for many years a JP in London, was highly sceptical of

Bowlby's theories: she ridiculed his popularisers in particular for con-
flating what she saw as the 'common-sense' notion that 'children (like
their elders) need to be dependably loved'[126] with the proposition of a
specific link between a child's separation from their mother and his or
her subsequent delinquency. More generally, Wootton also objected to
the predominance of individualised and psychological 'explanations' of
social pathology over sociological ones. Later, in the late 1960s and
1970s, the plans for the rebuilding of Holloway were also to prove controversial with the next generation of campaigners. But as this section
shows, feminist penal reformers of the 1920s–50s did raise their gaze
from the immediate consideration of the intricate details of prison life
to question the broader concept of carceral punishment and the treatment of women 'inside'.

Women and the campaign against the death penalty

Undoubtedly the most unfortunate of all the women detained in
Holloway, from its inauguration as a women's prison in 1902 until the
1950s, were the occupants of its 'condemned' cells. 15 women were executed in England and Wales between 1900 and the suspension of the
death penalty in 1965. Many more occupied the countries' condemned
cells after a death sentence had been pronounced upon them and before
their sentence was commuted: in all 130 women were sentenced to
death between 1900 and 1950.[127] As Ballinger points out, most of these
women were convicted of killing their own infant child, a crime for
which no women was executed in England and Wales after 1849. This
convention, however, did not spare them from being placed under sentence of death by the black-capped judge and held temporarily in the
condemned cell, before changes to the procedure were made under the
Infanticide Acts of 1922 and 1938. As this section shows, the first of
these Acts was a direct result of feminist pressure, which was arguably
particularly effective so soon after women's partial enfranchisement and
entry to the magistracy.

Narratives of the twentieth- century-campaign against the death
penalty seldom make much mention of its gendered aspects, perhaps
because the overwhelming majority of capital convicts were male. While
the value to the abolitionists of well-publicised and notorious executions
in the 1950s is generally acknowledged, including that of Ruth Ellis (executed in 1955 for the murder of her former lover and the last woman to
be hanged in England), several accounts surprisingly fail to recognise the
pivotal importance of the hanging of Edith Thompson in January 1923,

despite abundant evidence of a surge of interest in the question of the death penalty immediately following her execution.[128] While it is important for historical analysis to avoid the fallacy of 'post hoc, ergo propter hoc', Block and Hostettler are perhaps too tentative in their suggestion that the flurry of parliamentary questions about the death penalty in the early months of 1923 might or might not have been connected to Thompson's execution.[129] Thus some of the key gender issues in the campaign are neglected in their account. In addition, male parliamentarians tend to take centre stage in accounts of the anti-capital punishment campaign despite clear evidence of the close interest taken in this issue by women.

Feminist concern over the death penalty goes back at least to 1908 when the WFL and the WSPU took up the case of Daisy Lord, a young, working-class, unmarried woman who had been found guilty of murdering her newborn child. A sustained campaign was organised by the two militant suffrage societies as well as by the socialist paper, *The Clarion*, against Lord's death sentence.[130] However, petitions and letters calling for the reprieve of particular individuals were a regular feature of the narrative of capital cases: opposition to the *principle* of the death penalty was quite another matter. In the case of the WFL it seems that at least some of the women's suffrage movement had crossed that line, although opposition initially focused on the use of the death sentence in infanticide cases. As Daniel Grey points out, the feminist stance involved a critique of normative masculinity, and the perceived sexual 'double standards' that left poor, single women condemned by an unwanted pregnancy while their erstwhile male partners were unaffected by the consequences of their actions;[131] as well as an indictment of the then exclusively male criminal justice system, a theme which was to become a very familiar one in WFL propaganda over the coming years. In her speech to a WFL-organised public meeting in Trafalgar Square on the Lord case, one of the League's leaders, Charlotte Despard, objected both to the 'iniquity' of the sentence and to its imposition following a trial in a court 'composed entirely of men'. Other speakers argued for a change in the law of murder (presumably along the lines of the later Infanticide Act) while Mrs Cobden Sanderson focused her attention on the ceremony of the black cap and the pronouncement of the death sentence, which she likened to a form of torture.[132]

It seems that in the period up to 1922 the feminist campaign over the death penalty was inextricably linked to the infanticide issue, perhaps because the majority of killings by women fell into this category and because these cases so graphically illustrated the gender bias of the criminal justice system and women's inferior status. The 1922 Infanticide Act can therefore be seen as part of the general legislative improvement in women's rights within the legal system which took place in the years immediately after the First World War, and, notwithstanding its problematic assumption that childbirth in itself can cause psychological imbalance, it can be regarded as a success for the women's movement. It was certainly seen that way at the time, although not all feminists or women magistrates agreed with it – Mary Gordon for one had earlier objected to what she regarded as too light sentences for child murder, as did the Winchester prison visitor – later a JP – Florence Firmstone.[133] However, the majority of the women's movement, including the women's conference of the newly formed Magistrates' Association (MA), supported what they saw as a long-overdue and sensible amendment to the law of murder.

Previous attempts to change the law (for example in the period 1908–10) had failed[134] but once again, a specific case in which a young, working-class woman had a sentence of death passed upon her was to become the catalyst for a campaign; this time the conviction of Edith Roberts for the murder of her baby girl at Leicester Assizes in June 1921. Although her death sentence was soon commuted to penal servitude for life, this case continued to cause indignation in the women's movement, not least because empanelled women had been removed from the jury at the request of the defence barrister. Not surprisingly, women magistrates, intent on underlining the necessity for women to be in judgement in cases involving other women, led the protests. Two local women JPs addressed a protest meeting in Leicester, while Margaret Lloyd George (the first woman magistrate in Wales) and Gertrude Tuckwell took up the issue with the Home Office.[135] Their initial protests centred on the allegedly excessive life sentence placed on Roberts but the campaign soon moved on to more general proposals for legal reform. In January 1922 the MA (of which Tuckwell was already a leading member) resolved to recommend to the Home Secretary that in cases where a woman was charged with the murder of her infant child, if the evidence suggested that she had not fully recovered from giving birth, the judge could advise the jury to record a verdict of manslaughter instead.[136] As Chapter 1 points out, women magistrates with suffrage movement backgrounds were heavily over-represented among active members of the MA in its early years and their impact on the Association's policy can be detected here. The following month the Labour MP, Arthur Henderson, who had been a strong supporter of women magistrates as early as 1910, introduced the Child Murder (Trial) Bill, which effectively embodied the

MA proposals. Somewhat altered (not least in respect of its title) the bill became the Infanticide Act and received its Royal Assent in July 1922.[137] Nevertheless, feminist penal reformers continued to object when women whose cases fell outside the infanticide definition of this Act were still formally sentenced to death. Therefore during the 1930s the campaign was renewed for further legislation.[138] The law was duly amended in 1938 to include cases where the victim was up to one year old.

As has already been pointed out, no hanging of a woman convicted of killing her newborn child had taken place for over 70 years until 1920. The most recent execution of a woman had been in 1907 when the baby-farmer, Rhoda Willis (alias Leslie James) was hanged in Cardiff, the only woman to be executed in Wales during the twentieth century.[139] It is therefore highly probable that many people in the early 1920s assumed that the death penalty had been effectively suspended where women were concerned.[140] This view, however, was to be exposed as thoroughly unfounded when in January 1923 Edith Thompson was executed along with her lover, Freddy Bywaters, for the murder of her husband. As already suggested, this trial and sentence appears to have had a particularly profound effect in galvanising the movement for the abolition of the death penalty and especially the involvement of feminist women within it.

There are many accounts of the Thompson-Bywaters case in print – including some fictionalised versions, but it is worth mentioning a few salient points about the case here. Edith Thompson, a successful businesswoman, had had an affair with a younger man – Bywaters – who one evening attacked and killed her husband when the married couple were walking home in Ilford. Edith was accused of inciting the murder, the key evidence against her being in the form of letters she had previously written to her lover. In court and in the press, which reported the trial in salacious detail, it was generally assumed that Edith's guilt was greater because she was the older of the two: even Cicely Hamilton referred to them as 'the woman' and 'the boy'.[141] Although the initial public reaction therefore seems to have favoured a reprieve for Bywaters rather than Thompson, as Ballinger points out, an 'alternative truth' about this case was very quickly established afterwards.[142] In fact there were multiple 'alternative' readings of the evidence[143] some of which were constructed by feminist writers who suspected that Edith's un-Victorian sexual attitudes and her relative freedom as a 'modern', married woman with her own income and the ability to realise her consumer desires herself were her real crimes. Among these were the 'true crime' writer and novelist, Fryniwyd Tennyson Jesse. According to the defence barrister, Edith was hanged 'for immorality rather than murder',[144] a view with which Tennyson Jesse obviously concurred. She later based the plot of her best-known novel, *A Pin to see the Peepshow*, published in 1934, on the Thompson-Bywaters case, obtaining background information for the passages concerning Holloway from Mary Size.[145]

Tennyson Jesse was not the only contemporary feminist to see the raw material for fiction in the case. The first novelised version of the story was *Messalina of the Suburbs*, by E. M. Delafield.[146] As already pointed out, this was the penname of Elizabeth Dashwood, a Devon JP. Delafield's novel was written in 1923, the year of the executions, and published the following year, while the public's memories of its source material were still very fresh; yet its approach was markedly different to the newspaper trial accounts. As Delafield claimed in her dedication of the novel, she was trying to 'reconstruct the psychological develop-ments that led, by inexorable degrees, to the crime of murder'.[147] Her character, Elsie Palmer, is clearly an imaginative creation, and differs from Edith in important respects not least in that Elsie is not an inde-pendent career woman but a dissatisfied, shallow housewife. Yet the similarities to the 'real life' narrative as reported in the newspapers would have been clear to the novel's readers. Like Edith, Elsie's letters to her lover prove to be her undoing and in both tales there is a key inci-dent when the woman sees her co-accused by chance in the police sta-tion and inadvertently incriminates him.[148] Nevertheless, Delafield's implication is that, whatever her fictional creation is guilty of, it is not murder. The book ends with Elsie's discussion of her case with her solic-itor and a foreshadowing of her fate – the gallows: 'inexorable results would be suffered by herself, and she would never know how it was that these things had become inevitable – had happened'.[149]

While Delafield and Tennyson Jesse fashioned their reactions to the execution of Edith Thompson into novels that explored the sexual and gender politics of the specific case, other feminists reacted by question-ing the necessity for and morality of capital punishment as a whole. But women who had devoted years of their lives to fighting for equality before the law were careful not to suggest that Thompson should be reprieved just because she was a woman. In her comments on the case Cicely Hamilton made it plain she objected to hanging per se: 'I do not want women to have any legal privilege over men', she told the *Daily Sketch*.[150] She later expanded on her theme for *Lloyds Sunday News*, out-lining her four main objections to the death penalty; its irrevocability, its ineffectiveness as a deterrent, its immorality and the actual proce-dure of judicial murder. Hamilton regarded the Thompson-Bywaters trial as 'sordid' and objected to the 'horror', 'sensationalism' and 'morbid excitement' that the whole judicial process had occasioned in this case.[151] An editorial in the WFL paper, *The Vote*, adopted a similarly high-minded tone while denouncing the 'primitive barbarity' of the executions in Holloway and Pentonville and arguing that capital punishment should be abolished outright.[152] To these feminists in the 1920s the abolition of the death penalty, like equal rights for women, was an integral part of the march of progress towards a more 'civilised' state. Moreover, women were now conscious of their potential political power and ability to comment on affairs of state and public policy. Yet another woman writer, Clemence Dane, was moved by the first execution of a woman in 17 years to take up her pen and urge readers of *Good Housekeeping* to consider the capital punishment issue when choosing how to vote.[153]

Margery Fry was also among those deeply affected by the events of January 1923. She later claimed that although she had previously 'disliked' the idea of capital punishment, she did not feel very strongly about it at first.

> I came to hate it when as a visiting magistrate I went to see Edith Thompson whilst she was awaiting execution, and saw at close quarters the effect of this – to me, barbarous – affair on the people in the great prison building which I could see from my bedroom window. The woman herself struck me as a rather foolish girl who had romanticised her sordid love affair and genuinely thought she was innocent, discounting her own influence on her lover . . . [I]t comes as a shock to find flimsy personalities involved in dramas of life and death.[154]

Margery Fry was most struck by the impact of the execution on the prison and community as a whole. She later reasoned that the real problem with capital punishment was 'the amount of collateral suffering it brings, its fecundity of evil by-products', the suffering of relatives, of prison staff and the 'intolerable strain of reversing all those instincts of humanity which are at least as strong in the officer of our prisons as they are in the population as a whole'.[155]

In fact, there is evidence that Fry as HLPR secretary had raised the issue of the death penalty with the Lord Chancellor's office as early as 1921[156] and in the following year she organised a plebiscite of League members on the issue.[157] Yet the Thompson and Bywaters executions do seem to have had a galvanising effect on abolitionists, especially women. Margaret Wintringham, the second female MP to take her seat, argued in the *Howard Journal* that capital punishment was 'a subject which specially appeals to women, because their work is to bring life into the world, to tend life, to nurture it, to protect it and to see it grow in its different stages'.[158] Wintringham's case is unusual, as most feminist abolitionists preferred to avoid arguments about women's 'special mission', whereas she appeared to embrace them.

As explained in Chapter 1, in 1923 a new campaign group was set up to oppose capital punishment, which later became the National Council for the Abolition of the Death Penalty (NCADP). Individual feminists and women's organisations such as WILPF and the WCG played an important part in this development. In 1925 Margery Fry and Geraldine Cadbury encouraged Roy Calvert, a Quaker who had decided to refuse military service during the First World War on grounds of conscience, to give up his civil service job and work full-time for the NCADP.[159] Calvert's aim, in common with Margery Fry and the HLPR, to which he also belonged, was to research the subject thoroughly and put forward 'scientific' rather than emotive arguments for abolition – no mean feat given the highly charged atmosphere in which this debate was often held. To this end Calvert studied the penal policies of both abolitionist and death penalty states as well as the criminal justice system of the UK and produced many carefully constructed arguments, for example in the NCADP evidence to the House of Commons select committee (1931) and in his pamphlets and books, including *The Lawbreaker*, co-written by his wife, Theodora, and *Capital Punishment in the Twentieth Century*. Calvert's sudden death in 1933 at the age of 35 was not only a terrible shock to his family and friends but also a blow to the campaign.[160] Nevertheless, the NCADP continued and Theodora remained an important part of it, revising Roy's work for new editions and writing her own pamphlets[161] as well as serving on the campaign executive and later the capital punishment sub-committee of the HLPR. She lived to see both the suspension and the final abolition of the death penalty in Great Britain, although her jubilation at this success for penal reform was understandably tempered by the fact that Roy was not sharing the taste of victory with her.

Feminist penal reform activists played a greater role in the campaign against the death penalty than is generally recognised. Margery Fry in particular continued to make timely interventions in the public debate for the rest of her life and her former HLPR colleague, Lord Gardiner, invoked her memory during a 'long and brilliant'[162] speech in favour of suspension of the death penalty in 1965. But other members of Fry's network centred on the HLPR assisted the campaign as well and support was also enlisted from women associated with the wider feminist movement, including some, such as Esther Roper and Maude Royden, who were strongly identified with the peace movement. Therefore throughout its existence as a separate campaign group the NCADP was able to draw on the activism of seasoned campaigners who strove to keep the question of capital punishment at the forefront of public debate.

Pressure group campaigns that aim not only for legislative change but also to alter social and moral attitudes are necessarily long drawn out affairs. The campaign for women's suffrage took over 60 years from the petition presented to parliament by John Stuart Mill in 1866 to the achievement of equal franchise in 1928. The modern campaign for the abolition of the death penalty properly began in 1923 with the formation of the NCADP and achieved its landmark success in 1965 when parliament voted to suspend capital punishment. However, the death penalty is still a controversial matter today. An obvious feature of such long campaigns is that many of the initiators do not live to see the eventual success. Most of the feminists who rallied to the abolitionist cause in the 1920s were, as already shown, veterans of the women's suffrage campaign and well into the middle years of their lives. Therefore, with a few exceptions, such as the much younger Theodora Calvert, few of them lived to see the moment that they had worked so hard for. Nevertheless, they had endeavoured to promote the cause which so clearly matched their core beliefs in 'justice' and 'civilisation'.

The success of the anti-capital punishment movement is often interpreted as an example of penal-welfarism and/or humanitarianism in action: however it is clear that in the 1920s and 30s the campaign against the death penalty was also a cause dear to the hearts of many feminists. The feminist–criminal–justice reform network was careful never to imply that women should be treated differently from men except in the case of the infanticide law, which most abolitionists regarded as a gendered crime, and which could also be seen as a 'thin end of the wedge' towards total abolition. However it was inevitable that press attention would focus on the relatively rare cases in which women – especially the young and pretty ones[163] – were sentenced to death. Anti-death penalty campaigners also worked within a gendered culture in which it was often said that there was a 'special repulsion'[164] towards the hanging of women. Yet by and large they wished to avoid such emotional arguments preferring instead to portray their opponents as primitive and atavistic in their attitudes while grounding the abolitionist tactics firmly in the rational, scientific discourse of criminological 'facts'. Moreover, former suffragists in particular, were extremely wary of any debating point that might infer an

acceptance of chivalric attitudes – which was, they knew, the very same
discourse that was used to exclude women from juries and magisterial
benches during 'unpleasant' cases. Therefore feminists who opposed capital punishment opposed it absolutely, both for men and for women. As
the editorial in *The Vote* on the execution of Edith Thompson put it, 'we
are the last people to advocate any inequality between the sexes'.[165]
Nevertheless, it is clear that they perceived the death penalty to be a feminist issue and an integral part of their wider project for reform of state
and society.

Conclusion

Reform of the penal system, including the abolition of the death
penalty, was a key objective of the feminist–criminal–justice reform network in the decades between the introduction of women's suffrage and
the suspension of capital punishment in 1965. In many ways this was a
generally progressive cause, attractive to left-leaning or liberally minded
people, including some who were Conservative supporters. But the
activists should not be dismissed as ineffectual do-gooders, lacking in
any real knowledge or understanding of the criminal justice system and
its problems. Most of the key campaigners had detailed, practical knowledge of the system having undertaken voluntary service as JPs and
prison visitors, a few had been prisoners themselves. Many of them were
co-opted by the government as advisors, for example through membership of Home Office committees, sometimes serving as one of only a few
'token' or 'statutory' women. Belonging to a group sometimes termed
'the great and the good', they took their place on Home Office committees alongside civil servants, MPs, churchmen and representatives of the
relevant professions. For this elite, educated group of women at least, the
steps towards equal citizenship had brought them some opportunity to
promote a distinctively feminist approach to criminal justice policy,
albeit one that was sometimes apparently constricted by the gender attitudes of the time. Although invariably outnumbered by professional
men on the government's advisory bodies, they continued to provide a
feminist commentary on the penal system. This chapter has demonstrated that women activists in the HLPR in particular maintained a sustained critique of the penal treatment of women – and of men – and
sought more wide-ranging changes in the system than is sometimes
assumed. Clearly they had taken to heart Mary Gordon's reminder that
accountability for the criminal justice system lay with the country's citizens and voters.

5
Feminism and the Care of Victims

Human Sacrifice Today
A Victim
She is Five Years Old.
She is one of many. Shall these things be?[1]

In 1913 *The Vote* set out to shock its readers with the above headline. Seventy-five years later criminologist Jock Young argued that it was 1970s feminist studies that provided the beginnings of a 'radical victimology'.[2] Yet the 'second wave' feminists of the late twentieth century were not the first to emphasise the importance of the victim's perspective in any rounded consideration of criminal justice. Indeed, as the emotive tone of the quotation above suggests, much of the 'first wave' feminism's critique of criminal justice was driven by the treatment of the female and/or young victim of violence by the male-controlled courts. This chapter seeks to demonstrate that feminism was also relevant to the public debates in the mid-twentieth century surrounding the role and status of victims and what could be done for them, which led ultimately to the establishment of the Criminal Injuries Compensation Board in 1964. The chapter will argue that far from ignoring victims, the women's movement took a very great interest in them and played an important part in raising awareness of their needs, and suggests that a long-term effect of 'first wave' feminism's focus on female victimisation was to influence public perception of 'the victim' as a gendered being. It will also present evidence to demonstrate that women's organisations took a discernable interest in victims of crime throughout the twentieth century, including during the late 1950s and early 1960s, a period when their resources seemed stretched and feminism was supposedly dead, and that 1950s women were less reactionary on the issue of 'law and

139

order' than is sometimes supposed. The chapter will also analyse the ideas and influence of Margery Fry, the feminist who instigated the initial campaign for a criminal injuries compensation scheme. The subsequent fate of her proposals will be placed in the context of the political scene of the 1950s and contemporary debates about criminal justice, notably the concurrent debate concerning the re-introduction of corporal punishment for violent offenders.

Feminism and the victim in the early twentieth century

The victim has been described as the 'Cinderella' – or alternatively 'the forgotten man' – of the criminal law,[3] a 'below stairs' figure largely ignored by policy makers who concentrated their attention on the offender. Yet while official policy appeared to have little regard for the victim, women's organisations consistently showed a lot more interest. Arguably feminist engagement with the criminal justice system in the late nineteenth and early twentieth centuries largely arose out of concern for the (mainly female) victim. Indeed, the plight of young and/or female victims of male violence and the suspicion that they received unfair treatment in the all-male courts proved to be the initial spur to campaigners to call for the introduction of women police, magistrates and jurors. Women's organisations – including the National Union of Women Workers (NUWW) and the suffrage societies – continued to foreground the needs of victims in the years leading up to the First World War when there were frequent allegations in the feminist press of discriminatory treatment of women and young girls in the courts.[4] In addition philanthropic women were becoming increasingly indignant about the practice of clearing courts of all women when 'sensitive' (i.e., sexual) evidence was to be heard with the result that female victims – including young children – would have no one of their sex in court when they testified. The suffragist leader Millicent Fawcett raised this matter as early as 1897 when she headed a petition to the Lord Chief Justice on behalf of the National Vigilance Association (NVA) objecting to the exclusion of women from court.[5] The victims of sex abuse were uppermost in the minds of NVA activists, who, together with the National Society for the Prevention of Cruelty to Children (NSPCC), brought forward prosecutions of abusive fathers even before the specific criminalisation of incest in 1908.[6]

Since women were at that point still banned from any formal participation in the administration of justice, NUWW (later National Council of Women [NCW]) members decided to offer informal support to women and children brought before the magistrates by establishing court rotas. Volunteers would take it in turn to attend hearings and to act as 'friends' to young girls and women appearing before the court. The first police court rota was formed by members of the new Cambridge NUWW branch in 1913 and other towns soon followed this example.[7] The introduction of women magistrates and jurors after the War did nothing to convince activists that the rotas were unnecessary and new ones were established during the 1920s. In Tunbridge Wells the scheme, started in 1924, was still operating at the local magistrates' court in 1970.[8] The NCW official policy (as expressed in evidence to the Departmental Committee on Sexual Offences against Young Persons in 1925) was that if a court was cleared in order for a child to give evidence in a case of sexual assault, a 'suitable woman' should be present '*in addition* to Women Magistrates and Jurors'.[9] 'Suitable woman' was taken to mean a policewoman or probation officer, but if neither of these were available, a volunteer would be acceptable. Both the committee and the Home Office agreed that the presence of a woman in court was desirable, the latter having first made the recommendation to courts as early as 1909.[10]

Although the rota members usually worked with the support and co-operation of the authorities, there continued to be controversial incidents in which attempts were made to remove them and other women from hearings. In 1925, at Southport, a woman magistrate was asked to stay away from a case of indecent assault on two 12-year-old girls while members of 'The Ladies' Police Court Rota' were excluded by order of the Chief Constable, who claimed he was unable to give evidence relating to the offences in court if 'ladies' were present. Furious rota members protested in the local press about their removal but the Chief Constable remained unrepentant, claiming that they were a small, unrepresentative group who hampered the administration of justice.[11] Just for good measure, he claimed that women police were a waste of public money.[12] This incident received full coverage in a feminist press which was unsurprisingly unanimous in its outrage, not only regarding the Chief Constable's actions and stated opinions, but also with the woman magistrate's acquiescence with his request.

The NCW rotas could be seen as in some ways analogous to schemes for victims' support. However it is important to stress that the proffered assistance was not confined to victims, although the needs of abused women and (female) children had often prompted the establishment of these schemes in the first place. Rota members aimed to provide moral support to defendants, as well to witnesses because especially, but not only, in the case of women convicted of prostitution (who made up a significant proportion of women brought before the courts) there was a realisation that the dividing line between culprit and victim was by no means clear-cut. Victorian social purity activists often viewed prostitute women as more sinned against than sinning and placed the blame and responsibility for their 'fall' upon their clients and the moral 'double standard' that pervaded society.[13] This attitude continued to influence members of women's organisations in the early twentieth century, reinforcing their (and the public's) perception of 'the victim' as passive and feminine.

The women's movement's concentration on the needs of female and/or child victims, and witnesses arose from a mixture of motives including members' philanthropic interest in helping less fortunate 'sisters', consciousness of their 'maternal' responsibilities towards young girls and a perceived need to correct the seemingly rampant misogyny of the courts where a sexually abused girl could be portrayed as the real culprit – as a vicious 'little minx' who had led a decent man astray.[14] Carol Smart argues that feminists were engaged in a discursive struggle to frame 'the idea of child sex abuse as a recognisable, problematic and harmful behaviour'.[15] But the struggle was not merely to fix the notion of the offence, but also to establish a clear understanding of 'the victim' as innocent and damaged, and of the services of the woman 'professional' (be she a probation officer, JP, lawyer, social worker, police officer, doctor or volunteer) as vital to aid recovery and to ensure that justice was done. Rota members, like women magistrates and others in privileged situations, felt qualified to speak about the needs of women and children, especially those of lower social class. However, their emphasis upon female victimisation and their struggle to portray the victim as completely innocent may have contributed in the long run to the creation of gendered victim stereotypes and to the relative invisibility of male victims.[16]

Two ideal types of victim were clearly at the forefront of feminist discourse: the abused child and the battered wife. As Louise A. Jackson has demonstrated, the victims of child sexual abuse cases brought before the courts were overwhelmingly female. In her sample of cases tried in Middlesex and Yorkshire between 1830 and 1914 only 7 per cent of victims were male, although it is highly likely that a large amount of abuse – of both sexes – may have occurred without ever resulting in court appearances. Conversely, the alleged perpetrators (99 per cent) were overwhelmingly male.[17] As Jackson argues, sexual abuse was constructed as a product of a deviant form of masculinity, which was contrasted with the respectable, 'middle class codes of manliness'[18] favoured by the social purity movement and feminists. Smart argues that feminist perspectives regarding what is now termed child sexual abuse were minority opinions or 'counter-discourses' to the established, traditional views that prevailed in the legal and the medical professions.[19] Nevertheless, they were not without immediate influence or long-term impact. Importantly, Smart refutes the notion that the problem of sexual abuse was overlooked between the early 1900s and its 're'-discovery[20] in the 1970s by illustrating the ongoing interest of the NVA and the Association for Moral and Social Hygiene (AMSH) in particular. In the place of the sexually precocious, mendacious, 'little minx', feminists projected an image of the girl victim as innocent, vulnerable and in need of special treatment in court, or failing that, the support and protection of adult women. In addition to establishing rotas of volunteers, campaigners therefore sought to protect the child witness through the provision of separate waiting rooms at courts, the employment of women police to take statements and women doctors to conduct medical examinations, an increased use of the courts of summary jurisdiction in abuse cases and the presence of women magistrates in all cases of the sexual abuse of girls.[21]

Along with sexual assault, wife-beating was widely perceived as unacceptable; a product of a subordinate, unruly masculinity that 'undermine[d] patriarchy from within'.[22] Wiener suggests that a 'reconstruction' of gender attitudes in the nineteenth century contributed towards much lowering of society's tolerance generally regarding violence against women, albeit with judges adopting the new attitudes more readily than jurymen.[23] The protection of women from violence was a fundamental tenet of the women's movement since John Stuart Mill's denunciation of 'domestic tyranny' and was strongly associated (for example, by Frances Power Cobbe) with the need to raise the legal status of women as well as protect them in the courts.[24] In practice the 'protection' offered to victims of domestic violence in the late nineteenth century consisted of separation and maintenance orders, often issued for 'desertion' rather than assault.[25] By the early twentieth century some feminists (but by no means all) had reached the conclusion that divorce reform would afford victims of domestic violence better protection – or at least an escape route – but the prospect of easier divorce was highly controversial, even within suffrage societies. In 1911 the feminist Metropolitan Magistrate Cecil Chapman concluded, after adjudicating in many 'domestic' cases, that there should be a higher age of marriage for men and women, compulsory maintenance for a wife and children, reform of the bastardy laws, extension to the grounds for legal separation and an increase in divorce.[26]

In 1934 when the NCW voted to support an extension of the grounds for divorce to include desertion, cruelty, drunkenness and insanity, only one of its affiliates – the Mothers' Union – registered its opposition.[27] However, the authorities, including even women police and magistrates, continued to favour the reconciliation of couples where possible,[28] suggesting that concern for victims was often more rhetorical than practical, or that women's complaints of violent treatment by their spouses were not taken too seriously.

Of course better divorce prospects only addressed the long-term resolution of the problems of battered wives: in the short term they, like abused children, would need the services of women police, court rota volunteers and magistrates. Campaigners repeatedly affirmed that women JPs should always take part in the adjudication of any case involving a woman, including 'domestic' proceedings, so that 'a woman's point of view' could be heard – and given – on the bench.[29] For the most serious cases brought to trial at the Assizes they naturally argued that women should be on the jury. There was also some concern about the relatively light sentences handed down for violence: in May 1917 *Votes for Women* reported a penalty of two months' prison for a man who had attempted to murder his wife. However instances of grown-up women's victimisation generally took a very poor second place to those of sexual assaults on young girls in feminist propaganda, perhaps because of anticipated doubts among readers as to the possible culpability of older women in contrast to the assumed purity of children. Adult victims of reported sexual assault were anyway fairly scarce, perhaps because of under-reporting. Marital rape was not made a criminal offence until 1991[30] while prosecutions for rape and sexual assault committed by strangers were relatively rare.

As stated above, women's movement activists saw no contradiction in addressing the problems of both victims and offenders and perceived all women brought before the courts as potentially in social need. But while their construction of the archetypal victim as feminine had the advantage of confronting some of the ugliest manifestations of male power such as incest, rape and domestic violence, it did so at the expense of over-emphasis on women's physical weakness, vulnerability and 'otherness'. Consequently, in cases where the victim did not meet required standards of femininity there was a chance that she could be held responsible (or even blamed) for her predicament. Inevitably, given the long-standing debate over 'provocation' in the courts, the issue of culpability remained a live one.[31] This could be a problem for even the youngest of victims, as Jackson and Smart have shown. Girl victims of sex abuse often faced a 'Catch 22': if they were really as young and innocent as they seemed, how were they able to articulate their experiences so knowingly before the courts?[32] Beaten wives also were at risk of taking the blame for having nagged their husbands or even, sometimes, for being inadequate housewives.[33] Despite their interest in, and sympathy for, victims, early twentieth-century-feminists failed to mount a thorough challenge to suggestions that victims might be partly to blame for their predicament, although they unsurprisingly reacted strongly in extreme cases, such as when a seven-year-old victim of sexual assault was said to have 'importuned' her attacker.[34] Interestingly, the feminist-influenced Report of the Departmental Committee on Sexual Offences against Young Persons (1925), despite suggesting that 16-year-old girls could be 'excited', 'emotionally unstable' and already leading 'immoral lives', argued that even if they were sexually precocious and had 'led men on' they were not fully responsible and should therefore not be deprived of legal protection.[35] Thus the Report rejected the custom of regarding the girl to be at fault, even if she was near to, or over, the current age of consent (the committee's recommendation was that it should be raised to 17) while at the same time denying her any agency or ability to choose her own morality.

Sympathy for the victim did not necessarily preclude concern for offender, although the practical policies of the women's movement were aimed far more at the protection of the former than the treatment of the latter. In the case of sexual abuse charges, suggestions from women's organisations were usually limited to vague calls for tougher penalties, but these should be placed in the context of the many examples of acquittals, minimum fines and – in the view of campaigners – the derisory punishments that were handed down in courts which were collected by the feminist press and bodies such as the NVA. A typical example would be the £5 fine imposed on a 31-year old man for a 'serious offence' against a 'little girl' in 1930.[36] What women's organisations were seeking was justice, not necessarily vengeance. Adequate penalties for the sexual abuse of girls existed under the current law, (such as the Criminal Law Amendment Acts) and campaigners simply wished to see these enforced. In general, there was an understanding that a punitive sentence would do little in a practical way to help the victim, who was, after all, the chief concern.

Beyond the enforcement of the existing law (and excluding preventive measures,[37] which were also widely debated) three further possibilities were considered: the introduction of more overtly punitive sanctions such as corporal punishment for violent offenders, sterilisation 'of the mentally unfit' (who may or may not have included child abusers) and 'preventive' sentences, perhaps combined with psychiatric treatment. Calls for the first of these probably peaked in the 1950s (see below), but were not unheard of before the Second World War, especially in Conservative circles. But even there, the 'hangers and floggers' did not go unchallenged by women members with more progressive attitudes.[38] In the 1930s the influence of the eugenics movement ensured that the possibility of sterilisation was widely debated, but opinion on this matter among feminists and penal reformers was sharply divided. The Howard League took 'no corporate decision' while in Gloucestershire the Women Magistrates' Society rejected it as a policy option only by the chair's casting vote after an exhaustive discussion.[39] 'Preventive detention'[40] was favoured by reformers for repeat offenders in the 1920s, while by the 1930s reformers were calling for psychiatric treatment to be provided alongside a custodial sentence for a whole range of prisoners, including sex offenders.[41] The increasing tendency among penal reformers to view the latter as 'mad' rather than 'bad' was exemplified in the *Howard Journal* in 1958. Commenting on the Wolfenden Report, 'A Psychiatrist' offered the opinion that 'paedophiliacs' were often 'tragic figures, who did not understand what they had done wrong and who were not undeserving of sympathy'.[42] Reformers also maintained that justice for victims need not entail punitive treatment of the offender.

During the early twentieth-century discussions of victimisation, as well as in the context of debates on criminal injuries compensation during the 1950s and 60s, campaigners' rhetoric tended to dwell on the most obviously vulnerable and innocent categories of victims, the young, the old and (preferably also) female, in defiance of statistical evidence that revealed a different picture – that most recorded violent offences were male-on-male assaults involving young men who were known to each other. This tendency was, of course, merely a small part of a complex narrative about crime and punishment. The roots of this discourse are undoubtedly complicated, but the feminist campaigns of the late nineteenth and early twentieth century which aimed at exposing male violence against women and children and critiquing the decisions of the masculine agents of justice, undoubtedly played a part in the social construction of 'the victim' as feminine, and/or weak, young and disadvantaged. However, it should be stressed that this stereotyping of victims was based on reports of real suffering, whatever the police statistics suggested, and it is in any case highly probable that the victimisation of women (especially within the domestic context) was massively under-reported with only a minority of incidents resulting in legal proceedings.

As the detailed examination below (in [Margery Fry and victim's compensation, 1948–58]) of the public debate that took place on the compensation scheme in the 1950s and 60s reveals, competing discourses about the 'innocence' and culpability of victims still influenced discussions in the second half of the twentieth century. Nevertheless, and not withstanding feminists' interest in the reform of offenders, where the women's movement was concerned, 'the victim' was at the very least a significant figure whose interests should be considered, although it was apparently easier to extend sympathy to some victims than to others. At a later stage this chapter will consider to what extent campaigners for victims' compensation continued (rightly or wrongly) to construct 'the victim' as feminine, and the implications of the gendering of victims for the debate.

Margery Fry and victim's compensation, 1948–58

Margery Fry is widely acknowledged as the guiding spirit behind the scheme of criminal injuries compensation, which was the first major government initiative to address the issue of victimisation in modern times, even though the scheme was not enacted until several years after her death. No speech, press article or pamphlet supporting criminal injuries compensation in the decade after her death in 1958 was complete without a mention of her name. Yet her feminist credentials are rarely mentioned either in the contemporary tributes or in more recent accounts of the compensation campaign. In fact Miss Fry was not only a dedicated penal reformer, but was also active in the women's movement. While still in her twenties, Margery Fry was President of the Birmingham branch of the NUWW[43] and she retained links with the organisation, mainly through its Public Service and Magistrates' Committee, for most of her life. Along with the HLPR Secretary, Cicely Craven, and fellow JP Clara Rackham, Fry provided a vital connection between the worlds of penal reform and women's rights. Mawby and Walklate argue that the role of the women's movement in influencing social policy in the mid-twentieth century in the main took the form of 'welfare feminism'. Therefore they firmly place Fry's ideas on compensation in the context of the inception of the Welfare State in the years after 1945.[44] However, although Fry suggested that compensation scales be tied to other welfare benefits and was clearly influenced by Beveridge's social insurance model, her ideas on victim's compensation were not simply about the creation of another 'safety net'. Despite her close friendship with the pre-eminent 'welfare feminist' Eleanor Rathbone, Margery Fry was influenced by much more than just welfare considerations. Her vision of a victim-friendly policy was initially much wider and more philosophical than the 1964 compensation scheme that was a direct result of her campaign, and was closer to the concept of what is now termed 'restorative justice'. For her, state compensation was merely the first, and most readily attainable, step towards a more significant readjustment in the scales of justice that could work in favour of both victim and offender.

Margery Fry probably started to contemplate seriously some sort of novel approach to the needs of victims shortly after the passage of the 1948 Criminal Justice Act, which had enacted some of the proposals that she and her fellow reformers had been working on since the early 1930s. It is worth questioning why she embarked upon the compensation campaign at that particular moment. Her biographer suggests that the inspiration came from an account of tribal justice in Uganda given to her by Champion Russell, a long-serving HLPR ally, and from her own experience when a thief tried to snatch her handbag.[45] There has also been speculation that Fry's championing of the victim was motivated by an attempt to 'buy off' the supporters of corporal punishment, or 'keep the hangers and floggers at bay', by demonstrating that penal reformers cared about victims as well as offenders.[46] This interpretation of her intentions is far too crude: given the heated nature of the debate about crime and punishment in the 1950s, and the entrenched views of the Howard League's opponents, it is highly unlikely that they would have been 'bought off' by a modest compensation scheme or that Fry would have thought they would. The alternative explanation in this chapter of the intellectual genesis of Fry's ideas foregrounds principally her originality as a theoretician of justice, itself partly a result of her practical experience as a magistrate, together with her grasp of feminist perspectives regarding victimisation. To a lesser extent, her consciousness of the vulnerability of old age as she entered her ninth decade also influenced her thoughts on victimology and restitution.

When her book *Arms of the Law* (which contained the kernel of her thinking about victims) appeared in 1951, Margery Fry was already in her late seventies. Her approach to problems of criminal justice combined a theoretical understanding with practical experience and an ability to generate and carry forward policy innovations. Terence Morris described her as 'the dominant figure' in penal reform during the 1930s and 40s.[47] But although Fry was best known for her contributions to criminal justice policy, they formed only a part of a richly active life in which humanitarian causes in general figured greatly. Paul Rock argues that the Howard League's client had been the prisoner rather than the victim,[48] but Fry's interest was never going to be confined in such a way.

She did not believe that what was good for the victim was automatically bad for the perpetrator, or vice versa. Her arguments were founded in a holistic conception of the interests of the community and of justice. As her biographer points out, 'although the main business of her life was to seek humane treatment for criminals, she never forgot that lawbreakers hurt and destroy'.[49] Fry had very few illusions about offenders; Morris also recalled her view that a lot of them were 'very disagreeable people'.[50] On the other hand, she had no time for retribution or vengeance, which she regarded as primitive emotions that were ultimately unproductive.

Fry's experience as a JP – especially in the juvenile court, where it was sometimes possible for magistrates to order restitution by the offender – was influential on her thinking, as well as her wider philosophy of justice and her feminist standpoint. Writing in the mid-1960s, shortly before the emergence of the Women's Liberation Movement, her biographer claimed that Fry had little deep interest in equal citizenship.[51] Whether or not this is an accurate assessment, there is plenty of evidence to suggest that she fully appreciated the extent of inequality for women and had often taken practical steps to try to reduce it. During the 1950s listeners to the BBC could have heard her musing on the position of women, past and present, on old age and on the life of a single woman. A close reading of the scripts shows the quality of her reflections upon age, gender and spinsterhood and the extent to which, in the last years of her life, she was able to analyse her own socially constructed identity as a 'little old lady' and 'maiden aunt'.[52]

The first chapter of *Arms of the Law* drew upon a wide range of sources to outline what she perceived to be the historical evolution of the justice system from a time when private vengeance predominated, through a phase when voluntary 'compositions' were allowed, and a further period in which the community decided on a tariff of compensations, to one where the State punished criminals and private vengeance was no longer deemed acceptable.[53] Fry argued that 'the tendency of English criminal law . . . has been to "take it out of the offender" rather than do justice to the offended'. Bringing her experience as a juvenile court magistrate to bear she pondered, 'have we not neglected overmuch the customs of our earlier ancestors in the matter of restitution?' and argued that compensation orders were particularly beneficial to young offenders provided that the parents co-operated.[54] Restitution, she concluded, 'cannot undo the wrong, but it will often assuage the injury, and it has a real educative value for the offender, whether adult or child'.[55]

Significantly, despite (or because of) all her progressive, reforming campaign activities on behalf of offenders, Fry strongly believed in the importance of justice being done and being seen to be done. For example, she was highly sceptical of suggestions that juvenile courts could be replaced by child welfare councils run by local education authorities.[56] However, she believed that some form of restitution could play an important part in the offender's rehabilitation, hence her emphasis on its 'educative' value. While *Arms of the Law* only briefly touched on ways in which restitution could claim its place in the criminal justice system, it was resolute in its rejection of vengeance and of the use of fear as a deterrent to lawbreaking. Fry was only too aware that 'the greatest obstacle to the revision of penal administration is [the] mass of confused thought and emotion in the public mind'.[57] Her aim was to reveal that confusion as well as hint at a fresh approach.

Over the two years following the publication of Fry's book her ideas began to crystallise. She had probably had the question at the back of her mind for some years: Champion Russell's visit to Uganda, where he learned about a system of restitution in operation there, had been in the mid-1930s.[58] Fry was also aware – as Russell himself had emphasised back in 1931 – that the founding secretary of the Howard Association, William Tallack, had 'never ceased to advocate . . . restitution',[59] so the notion was far from alien to penal reform circles. However, a significant problem lay in the fact that the majority of offenders would not be in a position to pay the levels of monetary compensation that seemed the most appropriate form of reparation in the second half of the twentieth century, especially if they were in prison.[60] She therefore developed a proposal by 1953 – which she clearly envisaged as a first step towards a more complex system of restitution – for a scheme of state compensation. In a letter to the League's president, Lord Templewood, she outlined her ideas in some detail.

I have – this for your information only – a new iron in the fire. I am very anxious to put in the mind of the public the possibility of a return to the primitive idea that some compensation for injury is a first claim of justice for the victim of a crime. There seems no possibility of reviving the practice so far as injuries to property are concerned, but I do think the principle of the Industrial Accidents insurance should be extended in aid of those whom the forces of public law have failed to protect from bodily harm. Let the State get anything it can (it won't be much!) from the offender, but let its first concern be the wrongs of the victim! . . . I hope I have persuaded the BBC to run some talks on the whole interesting question.[61]

As a first step, Fry took her plan to the executive committee of the Howard League where it received a less than enthusiastic response, despite the Tallack 'tradition'. Although she admitted that the scheme was not strictly within the League's scope she had clearly hoped for some support: she was disappointed and may well have felt let down. She had, after all, practically created the organisation by joining the forces of the Penal Reform League to the older Howard Association in the early 1920s, and had remained its guiding spirit throughout the next three decades. In accounting for the Howard League's somewhat negative attitude, Rock cites the view of one of the executive members, C. H. Rolph, who recalled that his colleagues were influenced by the fact that the daughter of one of them had recently killed someone in a road accident.[62] However, perhaps understandably, the League's official minutes make no reference to this aspect. In any case, it is likely to have been just been one factor among several. The character and approach of the HLPR was anyway undergoing some alteration in the early 1950s following the retirement of Cicely Craven as secretary and her replacement by Hugh Klare. While Craven was very close to Fry, sharing much of the latter's philosophy concerning the nature of justice, Klare (the first salaried secretary of the League) had a very different, and arguably less consensual, style. Ryan contends that the Howard League was an 'acceptable', cautious pressure group that was already in Craven's day compromised by its close relationship with the Home Office.[63] Nevertheless it seems that in the 1950s the League became even more staid, indeed conservative, as not just Fry and Craven, but also more progressive members, were gradually removed from the scene for one reason or another. Klare actually boasted to Templewood of having 'quietly dropped Mr Fenner Brockway, a very left-wing Labour M.P' from the list of HLPR vice-presidents, and on another occasion described Gerald Gardiner (a close ally of Fry's on the victims' compensation issue and future Lord Chancellor) as 'extreme left'.[64] Thus changing personnel and a shift in political direction may have accounted for the less than enthusiastic initial reaction of the League to Fry's suggestions. Perhaps her proposals were simply too adventurous for the executive committee members at that point.

Despite the rebuff, Margery Fry continued to promote her ideas for victims' compensation, and told the HLPR executive that she would personally speak to the Home Office.[65] By the summer of 1954 her plan was on the agenda of the Advisory Council on the Treatment of Offenders (ACTO), on which she, the League's Chairman, George Benson MP and HLPR member Violet Creech Jones, all sat. She also instigated a media campaign, including letters to the press, newspaper features and, eventually, the radio broadcast mentioned in her letter to Templewood. Fry was a seasoned broadcaster who had been contributing to the BBC's talks since the 1920s and she evidently still retained excellent contacts at Broadcasting House.

The script of the broadcast, which was made in November 1956, reveals more of Fry's thinking. For practical and tactical reasons she had decided to concentrate on compensation for victims of violent offences in the first instance and in the talk she sought to present cases that were as innocent and vulnerable as possible. Given Fry's strong connections to the women's movement, it is interesting to assess the extent to which she shared feminists' emphasis on female victimisation. Morris's view was that she did adhere to 'the stereotypical image of the victim . . . as an essentially gentle, absolutely innocent, unsuspecting person'.[66] Although the examples she gave in her broadcast (with the exception of herself) *were not* 'little old ladies', they *were* predominately female: a young woman indecently attacked in her own home ('she couldn't bear to go back to her home'), a young girl raped on her way home and an old man 'flogged and coshed' in his shop. Her mastery of the intimate medium of radio by speaking personally to listeners was evident in the following confession:

> Two years ago a man snatched my bag in the street on a very dark night when nobody was about and he pulled and I pulled . . . and I was pulled right over. I tugged as long as I could: he got away with the bag and I slightly hurt my finger, but I suppose I could very easily be laid up with a broken hip for months.[67]

Although she emphasised that this incident was 'not the first thing that interested me in this question', the text of her radio talks indicate that she was very conscious of the double burden of age and gender and her own identity as an elderly woman. Fry picked mainly female examples in her broadcast and such a focus on feminine vulnerability was, of course, a recurrent theme of feminist discourse on victims. However, Home Office files reveal that in 1954 Fry collected data from the Old Bailey and Leeds Assizes that suggested a very different type of victim profile. She may well have also seen the examples of violent crime collated by the Chief Constable of Liverpool in which the majority of assault victims in cases brought to court were male.[68] As a shrewd judge of human nature and a long-serving magistrate she is as unlikely to have held illusions about the victims of crime as about the perpetrators, and her commitment to empirical, statistical research was paramount.

It is therefore highly probable that she chose such unimpeachably inno-cent examples for tactical and rhetorical reasons. On another occasion Fry told radio listeners that she believed that 'neither class nor sex nor colour must limit the emergence into world affairs of all that is out-standing in human nature'.[69] As a humanitarian she no doubt hoped her compensation scheme would help all those who required it, male or female, with the only proviso that the case against his or her assailant should be legally proven. But as a feminist, she would have also under-stood that women still lacked equality, especially in financial terms, hence the importance of monetary compensation.

Fry's overall aim was to focus attention on an aspect of justice that she felt had been neglected in recent decades. She was concerned mainly with the principles of restitution and compensation, and while she did flesh out the main points of her scheme in the last years of her life – to the extent of commissioning research on the likely cost – she did not con-front the devil that lay in the detail of it, except by emphasising that it would apply to cases proven in court and she did not think that collusion between alleged perpetrators and their victims would be a problem.[70] Therefore her role, even before her death, was as a campaign figurehead, in contrast to the part she had played in many of her earlier reform ini-tiatives which she had seen enacted. As she said to a supporter, 'this won't come in my time, but it will in yours'.[71] While Rock's observation that neither Fry, nor other supporters of compensation actually asked vic-tims what they wanted is insightful,[72] it is also clear that for campaigners like Fry the victims' views were largely irrelevant as they perceived the matter to be largely a political question of balance, justice and equity. Although her proposals for a criminal injuries compensation scheme were limited in scope, Fry seems to have seen them as merely a first step in a process of long-term change (or 'rebalancing') in criminal justice.

The politics of victims' compensation, 1958–62

After Fry's death in 1958 the campaign for compensation became less a matter of the principles of justice and more entangled in the public and political debates over 'law and order' that thrived in an era of increasing levels of recorded violent crime and mass media-led panics over delin-quency and 'teddy boys'.[73] To some extent the issue became linked not only to that of corporal punishment but also to capital punishment and to penal strategies in general. This section will examine the attitude of the Conservative Party and government, especially the Home Secretary from 1958 to 1962, R. A. Butler.

Although at first the Home Office was not keen on Fry's plan (arguing that compensation was a matter for civil rather than criminal courts, that the setting up machinery to collect it would be a difficult task and doubting whether public opinion would accept the idea of payment from public funds)[74] eventually Fry made some powerful converts to her ideas, perhaps the most important one being Butler. When he became Home Secretary, there was a perceptible change in the Home Office's attitude. Butler was the first Home Secretary since Herbert Morrison 14 years previously to attend a meeting of ACTO. Butler spoke to the Council immediately after he took over at the Home Office in 1958 and was also present at the next meeting (the first one to take place after Fry's death). He paid her a fulsome, but perhaps, given its wording, a slightly dubious, tribute claiming that 'many features of the penal system in this country already provide a fitting memorial to the work of this great lady'. However, it was evidently injudicious for him to make any firm commitment to criminal injuries' compensation at this point as the next words in speech were changed from 'I feel sure that for some time to come . . . her ideals and her known views on such questions as compensation for victims will influence your discussions' to ' . . . that mixture of idealism & realism which was so peculiarly her own will continue to influence your discussions'.[75] Nevertheless, soon afterwards Butler was to become much more proactive in support of the scheme, arguing in Cabinet committee that the government should make a commitment to it in principle in its 1959 White Paper, *Penal Practice in a Changing Society*, in the face of opposition from Treasury officials unwilling to make any spending commitment.[76]

Butler's enthusiasm for the scheme should be placed in the political context of increasing press and public debate over 'law and order' and stemmed to some extent from his uncomfortable position as a liberal Home secretary in a Conservative administration. His Cabinet memorandum urged that the government announce the establishment of a working party to consider the matter in view of increasing public concern about crimes of violence and 'the support that Miss Fry's scheme has attracted'. Butler argued that

> [t]he public suspicion that the government cares more for the offender than the victim makes it difficult to carry out necessary and socially useful measures of penal reform and encourages a dangerous feeling that the ordinary processes of criminal justice do not secure adequate reparation for the wrong done.[77]

Butler was mindful of what he termed the 'strong public demand for protection against victims of violence' but he rejected proposals for hanging, flogging or, as he put it, 'the application of draconian principles'.[78]

Butler's two biggest problems were his own party and the Treasury. In his memoirs he recalled his struggles against what he termed 'the Colonel Blimps of both sexes' of the Conservative Party who especially objected to his refusal to re-introduce corporal punishment.[79] This concurrent debate (see Chapter 2) was relevant to the victims' compensation scheme in several ways: supporters of corporal punishment such as the Conservative MP Thomas More made a good deal of use of the neglect of 'the victim' in their arguments and also focused on violent offenders as the group who were in their opinion most suitable for physical punishment. (Incidentally, whereas Butler, from his perspective as a party politician, saw victim's compensation as a useful distraction from the corporal punishment debate, there is no evidence that Fry had perceived it as such, despite her vehement dislike of flogging.) Certainly where the party conference was concerned, the compensation proposals did prove a useful decoy, and although the young lawyer and budding politician Geoffrey Howe was branded a Conservative Central Office 'stool pigeon' in 1961 when he proposed the amendment of a 'hanging and flogging' motion to include a specific mention of victim's compensation, Butler himself was apparently well received when he replied to the debate.[80]

Butler was especially mindful of the views of women in his party who he assumed were especially 'tough' on law and order. Butler's comment that the female 'Colonel Blimps' he faced at the party conference were 'more deadly, politically, than the male'[81] has been echoed by many commentators, especially on the left, who have tended to stereotype 1950s women, especially those in the Conservative Party, as rabid and reactionary opponents of 'progressive' penal policy. Peggy Duff, a left-wing veteran of many campaigns including for the abolition of the death penalty, alleged that 'the most virulent opponents of abolition [of capital punishment] were the affluent, beautifully hatted, tweedy Tory women who screamed for the rope and the cat at Tory Party conferences.'[82] Writing in the 1980s, at the height of Mrs Thatcher's power, Beatrix Campbell similarly argued that '[l]aw and order was the cauldron in which Tory women let off steam, a discourse which set them at odds with their own party leaders and set them apart from the preoccupations of women on the liberal or left wings of politics'.[83] Although Campbell qualifies her observation by drawing attention also to Tory women who supported penal reform[84] it is unfortunate that, in common with some other feminists on the left, she appears to confirm misogynist stereotypes concerning women's attitudes to 'law and order'. Evidence will be presented below (see, [Gender and 'the victim' in the 1950s]) showing that women's organisations maintained their traditional concern for the victim, especially the female one, but there is no strong indication of a simple correlation between gender and attitudes towards crime and punishment in this period, even within the Tory party. A close reading of reports of Conservative party conference debates show that in fact both men and women delegates were to be found on either side of the debate. However, interestingly, there was a strong tendency on the part of penal progressives to accuse their opponents of emotionalism over the problem of violent crime, thus signifying supporters of corporal punishment as in some way 'feminine' in attitude, whether or not they were actually female. Butler himself exemplified this tendency when he stressed to the Party Conference in 1961 that the decision not to reintroduce judicial corporal punishment had been a collective, cabinet one, based on evidence, not emotion.[85] Calls to reinstate corporal punishment were denounced as impulsive and irrational; compensation, in contrast, was portrayed as a measured and humane welfare-style response to human need.

The Treasury was a much more formidable obstacle to victims' compensation than the men and women of the party conference and its reluctance to take on another spending commitment was probably the main reason why the scheme was not set up during Butler's time as Home Secretary. Margery Fry had conducted some research into the likely cost before her death (based on the amounts of compensation given in industrial injuries claims) and her figures provided the basis of campaigner's estimates for some years. Although the supporters regarded the projected sum of around £150,000 as modest the Treasury was unconvinced and claimed any compensation scheme would remain low on its list of priorities. Butler argued that there was strong public support for helping victims and that the government was liable to be accused of 'cheeseparing insensitivity to the needs and wishes of the public' if no commitment was made in the White Paper. However, he accepted that it might take time for funds to be made available: 'a cat besides looking at a King may look ahead ten years', he wrote to the Chancellor, Heathcoat-Amory.[86] The Chancellor refused to make any spending commitment but agreed that a working party be set up to discuss the plans in detail, although he expressed an opinion that restitution should form part of the scheme.[87] Therefore the 1959 White Paper duly contained a brief mention of the possibility of the introduction of victims' compensation and the establishment of a working party and the whole matter was postponed until the latter reported in 1961, by which time Butler was about to leave the Home Office.

Rock quotes the opinion of Leslie Wilkins that the objection to criminal injuries compensation was not on the grounds of cost.[88] However, archive evidence does suggest that there was reluctance to spend in the Treasury (although not in the Home Office, which estimated the cost of the scheme as between £150,000 and £200,000). Furthermore, it suggests that Butler's support for criminal injuries compensation was stronger than Rock maintains, although ultimately he backed down in the face of the Chancellor's reluctance to commit money. Like Margery Fry, Butler had attempted to detach concern from the victim from vengeful and punitive treatment of the offender and place it within a 'modern', progressive penal policy. As such, the proposals attracted cross-party support and while the working party considered its report, backbench MPs kept up the pressure for action.

Gender and 'the victim' in the 1950s

Before, during and after the establishment of the Working Party, proposals for victims' compensation continued to attract press attention. This section will examine this continuing campaign and the attitudes of key pressure groups (mainly the feminist-influenced women's organisations of the day) towards the issue, and consider to what extent commentators, especially in the press, continued constructing 'the victim' as female. Walklate had argued that both positivist victimology and feminist work since the 1970s have contributed to the gendering of the archetypal victim as feminine.[89] As this chapter has demonstrated, this process can be traced much further back, at least to the 1870s and 80s when feminists in the social purity movement first emphasised the problem of male mistreatment of women and girls. Even in the 1950s, when feminism was apparently in its most quiescent state, women's organisations continued to hold their focus on the female victim of crime.

There was, however, some disagreement within women's groups as to whether the answer was compensation or corporal punishment. The plight of victims of violence may have become a leitmotif of many conferences and meetings but there was a clear division between supporters of retribution and those who combined concern for the victim with a strong commitment to improving the treatment of offenders. The split between progressives and reactionaries was most evident at the1958 annual meeting of the National Federation of Women's Institutes (NFWI) when (according to *The Times*) a 'lively debate' took place over a resolution calling for 'severe penalties' for crimes of violence and sexual assault. The mention of the latter type of offence is significant, as it suggests a continued gendering of 'the victim', and demonstrates the long-term salience of feminist discourse on male violence. However, the punitive resolution did not carry the day, as the eventual outcome was the passage of an amendment that merely called for 'government action' in preventing such crimes. Clearly the NFWI members present heeded the advice of one delegate that it would be a 'disgrace' if it 'allowed its name to be put on a resolution which was essentially a cry for vengeance'.[90]

The NCW was similarly divided between supporters and opponents of the reintroduction of corporal punishment for crimes of violence against the person. The resurgent popularity of corporal punishment with the NCW rank and file became evident in the early 1950s when local branches in Harrogate and Liverpool sent resolutions supporting its reinstatement to the Public Service and Magistrates' Committee: Harrogate's resolution was defeated only by the chairman's casting vote.[91] A similar resolution was put to the NCW annual conference in 1956 when the former president, Florence Earengey predicted that opinion would be equally divided. In the event, and most significantly, the NCW retained its tradition of penal progressivism by rejecting the call for corporal punishment to be introduced for crimes of violence by a large majority.[92] Likewise, four years later the conference supported a resolution calling for 'the early introduction of a scheme to provide compensation for the victims of crimes of violence' but voted against a recommendation that courts impose tougher, deterrent penalties for assault.[93] National Unions of Townswomen's Guilds (NUTG) also expressed support for victims' compensation at its annual gathering in 1959.[94] Thus, even in an era when feminism was apparently at a low ebb and concern over crime was heightened, women's organisations (although their rank-and-file were somewhat split between reaction and reform) nevertheless both retained their interest in the victim and rejected the knee-jerk reactions of the 'law and order' lobby by continuing to support policies that were broadly progressive in nature, such as crime prevention and victims' compensation. The coalition of women's organisations and penal reformers that had been built in the years after the Sex Disqualification (Removal) Act appears to have held firm, despite the mounting media-led panic about violent crime in the 1950s.

Nevertheless, despite their largely progressive stance, it is clear from the references to sexual crimes that members of the NFWI and other women's organisations had mainly female victims in mind and that they continued to be concerned about the crimes of rape and sexual assault in particular. With a disregard for statistics that might have upset Margery Fry, politicians, the press and members of the public continued to construct the victim as feminine. For example, when considering the type of victim deemed suitable for compensation, Butler told the Cabinet that 'the victims are ... often women' and were therefore unlikely to be carrying weapons.[95]

The press, too, seemed determined to cast women in the role of victims. Even when the primary victim was male, the secondary ones – the suffering family members – were not. In 1960 the *Star* featured the case of the widow of a murdered pawnbroker, who was 'desperately in need', and linked it to criticism of government delays in publishing the Working Party's report. The widow's MP, Barbara Castle, raised her case in parliament and topically pointed out that the compensation scheme would cost around £200,000 annually, 'about the cost of a tail end of a supersonic bomber'. The widow, the *Star* claimed, was 'desperately in need but all she gets from the Home Office is the usual expression of official sympathy'.[96]

Compared with the 1920s, there seems to have been far less emphasis on the child victim of sexual abuse in the 1950s–60s' discussions of victims. Although the possibility of long-term psychological damage in victims of sex crime was now recognised, it is likely that monetary compensation (which was the focus of the debate) was seen as less relevant to children than appropriate professional help: after all, loss of earnings was not an issue for the youngest victims. One exception might be compensation for pregnancy, which was discussed in some detail in the proposals of 'Justice', although in this hypothetical case the putative victim was an adult.[97] Some commentators have argued that a 'resurgence in domestic ideologies' by the 1940s had led to a more general denial of the existence of child sexual abuse and its ill effects.[98] More optimistically, perhaps reformers hoped that the Welfare State, in the form of better housing and education, would ensure the prevention of abuse. Sexual crime therefore appears to have been constructed by the press more as a problem of 'stranger danger' directed towards adult women rather than as abuse within families, while the sociological discourses surrounding 'the problem family' in the 1950s were overwhelmingly concerned with maternal neglect, not paternal abuse (an approach which, incidentally, was deprecated by Margery Fry).

Concern about rape, and the way in which it featured in discussions of victims' compensation, is evidenced by an emotive account of sexual violence that appeared in print in 1963. Under the heading 'Assaulted!' and accompanied by dramatic photographs 'posed by models', *Parade* magazine raised the issue of victims' compensation by telling the story of an MP's secretary ('Miss Smith') who was attacked and raped on her way home from work. Significantly, the article combined a sensational treatment of sexual crime with a plea to the Home Secretary to introduce a compensation plan. *Parade* detailed Miss Smith's financial losses – the cost of clothing, private hospital facilities ('to escape evil gossip'), a convalescent home and gynaecological treatment – while pointing out that the total bill of £350 did not include any compensation for 'all the pain, terror and anguish she suffered' or for 'the bitter memory of a bestial sex attack which will prevent Miss Smith from ever being a fully-happy bride'. The victim was presented to readers as a young, respectable, attractive virgin, wronged not only by her attacker but also by the criminal justice system that sentenced him to just three years in jail (at a cost to 'the taxpayer' of nearly £1000) and by the government which was taking far too long to decide on a compensation scheme.

The article gave a further example – again of a sex attack on an 'attractive blonde wife' who was alone at home. While the victims were female, their attackers (described rather salaciously as the 'passion-crooks') and their saviours were all male. Both the women – the wife and the secretary – clearly had male protectors who had not been able to prevent their misfortune, and in fact the article was critical of vigilantism, despite some sympathy expressed for a Yorkshire father who 'thrashed' his daughter's attacker and was then charged with assault himself. Luckily there was another chivalrous band of rescuers waiting to assist women, the men of the pressure group 'Justice', which had taken up the issue of compensation.[99] Thus, in this press coverage, the female victim was deprived of agency, was helpless and voiceless as well as innocent, needing the support of masculine pressure groups and the public to force the government to take notice of her plight. Interestingly, the article also conflated retribution with compensation: the subheading declared 'Jailing rapists and other violent criminals is not enough. They should be made to PAY for their crimes'. Graphic details of sexual assault and criticism of light sentences for offenders were presented as evidence in support of a fairly cautious plan for state compensation advanced by a group of mainly left-leaning lawyers, academics and politicians.[100] A further headline, 'Make them pay!' was, of course, completely at odds with the plan discussed in the article which was to make *the state* pay!

Blaming the victim

For campaigners the best examples of victims were the most innocent and blameless. As we have seen, claims of 'provocation' were often made in court and inevitably the notion that victims were in some way to blame for their predicament was often raised in discussions of the projected compensation scheme. The *Parade* article also raised the question of victim culpability, but instead of her moral turpitude, the victim was likely to be blamed more for her carelessness. Alongside a posed photograph of a young woman in a short skirt being seized from behind by a shadowy attacker, the caption asked, 'she may be partly to blame but should that exclude her from receiving compensation?' An anonymous 'leading criminologist' quoted in the article was critical of the suggestion that culpability should be taken into account when compensation amounts were fixed. The unnamed source argued that the scheme would lead to 'a lawyer's picnic'.

> You can just imagine barristers getting up to argue that if Miss X wore provocative fishnets, or hitched up her skirt, or was careless about the choice of strangers with whom she drove home after midnight, she should get less compensation than a more sensible or sophisticated girl.

A 'penal expert' (who clearly opposed the scheme) was also quoted saying that 'in many of these cases, the girls themselves are slightly to blame'.[101] The article failed either to resolve this issue clearly or to address the related problem of the low level of convictions for rape and sexual assault. 'Provocation' was simply regarded as a 'problem', but the terms in which it was discussed in *Parade* indicated that 'the victim' might not always be innocent, and suggests that women were separated into the categories of Madonna and whore. While the former was 'innocent', the latter might in some way have contributed to her misfortune, even if her faults were no greater than choosing the wrong clothes or the wrong companions.

Another feminine stereotype who could not automatically count on public sympathy was the nagging wife. Wiener argues that as far back as the eighteenth century the penalisation of women's verbal 'crimes' had been reduced and that by the nineteenth century, 'the fear of the shrew' had lessened.[102] Nevertheless, defendants accused of wife-beating or even murder continued to cite verbal provocation, although in the case of the latter offence it was extremely unlikely to secure acquittal. It is an indication of the persistence of this stereotype that in 1962 the Lord Chancellor, Lord Dilhorne, in reply to a debate on the compensation scheme instigated by Lord Longford, expressed concern about determining a level of compensation for a battered wife who 'may have nagged [her husband] beyond all endurance'.[103] Similarly, discussions of compensation scheme proposals often dealt with the issue of collusion and whether the victimised close relatives of offenders should receive payment.[104]

Of course, not all the hypothetical victims discussed in the many debates that took place over this time were female. The various official and unofficial reports that appeared on the proposals for compensation between 1960 and 1964 generally treated 'the victim' in a fairly gender-neutral way except when dealing with the effects of sexual crime. Naturally the issue of culpability was also often raised in relation to injuries suffered in bar-room brawls between men. Nevertheless, especially in the more emotional and salacious coverage such as the *Parade* article, female victims, especially those who suffered sexual assault, took centre stage. At a time of increasing public concern about violent crime, the little old lady and her virginal granddaughter served a purpose in that they represented the sort of blameless victim for whom political campaigners could show their care. Thereby progressive lawyers such as those in 'Justice', and politicians in both the Labour and Conservative Parties, hoped to deflect public support for more punitive measures such as corporal and capital punishment. Margery Fry had adopted a similar rhetorical device in her radio broadcast in the mid-1950s, but her motivation arguably was more associated with restitution and justice than with political calculation. Butler, Reg Prentice, Castle and other politicians, on the other hand, were probably mainly interested in providing some official response to the growing clamour surrounding law and order in general and violent crime in particular.

Conclusion

After several years of public discussion and a period of Treasury-led pre-varication, legislation was introduced in 1964 to establish the Criminal Injuries Compensation Board. After the death of Margery Fry, much of the running had been made by members of a new pressure group 'Justice', formed following the Russian invasion of Hungary in 1956 by a group of lawyers. However Fry remained an important influence. The 'Justice' membership included several former Howard League colleagues of hers, notably Hartley Shawcross, a former Attorney-General, who had served as her assistant secretary for the HLPR in the mid-1920s and Gerald Gardiner, who was not only a leading opponent of the death penalty but also a strong supporter of women's causes such as abortion law reform. Fry had apparently made contact with 'Justice' shortly before her death and in May 1958 Shawcross and other members of the group wrote to *The Times* arguing that the introduction of a compensation scheme for victims would be 'an entirely fitting memorial to the work of a remarkable woman'.[105] As already noted, supporters of compensation routinely mentioned Fry as the instigator of the plan. However, in the case of 'Justice', there really was a close connection and she would surely have worked with this group had she lived longer.

In the House of Commons MPs such as Reg Prentice had pressed the compensation issue through private members' bills and parliamentary questions and, as we have seen, Butler was by no means unsympathetic when he was Home Secretary, although the Treasury was less enthusiastic. Butler also encouraged the Conservative Political Centre to produce its own report, which was submitted to the new Home Secretary, Henry Brooke, in 1962 a few months before the 'Justice' report.[106] Then in 1964 the government finally published its White Paper, the scheme was debated in Parliament, and commenced on 1st August.

Although women's organisations such as the NCW expressed support for victims' compensation in their resolutions and resisted calls for punitive measures to be taken against offenders, they did not campaign very actively for the scheme in the years leading up to its introduction. However, this was probably not because feminism was completely quiescent in the early 1960s, but rather because activists' energies were focused elsewhere at this point, namely on the campaign for women jurors and in dealing with the aftermath of Wolfenden Report recommendations on the law regarding prostitution and the resultant Street Offences legislation of 1959 (see Chapter 3). Nevertheless, they continued to be interested in justice for victims, especially young and/or female ones, a concern often made manifest in their ongoing campaign for women police. There was a characteristic complaint at the NCW Public Service and Magistrates' Committee in 1962 when an episode of the new BBC drama series *Z Cars* showed a young female victim being questioned without there being a woman police officer present.[107]

More broadly, feminist discourse had probably helped to shape popular (mis)conceptions about 'the victim' over many decades, even before male violence against women became a major concern of 'second wave' feminism. Although Margery Fry did not live to see the implementation of her plans in 1964, the influence, and practical campaigning in her last years, of this veteran of the suffrage generation was deeply significant in bringing about the first major policy initiative of the twentieth century to address the needs of the victim of crime. The Cinderella of the legal system had not lacked a fairy godmother.

Conclusion

> I am a feminist because I dislike everything that feminism implies. I desire an end to the whole business, the demands for equality, the suggestion of sex warfare, the very name of feminist . . . But while inequality exists, while injustice is done and opportunity is denied to the great majority of women, I shall have to be a feminist with the motto 'Equality First'.

This declaration, adapted from the words of the author Winifred Holtby, was chosen by Maureen Colquhoun to preface her own memoir, published in 1980.[1] Originally written in the context of the debate between 'old' and 'new' feminism that had erupted in the mid-1920s, the quotation nevertheless provided a suitable text for a feminist of a different generation. Colquhoun recognised the relevance of Holtby's manifesto to the struggles she participated in as a feminist and openly gay MP during the 1970s heyday of the Women's Liberation Movement. But Colquhoun was not one of the younger women of the 'second wave' of feminism. Born in 1928, she came to political maturity in the aftermath of the Second World War, at a time when feminism was supposedly at its lowest ebb.

This book has tried to achieve a number of objectives. On one level, it has attempted to bring to light a previously neglected aspect of feminist political activity between the 1920s and 60s, involvement in campaigns concerning criminal justice policies in general and those concerning women in particular. Evidence has been presented to support the assertion that the women's movement maintained a deep concern about many aspects of the criminal justice system, ranging from the overtly gendered operations of the courts and prisons to the problems of youth justice and the debate about the death penalty. Strong connections between women's organisations and the penal reform movement have been revealed, and the significance of a substantial number of women activists who crossed between these two overlapping worlds has been established. Margery Fry, whose work and personality were of central importance in the feminist–criminal–justice network until her death in 1958, would have heartily endorsed Winifred Holtby's sentiments quoted above. In Fry's own words: 'Women do their best work when they are allowed to do it, not as women, but as human beings'.[2] Fry and her allies in the Howard League for Penal Reform (HLPR) certainly did not limit their interests to the problems of women in the criminal justice system, although they were always mindful of its gendered impact and consistently applied a feminist analysis to its problems. Involvement in this area of policy was not a denial of their feminist principles, but an expression of them, the assertion of a woman's right to be politically engaged. Perhaps my biggest surprise in undertaking the research for this book was just how important the activism of a small group of women was to the operation of the HLPR between the early 1920s and the mid-1950s. Margery Fry's significance in this context is fairly well known, but the agency of her friends and allies Clara Dorothea Rackham, Cicely Craven, Winifred Elkin, Madeleine Robinson, Theodora Calvert, Gertrude Eaton and Marjorie Franklin (among many others) has not been fully appreciated. It is hard to imagine what Britain's penal reform movement would have achieved in this period without the work and dedication of its female volunteers.

In addition to recovering the story of feminist engagement with the problems of criminal justice this book has attempted to contribute further to an already well-established historiographical theme regarding the continued vitality of the women's movement in the so-called 'intermission' between the 'first' and 'second waves' of feminism. Rather than seeing the suffrage era before the First World War and the 1970s as the only moments when the women's movement had widespread support and political salience, these periods are better envisaged as spells of hyperactivity surrounded by decades of dogged, perhaps unspectacular, but nevertheless determined campaigning. This can be detected even in the 1950s, so long regarded as a low point in feminist activity. The period between the end of the Second World War and the early 1960s did pose particular problems for the feminist movement; but these were more of a practical nature than an ideological one in that the suffragist generation, whose members' awareness of gender inequality had been so heightened by their battle for the vote, was dying out. The women's movement did gain a new generation of leaders, but arguably their priorities were the consolidation of earlier gains rather than the attainment of fresh goals. The evidence covered in this book also indicates that feminists in the 1950s and early 1960s were highly selective in choosing to put their energies into campaigns that were both significant in terms of women's rights and winnable. The social climate of that period (or any time since) was not conducive to much improvement in the human rights of prostitutes but a sustained, and ultimately successful, campaign for equality in jury selection was run with support from across the women's movement. In short, feminism in 1950s Britain may have become a cautious and conservative beast in the political jungle of the time, but it was far from extinct.

The historiography of Britain in the 1950s is clearly still a work under construction, but already it seems possible to challenge some of the popularly imagined clichés about the period. It is conventional to portray the 1950s in terms of contrasts with the 1930s, as an age of affluence, consumerism and welfare as opposed to economic depression, poverty and unemployment. But when the state of the criminal justice system and the position of women in society are both considered, there is far greater similarity between the decades. The ten years after 1948 saw the implementation of a Criminal Justice Act which was based on policy discussions that had taken place 20 years before. Penal welfarism, which had its origins in the early twentieth century, was arguably at its zenith and was able to resist easily the rearguard action for a return to corporal punishment; while penal reformers in the 1950s were fighting for the same causes as 20 years previously, notably for the abolition of the death penalty. Meanwhile, feminists were still trying to get the law on jury selection reformed. Joan Kelly pointed out some years ago that feminist historiography is very capable of upsetting 'accepted evaluations of historical periods' and periodisation.[3] Criminal justice history likewise has its own narrative and 'turning points'.

Another, related aim of this book has been to probe the eternal, irresolvable historical conundrum of continuity versus change. It has been suggested that there was much more continuity between the feminisms of the different 'waves' and eras than is often assumed, especially regarding feminist discourse concerning women, crime and criminal justice. Most accounts of the relationship between feminism and criminology in Britain start with the 'second wave', often with the publication of Carol Smart's *Women, Crime and Criminology* in 1976.[4] Oddly, feminist criminologists in the last quarter of the twentieth century often began with the premise that criminology had neglected women offenders.[5] While this may be the case if one considers only the narrow discipline of academic, 'scientific' criminology from which women had been effectively excluded due in the main to gender inequality in universities, it is not a criticism that can be sustained if the work of feminists outside the academy is taken into account. For example, Chapter 4 highlights the extent to which a detailed feminist critique of the penal system was developed in the half-century following the imprisonment of suffragettes and was published in a variety of places, including feminist periodicals and penal reform journals. The real repository of detailed knowledge and understanding about women and crime was not to be found in male-dominated academia, where criminology was anyway a relatively small and underfunded pursuit at least until the 1960s, but among women JPs and prison visitors who had day-by-day contact with the criminal justice system and a network of voluntary organisations in which to discuss its problems. Despite their generally middle-class backgrounds and the role they played in the courts effectively 'policing' and controlling less fortunate men, women and children on behalf of the state, prominent women magistrates developed a powerful liberal feminist critique of criminal justice largely based on their understanding of the discourse of 'rights'. This was evident as much in their concern for 'the victim' as in their misgivings concerning the effectiveness of the prison system. Moreover, as Chapter 2 shows, leading women JPs and their organisations were important architects and promoters of penal welfarism in the youth justice system.

Chapter 4 hinted at discernable parallels between the 'first wave' feminist critique of the penal treatment of women and some of the campaigns that have emerged on this issue since 1970. The initial ten demands of the campaigning group Women in Prison,[6] founded in 1982, would have been perfectly comprehensible to HLPR campaigners in the 1930s and 40s, with the exception of references to the cessation of discrimination against lesbians. Even more recently in 2004, the Fawcett Society Commission on Women and the Criminal Justice System concluded that 'prison is rarely the solution for the complex issues faced by women offenders',[7] a statement with which Mary Gordon would have concurred 90 years ago. The Commission's report found that '[f]emale prisoners are a disproportionately disadvantaged population with high levels of poverty, low levels of educational attainment, and poor employment histories'. It also reported high levels of self-harm among women in prison, a high incidence of drug dependency and mental health problems, increasing amounts of re-offending by women and a lack of constructive training courses for them in comparison with men in prison.[8] The report concluded, '[w]e believe that there is an urgent need for the establishment nationally of non-custodial provision designed with women's needs in mind'.[9] If 'drink' is substituted for 'drugs' none of these points would have been unfamiliar to a regular attendee of meetings of women magistrates in the 1930s.

Of course, it would be a distortion to take the 'continuity' argument too far. Crucially, the social and moral attitudes which form such a vital influence over the practices of the criminal justice system were very different in the early part of the twentieth century than in the last 30 years. The ways in which the women's movement before the 1960s reflected and even reinforced the gender norms of the time has been criticised, for example the embracing of 'new' feminism by National Union of Societies for Equal Citizenship (NUSEC) in the 1920s and 30s has been interpreted as acceptance of the patriarchal system and acquiescence with the notion of 'separate spheres'. But to a large extent this was the result of pragmatism on the part of the advocates of 'new' feminism. For example, the frequent suggestion that the ideal rehabilitation for a young female offender was a stable, companionate marriage could be interpreted as support for patriarchal relations, but was equally likely to be the outcome of a realisation that the alternatives for many of the women were poverty, unstable relationships or even a return to jail. The women's movement in the first half of the twentieth century was anyway a 'broad church' that included many people who, despite fighting for improvements in the lot of women, rejected identification as 'feminists', for example Gertrude Tuckwell, whose 'political work for women . . . might be considered by others to identify her with the communitarian socialist mode of feminism'[10] despite her own denial of the label at the height of the debate over protective legislation for women workers during the mid-1920s.

Notwithstanding the heat of the debate during the 1920s between the 'old', equalitarian feminists and the supporters of 'new', welfare-orientated policies, there remained a lot of common ground between the two groups and they often continued to collaborate on campaigns. Members of the equalitarian camp were just as apt as 'new' feminists to make statements concerning women's 'special' abilities, for example in arguments they employed in favour of women magistrates for juvenile courts. However, in general the feminists featured in this book tended to avoid the type of claims made in the Victorian period about women's 'nature', instead placing their arguments in the name of 'common humanity' as the quote from Holtby at the start of this chapter suggests. Women's 'special' abilities were envisaged as more a matter of nurture than nature: although campaigners would not have used the term, they perceived that gender roles were socially constructed. Moreover, although maternal ideology had some rhetorical utility and provided a useful key to opening up the masculine world of criminal justice to women, activists clearly refused to confine their concern to women and children. The differences between feminists therefore seem less significant in the context of criminal justice than the common ground between them. It is also important to recognise that the generation of liberal feminists typified by Margery Fry were great optimists and believers in progress. Fry, looking back over her life when she was in her late seventies, was mindful of and thankful for the significant changes she had witnessed in the status of women, recalling that when she was young, '[s]uch creatures as women lawyers, or MPs or directors of businesses, or soldiers or policemen were undreamt of, or only dreamt of as familiar figures of fun in farces.'[11]

Although their ideas were naturally shaped by the era they lived in, members of the feminist–criminal justice network were not necessarily lacking in imagination, nor were they as cautious or conservative as they might have appeared. Women JPs, most obviously those with left-wing views, could be audacious, even outspoken in their criticism of the criminal justice system. In the early 1920s the South Wales suffragist and Liberal parliamentary candidate Mrs Coombe Tenant, claimed after only three years as a JP to be 'appalled' at the amount of power in the hands of untrained local magistrates.

> Any two magistrates may order the removal of a child . . . to an industrial school against the will of its parents . . . Can anyone suppose if this power had been exercised against the children of well-to-do parents it would have remained without safeguards?[12]

Although her statement could be interpreted simply as a plea for more training for JPs, it also hints at a deeper unease with the social bias of the criminal justice system. Socialist woman especially were apt to reflect upon class as well as gender inequalities in the system. Speaking at a conference of magistrates in 1927 Gertrude Tuckwell admitted that there appeared to be 'one law for the rich and another for the poor'.[13] Later in the century Barbara Wootton, a feminist and a socialist, was critical of many aspects of the system as she surveyed it after retirement from the bench in the 1960s, claiming that 'in my later days as a juvenile court chairman I began to feel more and more as if we were all enacting scenes from Dickens'.[14] Wootton also expressed doubts about the sexual mores she was supposed to enforce in the juvenile court, recalling that she had 'great difficulty in producing convincing reasons why young people should not behave as they preferred provided always that they took adequate precautions'.[15] Perhaps doubts such as these were confined to a minority of women predisposed to question society's moral standards and the criminal justice system which was a reflection of those values. But these were the very women who played such a central part in the feminist–criminal–justice reform network and some of them, including Wootton, were widely acknowledged as experts and were even recruited by the government as policy advisers.

Finally, it is necessary to address the problem regarding why the myth persists that 'first wave' feminism had died long before the advent of the 'second wave'. Largely this has been a question of historical amnesia, coupled with the inevitable fact that less attention is accrued by patient, dull committee work than the spectacle of street protest. As Cheryl Law pointed out regarding the contrast between the state of the women's movement in the 1920s and before the First World War, 'using the militant phase [of the women's suffrage movement] as a yardstick for all subsequent political activity has undermined a sincere portrayal of women's participation'.[16] However, the idea that there was a historical pause between the 'waves' is often perpetrated by feminists themselves. For example, Daly and Chesney-Lind proposed that 'first wave' feminism had ended with the granting of women's suffrage, yet acknowledged 'that the conventional dating of the first- and second-wave is rightly challenged by several scholars who find greater continuity in feminist thought and action'.[17]

Maggie Humm argues that second wave feminism 'takes as its starting point the politics of reproduction, while sharing first wave feminism's politics of legal, educational and economic equal rights for women'.[18] However, this seems to be a very fine distinction, given the admission of so much common ground and in view of abundant evidence that 'first wave' feminism in the late nineteenth and early twentieth centuries by no means ignored the 'politics of reproduction'. The common ground is, of course, the territory of liberal feminism, the ideological underpinning of key campaigns for women's rights fought in all 'waves'. Although often reduced to the status of one feminist 'perspective' among many, liberal feminism has nevertheless delivered some tangible improvements in the status of women in Britain: notions of 'rights', 'duties' and 'equality' have proved to be powerful ideological weapons. But with their new ideas and fresh perspectives, some 'second wave' feminists in the 1970s may have been unable to recognise their affinity with an older, more cautious generation and instead chose to reinvent feminism as if from scratch. Inspired by socialist philosophy, many British 'second wave' feminists felt they had little in common with the older, more conservative, generation. Thus the old lobbying methods of a traditional pressure group were swept aside by the energetic, young enthusiasts for a 'new social movement'.

More than 30 years later, as the young women of the 1970s have become the older generation themselves, a reappraisal of feminism in the mid-twentieth century has been largely achieved. In many ways the period offers parallels with the present day. Once again the mass media treats feminism as 'dead', as a thing of the past,[19] and young women are encouraged to assume that the battles for rights have all been won. Yet there is plenty of evidence that neither of these suppositions is true. The vibrancy of a good deal of the women's movement in working for the reform of criminal justice between 1920 and 1970 suggests that these contentions were as untenable then as they are now.

Notes

Introduction

1. 'When I am MP', *The Vote* (paper of the Women's Freedom League), 15 June 1928, p. 186.
2. A. Logan, 'In search of equal citizenship', *Women's History Review*, 16, 4 (2007) 501–18.
3. N. Naffine, *Feminism and Criminology* (Cambridge: Polity Press, 1997), p. 11.
4. J. Walkowitz, *Prostitution and Victorian Society* (Cambridge: Cambridge University Press, 1980).
5. For a discussion of Frances Power Cobbe's 'Wife Torture in England' article, see B. Caine, *Victorian Feminists* (Oxford: Oxford University Press, 1992). For child abuse, see S. Jeffreys, *The Spinster and Her Enemies: Feminism and Sexuality 1880–1930* (London: Pandora Press, 1985); L. A. Jackson, *Child Sex Abuse in Victorian England* (London: Routledge, 2000).
6. For example, C. Lytton, *Prison and Prisoners* (London: Virago, 1988, first published 1914). See also J. Purvis, 'The Prison Experiences of the Suffragettes in Edwardian Britain', *Women's History Review*, 4, 1 (1995) 103–33.
7. O. Banks, *Faces of Feminism: A Study of Feminism as a Social Movement* (Oxford: Martin Robertson, 1981), Part III.
8. C. Law, *Suffrage and Power, The Women's Movement, 1918–28* (London: I. B. Tauris, 1997), p. 225.
9. M. Pugh, *Women and the Women's Movement in Britain*, 2nd edn (Basingstoke: Macmillan, 2000), pp. 108–10.
10. Law, *Suffrage and Power*, p. 177.
11. M. Andrews, *The Acceptable Face of Feminism: The Women's Institute as a Social Movement* (London: Lawrence and Wishart, 1997); C. Beaumont, 'Citizens not Feminists: the boundary negotiated between citizenship and feminism by mainstream women's organisations in England, 1928–39', *Women's History Review*, 9, 2 (2000) 411–29. S. Innes, 'Constructing Women's Citizenship in the Interwar Period: the Edinburgh Women Citizens' Association', *Women's History Review*, 13, 4 (2004) 621–47. For full discussion of this point, see Chapter 1.
12. H. Jones, *Women in British Public Life, 1914–50: Gender, Power and Social Policy* (Harlow: Longman, 2000).
13. J. Liddington, *The Road to Greenham Common: Feminism and Anti-Militarism in Britain since 1820* (London: Virago, 1989).
14. D. Garland, *The Culture of Control* (Oxford: Oxford University Press, 2001), p. 3; V. Bailey, *Delinquency and Citizenship: Reclaiming the Young Offender, 1914–1948* (Oxford: Clarendon Press, 1987); D. Garland, *Punishment and Welfare* (Aldershot: Gower, 1985).
15. Excellent recent examples on these topics are H. J. Self, *The Fallen Daughters of Eve: Prostitution, Women and Misuse of the Law* (London: Frank Cass, 2003) and L. A. Jackson, *Women Police: Gender, Welfare and Surveillance in the Twentieth Century* (Manchester: Manchester University Press, 2006).

16. Fawcett Society Commission on Women and the Criminal Justice System, *Report* (London: Fawcett Society, 2004).
17. Pugh, *Women and the Women's Movement*, Chap. 10.
18. C. Dyhouse, *Feminism and the Family in England, 1880–1939* (Oxford: Blackwell, 1989), p. 4.
19. Beaumont, 'Citizens not Feminists'.
20. B. Harrison, *Prudent Revolutionaries* (Oxford: Clarendon Press, 1987).
21. S. Kemp and J. Squires (eds), *Feminisms* (Oxford: Oxford University Press, 1997), p. 3.
22. Banks, *Faces of Feminism*, pp. 169–72.
23. S. K. Kent, *Making Peace: The Reconstruction of Gender in Interwar Britain* (New Jersey: Princeton University Press, 1993).
24. See P. Thane, 'Women of the British Labour Party and feminism, 1906–45', in H. L. Smith (ed.) *British Feminism in the Twentieth Century* (Aldershot: Edward Elgar, 1990).
25. J. Hinton, *Women, Social Leadership and the Second World War* (Oxford: Oxford University Press, 2002), p. 4.
26. J. Liddington and J. Norris, *One Hand Tied Behind Us* (London: Virago, 1978).
27. J. Gaffin and D. Thoms, *Caring and Sharing: The Centenary History of the Co-operative Women's Guild* (Manchester: Co-operative Union Ltd, 1983), p. 88.
28. Pugh, *Women and the Women's Movement*, Chap. 10.
29. S. Spencer, *Gender, Work and Education in Britain in the 1950s* (Basingstoke: Palgrave Macmillan, 2005).
30. Ibid., p. 2.
31. A. Logan, 'Making Women Magistrates: Feminism, Citizenship and Justice in England and Wales, 1918–1950' (unpublished PhD thesis, University of Greenwich, 2002).
32. L. Zedner, *Women, Crime and Custody in Victorian England* (Oxford: Clarendon Press, 1991) p. 123.
33. E. B. Freedman, *Their Sisters' Keepers: Women's Prison Reform in America, 1830–1930* (Ann Arbor: University of Michigan Press, 1981).
34. J. Manton, *Mary Carpenter and the Children of the Streets* (London: Heinemann, 1976) p. 164.
35. Zedner, *Women, Crime and Custody*, p. 120.
36. For full details of Carpenter's 'conversion' to feminist causes, see Manton, *Mary Carpenter*, pp. 217–9.
37. Walkowitz, *Prostitution*, p. 125.
38. Ibid., p. 117.
39. M. J. Wiener, *Men of Blood: Violence, Manliness, and Criminal Justice in Victorian England* (Cambridge: Cambridge University Press, 2004), pp. 3, 156.
40. See J. Jordan, *Josephine Butler* (London: John Murray, 2001), pp. 222–9.
41. Jeffreys, *Spinster and Her Enemies*, p. 62. See also L. Bland, *Banishing the Beast: English Feminism and Sexual Morality, 1885–1914* (Harmondsworth: Penguin, 1995) p. 253.
42. WL 4NVA, minutes, 12 November 1886.
43. Ibid., 4 October 1887; 1 November 1887. The superintendents' responses were mostly negative (minutes, 3 January 1888). Although some historians have claimed the NVA were requesting the appointment of women police, the exact

wording of their demand was 'women attendants at police cells'. For the campaign for women lawyers, see Chap. 3.

44. TNA HO45/24609, cutting from *Common Cause*, October 1910. A reader sent the cutting to the Home Secretary, Winston Churchill, adding 'it is high time [women] had some share in the administration of the criminal law where women and young girls are concerned'.
45. H. Frances, '"Dare To Be Free!" The Women's Freedom League and its legacy', in J. Purvis and S. Holton (eds), *Votes For Women* (London: Routledge, 2000), p. 193.
46. *Votes for Women*, May 1917; August 1917.
47. Purvis, 'Prison experiences', 109–10.
48. Lytton, *Prisons and Prisoners*, p. 56.
49. *Howard Journal*, III, 1, (1930) p. 39. The Penal Reform League later merged with the Howard Association to form the HLPR. See Chap. 1.
50. WMRC MSS16C/6/P/6, PRL 4th Annual Report 1911.
51. G. Rose, *The Struggle for Penal Reform* (London: Stevens, 1961), p. 75.
52. WMRC MSS16C/6/P/6, PRL 6th Annual Report, 1913.
53. *The Times*, 21 July 1913, p. 10.
54. Ibid., 12 April 1912, p. 10. The NUWW was the forerunner of the NCW.
55. Ibid., 29 March 1919, p. 4.

1   Feminism and Criminal Justice Reform

1. TNA LC02/463, press release 27 July 1920.
2. Ibid., undated memorandum from Schuster to Sir Edward Troup.
3. The Hampshire Women Magistrates' Association (HWMA) allowed men to attend their meetings as 'honorary members', but the response from male colleagues appears to have been poor. See HRO 23M57/1.
4. M. Morgan, 'The Women's Institute Movement – The Acceptable Face of Feminism?', in S. Oldfield (ed.) *This Working Day World: Women's Lives and Culture(s) in Britain 1914–1945* (London: Taylor and Francis, 1994), p. 30; S. Innes, 'Constructing Women's Citizenship in the Interwar Period: the Edinburgh Women Citizens' Association', *Women's History Review*, 13, 4 (2004), 621–47; C. Beaumont, 'Citizens Not Feminists: The Boundary Negotiated Between Citizenships and Feminism by Mainstream Women's Organisation in England 1928–39', *Women's History Review*, 9, 2 (2000), 411–29.
5. A. Logan, 'In Search of Equal Citizenship', *Women's History Review*, 16, 4 (2007), 501–18.
6. For the role of mutual improvement in the self-education of the British working class, see J. Rose, *The Intellectual Life of the British Working Classes* (New Haven: Yale University Press, 2001).
7. These were Margaret Wynn Nevinson (Hampstead), *The Vote*, 30 July 1920, Mrs E. J. Smith (Brighton) Ibid., 27 August 1920 and Miss Tooke (Gateshead) Ibid., 17 September 1920.
8. For example, *The Vote*, 20 January 1933, p. 18.
9. See Chapter 3.
10. For example, 'A Magistrates' Task', by 'ASC' (Alice Schofield Coates, League president and Middlesbrough magistrate), *The Vote*, 21 September 1928, p. 303.

11. E. Wilson, *Only Halfway to Paradise: Women in Postwar Britain: 1945–1968* (London: Tavistock, 1980) p. 183.
12. C. Eustance, 'Daring to be Free!' (unpublished D Phil thesis, University of York, 1993), p. 327.
13. Ibid., p. 386.
14. Ibid., p. 327.
15. See Chapter 5.
16. *The Vote*, 24 April 1925, pp. 130, 135.
17. TNA PCOM9/409, letter from Margery Fry to Alexander Paterson, 18 July 1930.
18. *Woman's Leader*, 26 November 1920, p. 915 and 3 December 1920, p. 948; *The Times*, 1 December 1920, p. 9.
19. *Woman's Leader*, 11 August 1922, p. 218.
20. Ibid., 1 September 1922, p. 241 and 8 September 1922, pp. 254–5.
21. GCRO 06165/1, GWMS minutes, 30 September 1922.
22. *Woman's Leader*, 22 May 1925, p. 134; 5 June 1925, p. 150.
23. *Howard Journal*, I, 1 (1921), pp. 4; 63–4.
24. TNA PCOM/409; *Woman's Leader*, 17 October 1931.
25. *Howard Journal*, IV, 4 (1937).
26. B. Harrison, *Prudent Revolutionaries: Portraits of British Feminists between the Wars* (Oxford: Oxford University Press, 1987), p. 8.
27. Ibid., p. 17.
28. D. Spender (ed.), *Time and Tide Wait for No Man* (London: Pandora Press, 1984), p. 170.
29. Ibid., p. 178.
30. Wilson, *Halfway to Paradise*, p. 182.
31. WL 5/SPG.
32. See Chapter 5.
33. H. J. Self, *The Fallen Daughters of Eve: Prostitution, Women and Misuse of the Law* (London: Frank Cass, 2003), pp. 50, 88, 102. The Josephine Butler Society (JBS) is still a NCW affiliate.
34. D. Glick, *The National Council of Women: The First One Hundred Years* (London: National Council of Women, 1995), pp. 125–8.
35. For example, by J. Alberti, *Beyond Suffrage: Feminists in War and Peace, 1914–1928* (London: Macmillan, 1989), p. 123. For a recent analysis of NUWW political attitudes, see J. Bush, *Women Against the Vote: Female Anti-Suffragism in Britain* (Oxford: Oxford University Press, 2007), pp. 57–65.
36. N. and J. MacKensie (eds), *The Diary of Beatrice Webb Volume 2* (London: Virago, 1983), pp. 124–5.
37. M. Pugh, *The March of the Women* (Oxford: Oxford University Press, 2000), p. 102.
38. P. Hollis, *Ladies Elect: Women in English Local Government, 1865–1914* (Oxford: Oxford University Press, 1987), p. 237.
39. A description of Lady Selborne JP, sister of Lord Salisbury and NCW president 1920–1: C. Sykes, *Nancy: The Life of Lady Astor* (London: Collins, 1972), p. 201.
40. Glick, *National Council of Women*, p. 121.
41. LMA ACC/3613/1/77, PSMC minutes, 25 January 1914.
42. Ibid., 23 June 1921.
43. Ibid., 15 May 1927.
44. See Chapter 3.
45. LMA ACC/3613/1/77, PSMC minutes, 7 December 1922.

46. See TNA HO73/116, evidence of Miss Kelly to the Committee on the Treatment of Young Offenders (1925).
47. In her evidence to the committee (ibid.) Miss Kelly admitted, 'I have not got the correct feminist idea that women police will do everything that is not done at the present time.' However, her views could be seen as incorporating feminist sentiments.
48. Later known as Madeleine Robinson.
49. She was also a member of the Executive of the Magistrates' Association.
50. TNA HO73/116.
51. LMA 3613/01/079. The juvenile court rules allowed cases to be tried by men justices without the presence of women, but not vice versa.
52. Ibid., PSMC minutes, 17 November 1965. Wembley branch objected to the suggestion, apparently later dropped, that the country's first woman judge should be addressed in this way.
53. C. Frankenberg, *Not Old Madam, Vintage: An Autobiography* (Lavenham: Galaxy Books, 1975), p. 49.
54. Ibid., p. 134.
55. *Guardian*, 5 January 1967 (cutting in WL).
56. M. Pugh, *Women and the Women's Movement in Britain 1914–1959*, 2nd edition (Basingstoke: Macmillan, 2000), p. 302.
57. Glick, *The National Council of Women*, p. 149.
58. Ibid., p. 120.
59. http://fp.ncwgb.f9.co.uk/index.htm (accessed 30 August 2007).
60. Self, *Prostitution*, p. 183.
61. G. Rose, *The Struggle for Penal Reform* (London: Stevens, 1961), p. 97.
62. Ibid., p. 101.
63. Ibid., p. 156.
64. Margery Fry Papers (MFP), transcript of 'The Most Important Things', (BBC broadcast, 12 May 1957).
65. Shawcross was a barrister, politician and businessman, serving as attorney-general in the Atlee government. M. Beloff, 'Shawcross, Hartley William, Baron Shawcross, 1902–2003', *Oxford Dictionary of National Biography* (online edn: Oxford University Press, Jan. 2007, accessed 3 Sept. 2007).
66. E. Huws Jones, *Margery Fry: The Essential Amateur* (Oxford: Oxford University Press, 1966), p. 149.
67. D. Wills, 'Marjorie Franklin', *British Journal of Criminology*, 15, 2 (1975), p. 110.
68. *Newnham College Register, Volume I* (Cambridge: Newnham College, 1979).
69. WMRC MS16B/ADP/1/1. Gore Booth and Roper were leading suffragists in the north west of England who have been credited with reviving the women's suffrage movement in the region and with encouraging Christabel Pankhust to play an active part in it. See J. Liddington and J. Norris, *One Hand Tied Behind Us* (London: Virago, 1978), pp. 170–1. For a full account of their lives, see G. Lewis, *Eva Gore Booth and Esther Roper: A Biography* (London: Pandora Press, 1988).
70. WMRC MS16B ADP/4/2/4, list of vice presidents of the NCADP.
71. TNA HO45/16943.
72. *The Times*, 20 July 1920, p. 14.
73. WUMRC MSS16C/4/21.
74. *The Times*, 27 October 1920, p. 9.

75. Huws Jones, *The Essential Amateur*, p. 118; Minutes of Evidence to the Royal Commission on Justices of the Peace (1948), Cmd 7463, appendix III, para. 2334.
76. The six being Miss Fry, Miss Kelly, Mrs Rackham, Mrs Dowson, Miss Tuckwell and Miss Rathbone. See MA Second Annual Report (1923), p. 2.
77. Ibid., p. 5; Third Annual Report (1924), p. 5.
78. GCRO D6156/2, GWMS minutes, 25 February 1947.
79. *The Magistrate*, V, VII, (Jan.–Feb. 1939), p. 166.
80. J. P. Eddy, *Justice of the Peace* (London: Cassell, 1963), p. 181.
81. The work of Sue Innes is an obvious exception, but concerns Scotland, not England and Wales.
82. M. Pugh, *Women and the Women's Movement*, pp. 50–1.
83. WL 5NWC, Maidstone WCA minute book 1918–1927.
84. Morgan, 'The Women's Institute Movement', p. 31.
85. Pugh, *Women and the Women's Movement*, p. 242.
86. CCRO RS84/91, Cambridge and District WCA programmes. This WCA was not wound up until 1984.
87. Women's Library: 5NWC, 'A Job in Each Hand'; report on members' survey (1956–7).
88. D. Spender, *There's Always Been a Women's Movement This Century* (London: Pandora Press, 1983), p. 159.
89. The following section is based upon the GWMS minute book in Gloucestershire County Record Office: GCRO 06156/1.
90. GCRO D6156/2, cutting from *Birmingham Evening Dispatch*, 28 September 1937.
91. Ibid., *Birmingham Evening Dispatch*, 14 October 1937.
92. Ibid., *Birmingham Mail*, 23 September 1937.
93. LMA ACC/3613/1/77, PSMC minutes, 15 May 1930; HRO 23M57/1 and 23M57/5/2.
94. GCRO D61562, *Birmingham Post*, 14 October 1937.
95. GCRO D6156/1, GWMS minutes, 9 April 1935 and 30 June 1936.
96. *The Times*, 23 October 1935, p. 15.
97. E. Burney, *Magistrate, Court and Community* (London: Hutchinson, 1979), p. 209.
98. HRO: 23M57/9.
99. WUMRC MSS 16C/4/2.
100. Pugh, *Women and the Women's Movement*, p. 248.
101. Rose, *The Struggle for Penal Reform*, p. 102.
102. WL 3/AMS/B/04/11, Pethick Lawrence to Alison Neilans, 25 January 1937.
103. Frankenberg, *Not Old Madam, Vintage*, p. 166.
104. Pugh, *Women and the Women's Movement*, p. 284.

2   Juvenile Justice

1. TNA LCO2/463, letter from Schuster to the Home Office, 16 February 1920.
2. Royal Commission on Justices of the Peace, *Evidence* (London: HMSO, 1910) Cd 5358, paragraphs 1013–15 and 1196–1200.

3. Gertrude Tuckwell Papers (GTP), cutting from the *Times Educational Supplement* (1919?).

4. S. Koven and S. Michel, *Mothers of a New World: Maternalist Politics and the Origins of Welfare States* (London: Routledge, 1993), p. 2.

5. F. Prochaska, *Women and Philanthropy in Nineteenth-Century England* (Oxford: Clarendon Press, 1980), pp. 149–50.

6. K. Bradley, 'Juvenile Delinquency, the Juvenile Courts and the Settlement Movement 1908–1950: Basil Henriques and Toynbee Hall', *Twentieth Century British History*, 19, 2 (2008), pp. 133–55.

7. For the relationship between social activism and suffragism, see J. Lewis, *Women and Social Action in Victorian and Edwardian England* (Aldershot: Edward Elgar, 1991); O. Banks, *Faces of Feminism: A Study of Feminism as a Social Movement* (Oxford: Martin Robertson, 1981), pp. 95–6.

8. For example, E. Macadam, *The Social Servant in the Making* (London: George Allen and Unwin, 1945).

9. E. Macadam, *The Equipment of the Social Worker* (London: George Allen and Unwin, 1925), p. 206.

10. E. B. Freedman, *Maternal Justice: Miriam Van Waters and the Female Reform Tradition* (Chicago: University of Chicago Press, 1996), p. xiii.

11. A. Platt, *The Child Savers* (Chicago: University of Chicago Press, 1969), pp. 77–9.

12. J. Lewis, 'Gender, the Family and Women's Agency in the Building of "Welfare States": the British Case', *Social History*, 19, 1 (1994), pp. 37–55.

13. L. Mahood, *Policing Gender, Class and Family* (London: UCL Press, 1995), pp. 72–5.

14. L. Gordon, *Heroes of Their Own Lives, the Politics and History of Family Violence: Boston 1880–1960* (London: Virago, 1988), p. 62.

15. M. Tims, *Jane Addams of Hull House, 1860–1935: A Centenary Study* (London: Allen & Unwin, 1961), pp. 64–5.

16. L. Martindale, *A Woman Surgeon* (London: Gollancz, 1951), p. 95.

17. J. Whitney, *Geraldine S. Cadbury 1865–1941* (London: Harrap, 1948), p. 109.

18. H. Hendrick, *Images of Youth: Age, Class and the Male Youth Problem* (Oxford: Clarendon Press, 1990).

19. J. Springhall, *Coming of Age: Adolescence in Britain, 1860–1960* (Dublin: Gill & Macmillan, 1986), pp. 28–9.

20. Youth movements were established partly in order to divert youthful energies away from harmful activities. See J. Springhall, *Youth, Empire and Society 1883–1940* (London: Croom Helm, 1977).

21. *The Vote*, 12 September 1913, p. 326.

22. N. Adler, *Separate Courts of Justice for Children* (London: Women's Industrial Council, 1908). Miss Adler later served on the London County Council and as a London JP.

23. D. Bochel, *Probation and Aftercare: its Development in England and Wales* (Edinburgh: Scottish Academic Press, 1976), p. 40–1.

24. Whitney, *Geraldine S. Cadbury*, pp. 72–86.

25. G. Cadbury, *Young Offenders Yesterday and Today* (London: George Allen & Unwin, 1938), p. 97.

26. The Barrow Cadbury Trust was one of the sponsors of the 2004 Report of the Fawcett Society Commission on Women and the Criminal Justice System.

27. T. Skyrme, *History of the Justices of the Peace Volume 2* (Chichester: Barry Rose, 1991), p. 255.
28. Adler, *Separate Courts*, p. 5.
29. Ibid., p. 6.
30. Jane Lewis, 'Anxieties about the family and the relationships between parents, children and the state in 20th Century England', in M. Richards and P. Light (eds.), *Children of the Social World* (Oxford: Blackwell, 1986), p. 38.
31. *House of Commons Debates*, 1 November 1920, column 153.
32. GTP, cutting from *Daily Express*, 21 December 1918.
33. *House of Lords Debates*, 15 June 1920, column 594.
34. Banks, *Faces of Feminism*, p. 89.
35. J. Lewis (ed.), *Labour and Love: Women's Experience of Home and Family, 1850–1940* (Oxford: Blackwell, 1986), p. 6.
36. Banks, *Faces of Feminism*, pp. 98–9, p. 167.
37. LMA ACC/3613/1/77, PSMC minutes, 12 May 1920.
38. Ibid.; *NCW Occasional Paper 91*, July 1920.
39. GTP, cutting from *Reynold's News*, 16 June 1919.
40. Ibid., cutting from *Daily Chronicle*, 14 April 1926.
41. Prochaska, *Women and Philanthropy*, p. 1.
42. Juvenile Courts (Metropolis) Act, 1920 (10 & 11 Geo. 5.), pp. 1–2.
43. Skyrme, *History of the Justices of the Peace Volume 2*, p. 149.
44. TNA LCO2/897066; WL 5NCW, recruitment leaflet n. d. (c. 1968).
45. *The Times*, 27 April 1923, p. 9.
46. *House of Commons Debates*, 1 November 1920, columns 148–9.
47. TNA LC02/463.
48. *The Times*, 29 October 1932, p. 12.
49. TNA LCO2/463, memorandum from Clarke Hall, 20th February 1920.
50. Ibid., letter from Biron, 31 July 1920. This description is reminiscent of similar terms used for women's suffrage supporters.
51. TNA LC02/463, reply to Schuster from Home Office, n. d.
52. Ibid., report from Chief Metropolitan Magistrate, 25 February 1920.
53. Ibid., letter from Schuster to the Home Office, 19 March 1920.
54. Lord Birkenhead specifically rejected the plan when proposing the Bill's second reading. *House of Lords Debates*, 15 June 1920, columns 596–7.
55. TNA LCO2/463, letter to Lord Chancellor from Robert Parr, NSPCC Director, 20 March 1920.
56. Ibid., cutting from *Westminster and Pimlico News*, n. d.
57. *The Times*, 10 May 1920, p. 13.
58. Ibid.
59. Ibid., 12 May 1920, p. 12.
60. Ibid., 13 May 1920, p. 12.
61. Ibid., 21 May 1920, p. 11.
62. TNA LCO2/463, letter to Claud Schuster from Gertrude Tuckwell, 16 June 1920.
63. TNA HO45/10970/404139.
64. TNA LCO2/463, memorandum from 'B.S.', 27 May 1920.
65. *The Times*, 21 May 1920, p. 11.
66. *House of Lords Debates*, 15 June 1920, columns 601–12.
67. Ibid., columns 593–9, 624.
68. Ibid., 21 June 1920, columns 809–11; 6 August 1920, column 921.

69. Ibid., 6 August 1920, column 918.
70. TNA LCO2/463, letters from Schuster to Tuckwell 17 June and 26 July 1920; Tuckwell to Schuster 25 July 1920.
71. For the full list, see *The Times*, 20 July 1920, p. 14.
72. TNA LCO2/463, letter from Schuster to Tuckwell, 26 July 1920.
73. Ibid., letter from Biron, 31 July 1920.
74. *House of Commons Debates*, 1 November 1920, columns 134–52.
75. Ibid., column 146.
76. *The Times*, 11 January 1921, p. 7.
77. Ibid., 17 January 1921, p. 7.
78. TNA HO45/13777, minutes of evidence of the Home Office committee on the Metropolitan Courts and Juvenile Courts, 10 December 1928.
79. TUC Library, copy of Home Office memorandum, 17 December 1929.
80. TNA HO45/13777/27.
81. TNA HO45/13403/12.
82. J. Lovat Fraser, *Child Offenders* (London: State Children's Association, 1928), pp. 3–4. Lovat Fraser was a barrister on the South Wales circuit, a Cardiff councillor and Labour MP.
83. *Woman's Leader*, 14 August 1925, p. 230.
84. Departmental Committee on the Treatment of Young Offenders, *Report* (1927), Cmd. 2381, Appendix 1, p. 131.
85. Ibid., pp. 26–7.
86. TNA HO45/13402/2.
87. TNA HO45/13402/6. With very few exceptions, notably Clarke Hall and Mullins, stipendiaries did not involve themselves in the Magistrates' Association.
88. TNA LCO2/1955.
89. TNA HO45/15746/59.
90. TNA LCO2/1955.
91. LMA/3613/01/079, PSMC minutes, 17 June 1948; 15 October 1955.
92. TNA HO45/15746/74.
93. A. Logan, 'Professionalism and the Impact of England's First Women Justices', *Historical Journal*, 49, 3, (2006), pp. 833–50.
94. TNA HO45/15746/51.
95. H. Mannheim, *Juvenile Delinquency in an English Middletown* (London: Kegan Paul, 1948).
96. *The Vote*, 22 May 1931, p. 165.
97. *The Vote*, 22 May 1931, p. 165.
98. A. Logan, "A Suitable Person for Suitable Cases": The Gendering of Juvenile Courts in England, c. 1910–39, *Twentieth Century British History*, 16, 2 (2005) 129–145.
99. Bradley, 'Juvenile Delinquency'.
100. Cadbury, *Young Offenders*, pp. 116–7. The age of criminal responsibility was eight.
101. Cadbury, *Young Offenders*, pp. 73–4.
102. Whitney, *Geraldine S. Cadbury*, p. 124. The hostel ceased to be used after the Second World War.
103. Ibid., p. 119.
104. *Woman's Leader*, 26 December 1927, p. 359.

105. *The Magistrate*, I, X (March 1926), pp. 119–20; *Howard Journal*, I, 3 (1924), pp. 121–8.
106. D. Wills, 'Marjorie Franklin', *British Journal of Criminology*, 15, 2 (1975), 109–10.
107. Departmental Committee on Corporal Punishment, *Report*, (1938), Cmd 5684, p. 19. Hereafter Cadogan Report.
108. *The Times*, 13 January 1928, p. 8 (letter from Lovat Fraser).
109. Cadogan Report, p. 44.
110. *The Magistrate*, II, XXXIX (April–May 1932), pp. 577–80.
111. See, for example, J. L. Gibbin, 'Recollections of a Magistrate', *Labour Woman*, (March 1932).
112. Cadogan Report, p. 40.
113. Powys Archive B/PS/Y/JCP/01. Justices were supposed to establish Probation Committees to oversee the work of probation officers with both adult and young offenders. I am grateful to John Minkes who gave me this reference and an example of a 'voluntary honorary' probation officer in Wales who, unpaid, handled a very small caseload in the 1930s.
114. P. Cox, *Gender, Justice and Welfare: Bad Girls in Britain, 1900–1950* (Basingstoke: Palgrave Macmillan, 2003), pp. 167–8.
115. *The Times*, 18 March 1938, p. 17.
116. A joint meeting of the PSMC and the NCW legislation committee met to discuss this issue in 1939. Mavis Tate MP spoke in favour of corporal punishment and Cicely Craven JP of the Howard League against. No vote was recorded. LMA ACC/3613/03/002/A PSMC minutes, 19 April 1939.
117. *The Times*, 29 October 1938, p. 8.
118. *The Magistrate*, IV, LXIX (Sept/Oct.1936) p.1052; V, VII (January 1937), p. 1114.
119. *House of Commons Debates*, 9 November 1937, column 1591.
120. *The Vote*, 14 November 1930, p. 366.
121. Ibid., 21 February 1930, p. 60.
122. See, for example, *House of Commons Debates*, 18 February 1937, 15 March 1937, 29 April 1937.
123. TNA: LCO2/1955, comment by 'FML', n. d.
124. *The Times*, 3 June 1936, p. 10.
125. See list in Appendix I of the Cadogan Committee Report.
126. *The Times*, 22 June 1940, p. 3; 16 June 1941, p. 2.
127. J. B. Thompson, *Justice of the Peace in Juvenile Courts* (London: Labour Research Department, 1944), p. 1.
128. Cicely Craven in *The Times*, 7 December 1948, p. 5.
129. *The Times*, 28 February 1950, p. 5.
130. G. Pearson, *Hooligan: A History of Respectable Fears* (London: Macmillan, 1983), p. 15.
131. TNA HO291/20, MA memorandum, April 1960.
132. Ibid., views of Oxford undergraduates, June 1960.
133. Ibid. AC216, memorandum on public opinion.

3 Women in the Criminal Courts

1. *The Vote*, 9 May 1913, p. 23.
2. Lytton, *Prisons and Prisoners*, pp. 56, 223–4, 257.

3. *The Vote*, 28 November 1913, p. 62.
4. For discussion of 'double deviance', see F. Heidensohn and L. Gelsthorpe, 'Gender and Crime', in M. Maguire, R. Morgan and R. Reiner (eds), *Oxford Handbook of Criminology*, 4th edn (Oxford: Oxford University Press, 2007), p. 400.
5. For women's entry to the legal profession, see J. C. Albisetti, 'Portia Ante Portas: Women and the Legal Profession in Europe, ca 1870–1925', *Journal of Social History*, 33, 4 (2000), 825–57. A detailed analysis of legal arguments can be found in C. A. Corcos, 'Portia Goes to Parliament: Women and their Admission to Membership in the English Legal Profession', *Denver University Law Review*, 75, 2 (1997), 307–417.
6. Albisetti, 'Portia', p. 845.
7. L. Schwarz, 'Professions, Elites and Universities in England, 1870–1970', *Historical Journal*, 47, 4 (2004), p. 942.
8. L. Howsam, 'Orme, Eliza (1847–1937)', *Oxford Dictionary of National Biography* (online edn: Oxford University Press, Jan. 2004, accessed 5 June 2006).
9. I am grateful to Rosemary Auchmuty for this information.
10. D. Mitchell, *Queen Christabel* (London: MacDonald and Jane's, 1977), p. 43.
11. Ibid., pp. 55–6.
12. *The Vote*, 11 July 1913, p. 177.
13. *The Vote*, 17 October 1913, p. 405.
14. *New Statesman*, 5 May 1917 (cutting in WL 5HLN). A 1914 deputation, reported in *The Times* on 28 March 1914 included Dr Elizabeth Garrett Anderson, Fawcett's sister.
15. TUC library, GTP.
16. WL 7HLN, speech notes.
17. WL, cutting from *The Times*, 30 December 1988.
18. Ibid.
19. *The Vote*, 15 April 1921, p. 434.
20. WL 7HLN.
21. Videotaped interview with Theodora Calvert (recorded c. 1987).
22. *Woman's Leader*, 16 December 1927, p. 359.
23. Quoted in Corcos, 'Portia goes to Parliament', p. 396.
24. Ibid., p. 398.
25. A. Logan, 'In Search of Equal Citizenship', *Women's History Review*, 16, 4 (2007), 501–18.
26. WL 7HLN, letter from Helena Normanton to the Open Door Council, 1938.
27. WL 5/SPG/C/09.
28. H. Sommerlad and P. Sanderson, *Gender, Choice and Commitment: Women Solicitors in England and Wales and the Struggle for Equal Status* (Aldershot: Ashgate, 1998), p. 89.
29. H. Kennedy, *Eve was Framed: Women and British Justice* (London: Random House, 1993), p. 59.
30. Logan, 'In Search of Equal Citizenship', p. 512.
31. *The Vote*, 16 April 1920, p. 20.
32. Ibid., 14 January 1921, p. 332.
33. Ibid., 16 April 1920, p. 20.
34. *Woman's Leader*, 11 February 1921, p. 35.
35. Ibid., 4 February 1921.

36. M. Takayanagi, 'Widening Opportunities for Women: The Passage of the Sex Disqualification (Removal) Act 1919' (unpublished paper, 2007), p. 26.
37. Ibid., p. 46.
38. Ibid., p. 47.
39. *Kent and Sussex Courier*, 7 January 1921.
40. *The Vote*, 15 April 1921, p. 434.
41. *The Times*, 1 February 1921, p. 10.
42. Ibid., 2 February 1921, p. 6.
43. *Woman's Leader*, 11 February 1921, p. 35.
44. *The Times*, 1 February 1921, p. 10.
45. *The Vote*, 15 April 1921, p. 463.
46. Ibid., 20 January 1933, p. 36.
47. WL 5/SPG/J67 SPG Newsletter, December 1962; *The Townswoman*, XXIX, 2 (February 1962), p. 32.
48. Departmental Committee on Jury Service, *Report* (London: HMSO, 1965) Cmnd 2627. Hereafter Morris Report.
49. *House of Commons Debates*, 20 March 1962, column 212.
50. *The Times*, 16 November 1962, p. 12.
51. *The Times*, 6 December 1966, p. 11.
52. Ibid., 20 April 1966, p. 12.
53. WL 5/SPG/J84.
54. *The Times*, 14 November 1967, p. 2.
55. *The Townswoman*, XXIX, 2 (February 1962), p. 32.
56. *The Times*, 22 October 1965, p. 17.
57. Ibid, 15 July 1966, p. 13; 19 July, p. 19.
58. Ibid., 22 November 1966, p. 9.
59. Morris Report, p. 12.
60. Ibid., p. 17.
61. Ibid., pp. 15-7.
62. Ibid., p. 17.
63. Ibid., pp. 103-4.
64. WL 5/SPG/J80.
65. LMA/3613/01/079 PSMC minutes, 29 April 1965.
66. *The Times* 15 April 1965, p. 13; 24 April 1965, p. 9.
67. *House of Commons Debates*, 28 April 1966, col. 42.
68. Ibid., 18 March 1971, col. 367.
69. See M. Rendel, 'Legislating for Equal Pay and Opportunity for Women in Britain', *Signs*, 3, 4 (1978), 897-908.
70. WL 5SPG/J74.
71. D. Spender, *There's Always Been a Women's Movement*, (London: Pandora Press, 1983), p. 42.
72. L. Zedner, *Women, Crime and Custody*, (Oxford: Oxford University Press, 1991), p. 35.
73. For a summary of the police forces' role, see D. Taylor, *Crime, Policing and Punishment in England, 1750-1914* (Basingstoke: Macmillan, 1998), p. 81.
74. For a succinct summary of the law, see J. Laite, 'Paying the Price Again: Prostitution Policy in Historical Perspective' (2006) www.historyandpolicy.org/papers/policy-paper-46.html
75. H. J. Self, The Fallen Daughters of Eve: Prostitution, Women and Misuse of the Law (London: Frank Cass, 2003).

76. The introduction of fingerprinting in the early 20th century made the labelling more official still. See Laite, 'Paying the Price Again'.
77. Self, *Prostitution*, p. 105. Lady Nunburnholme was also president of the National Vigilance Association.
78. Readers should refer to J. Walkowitz, *Prostitution and Victorian Society* (Cambridge: Cambridge University Press, 1980); L. Bland, *Banishing the Beast: English Feminism and Sexual Morality 1885–1914* (Harmondsworth: Penguin, 1995); J. Jordan, *Josephine Butler* (London: John Murray, 2001).
79. Bland, *Banishing the Beast*, p. 299.
80. Ibid., pp. 99–100.
81. For a detailed summary of the law on prostitution and the changes to it in the nineteenth and twentieth centuries, see Self, *Prostitution*, pp. 37–58.
82. E. Crawford, *The Women's Suffrage Movement: A Reference Guide 1866–1928* (London: Routledge, 1999), p. 444.
83. WUMRC, MS16B/1/1; *Howard Journal*, II, 3 (1927), pp. 214–9.
84. Self, *Prostitution*, p. 39.
85. *Howard Journal*, II, 3, (1927) p. 182.
86. Self, *Prostitution*, p. 54.
87. This had broken away from the Pankhurst-led WSPU during the Great War. Members included Dorothy Evans, later of the Six Point Group.
88. WL 7/ASC/4/2/1 Handbill in the papers of Amelia Scott, n. d.
89. WL 3/AMS/B/04/3, cutting from *The Shield*, April 1949.
90. Self, *Prostitution*, pp. 4–5.
91. *Woman's Leader*, 24 October 1924, p. 312.
92. WL 3/AMS/B/04/3 cutting from *The Shield*, April 1949.
93. For a brief account of the Savidge Case, see Self, *Prostitution*, pp. 5–6.
94. *Howard Journal*, II, 4, (1929), p. 286.
95. E. Huws Jones, *Margery Fry: The Essential Amateur* (Oxford: Oxford University Press,1966), p. 156. 'Jix' was the Home Secretary's nickname.
96. *Howard Journal*, II, 4, (1929), p. 286.
97. Departmental Committee on Street Offences, *Report* (London: HMSO, 1928) Cmd 3231.
98. WL 3AMS/B/04/10, Critique of the Street Offences Committee Report by Helen Wilson MD, president, W. C. Roberts, chairman and Alison Neilans, secretary, AMSH, 11 December 1928.
99. Self, *Prostitution*, p. 7.
100. WL 3/AMS/B/04/3, cutting from *The Shield*, April 1949.
101. WL 3AMS/B/04/11, letter from Neilans to Pethick-Lawrence, 13 January 1937.
102. Ibid., 'Liberty of the Subject: How Prostitutes are Treated' (AMSH leaflet, 1937).
103. WL 3/AMS/B/04/12.
104. Ibid. The file contains a cutting of a report of the Conference which appeared in *The Woman Teacher*, 12 March 1948.
105. *Howard Journal*, VI, 3 (1943), p. 167.
106. WL 3/AMS/B/04/3, letter from Margery Fry to Chave Collisson, 26 April 1950.
107. WUMRC MSS16B/1/5, HLPR minutes, 18 February 1955.
108. *Howard Journal*, X, 1 (1958), p. 1.
109. Self, *Prostitution*, p. 268.
110. *House of Commons Debates*, 13 December 1950, columns 1175–8.

111. Ibid., 4 May 1951, column 1514.
112. See, for example, the remarks of Sir Michael Havers quoted in S. M. Edwards, 'Prostitutes: Victims of Law, Social Policy and Organised Crime', in P. Carlen and A. Worral (eds), *Gender, Crime and Justice* (Milton Keynes: Open University Press, 1987), p. 49.
113. Self, *Prostitution*, pp. 100–1.
114. *House of Commons Debates*, 4 May 1951 columns 1514–6.
115. A. Perkin, *Red Queen* (London: Macmillan, 2003), p. 379.
116. M. Pugh, *Women and the Women's Movement in Britain 1914–1959*, 2nd edition (Basingstoke: Macmillan, 2000), pp. 308–9.
117. B. Castle, *Fighting all the Way* (London: Macmillan, 1993).
118. Richardson was one of the sponsors of Maureen Colquhoun's Protection of Prostitutes Bill, discussed later in this chapter. Later, in the 1980s she was Labour's Shadow Minister for Women.
119. Perkins, *Red Queen*, p. 355.
120. Self, *Prostitution*, p. 88.
121. Ibid., p. 90.
122. Ibid., p. 91.
123. Laite, 'Paying the Price Again'.
124. Self, *Prostitution*, p. 96, n. 38.
125. Ibid., pp. 223, 254.
126. Ibid., p. 259. In 1959 25 women were elected to the House of Commons, making up 4 per cent of MPs.
127. J. Kelley, *When the Gates Shut* (London: Longman, 1967), pp. 42, 115–6.
128. P. Bartley, *Prostitution: Prevention and Reform in England, 1860–1914* (London: Routledge, 2000), p. 36.
129. Kelley, *When the Gates Shut*, pp. 116, 43.
130. LMA/3613/01/079, PSMC minutes, passim.
131. This was achieved in the 1982 Criminal Justice Act. See Self, *Prostitution*, p. 271 for a full discussion.
132. M. Colquhoun, *A Woman in the House* (Shoreham by Sea: Scan Books, 1980), pp. 130–4. Paisley claimed the bill would 'undermine the moral fabric' of society.
133. WL, cuttings from the *Independent* and the *Daily Telegraph*, 25 April 1994.
134. Edwards, 'Prostitutes: Victims of Law, Social Policy and Organised Crime', pp. 52–3.
135. Ibid., p. 43.
136. Self, *Prostitution*, p. 272.
137. Laite, 'Paying the Price Again'.
138. Fawcett Society, *Report*, pp. 22–5.

4 Women in the Penal System

1. M. Gordon, *Penal Discipline* (London: George Routledge and Sons Ltd, 1922), pp. ix–x.
2. E. Crawford, 'Police, Prisons and Prisoners: the view from the Home Office', *Women's History Review*, 14, 3/4 (2005), p. 498.
3. J. Bush, *Women Against the Vote* (Oxford: Oxford University Press, 2007), p. 65.

4. B. Forsythe, 'Russell, Adeline Mary, Duchess of Bedford (1852–1920)', *Oxford Dictionary of National Biography* (online edn: Oxford University Press, 2004, accessed 1 Feb 2008).

5. E. B. Freedman, *Their Sisters' Keepers: Women's Prison Reform in America 1830–1930* (Ann Arbor: University of Michigan Press, 1981), p. 24.

6. B. Harrison, 'State Intervention and Moral Reform in Nineteenth Century England' in B. Harrison and P. Hollis (eds) *Pressure from Without* (London: Edward Arnold 1974).

7. Holloway housed just over one-third of female prisoners in England and Wales in the 1960s. See P. Rock, *Reconstructing a Women's Prison* (Oxford: Oxford University Press, 1996), p. 22.

8. Freedman, *Their Sisters' Keepers*, p. 48; *Maternal Justice: Miriam Van Waters and the Female Reform Tradition* (Chicago: University of Chicago Press, 1996), pp. 185–6.

9. L. Zedner, *Women, Crime and Custody in Victorian England* (Oxford: Oxford University Press, 1991), p. 128; B. Forsythe, 'Gordon, Mary Louisa (1861–1941)', *Oxford Dictionary of National Biography* (online edn: Oxford University Press, Sept. 2004, accessed 1 Feb. 2008).

10. Forsythe, 'Duchess of Bedford'.

11. E. Gore, *The Better Fight: The Story of Dame Lilian Barker* (London: Bles, 1965), p. 208.

12. A. D. Smith, *Women in Prison: A Study in Penal Methods* (London: Stephens, 1962), pp. 142–3.

13. Size came out of retirement to take charge of Askham Grange Open Prison. M. Size, *Prisons I Have Known* (London: Allen & Unwin, 1958).

14. C. McCall, *They Always Come Back* (London: Methuen, 1938), p. 51. McCall probably had Mary Size in mind.

15. Ibid.

16. Morrison appointed the first woman stipendiary magistrate in 1945. See P. Polden, 'The Lady of Tower Bridge: Sibyl Campbell, England's first woman judge', *Women's History Review*, 8, 3 (1999), 505–26. His appointments to the first Advisory Council on the Treatment of Offenders (1944) included seven women among the 20 members.

17. Gore, *The Better Fight*, p. 117.

18. Four successive governors 1910–47 were medically trained. Rock, *Reconstructing a Women's Prison*, p. 25.

19. For a discussion of the meaning of 'professionalism' in the context of voluntary work, see A. Logan, 'Professionalism and the Impact of England's First Women Justices, 1920–1950'. *Historical Journal*, 49, 3 (2006), pp. 833–50.

20. T. Skyrme, *History of the Justice of the Peace Volume 2* (Chichester: Barry Rose, 1991), p. 235.

21. E. Huws Jones, *Margery Fry: The Essential Amateur* (Oxford: Oxford University Press,1966), p. 118.

22. *The Vote*, 28 March 1930, p. 97.

23. Size, *Prisons*, p. 114. Earengey was married to a judge.

24. F. Prochaska, *Women and Philanthropy in Nineteenth Century England* (Oxford: Clarendon Press, 1980), Chapter V.

25. *Woman's Leader*, 8 September 1922, p. 248.

26. *Howard Journal*, II, 1 (1926), p. 86.
27. GCRO 06156/1, GWMS minutes 3 July and 16 October 1923, 1 January 1924.
28. *Woman's Leader*, 8 September 1922, p. 248.
29. L. Martindale, *A Woman Surgeon* (London: Gollancz, 1951), pp. 202–3.
30. H. Dowson, 'The League of Honour in Nottingham', *The Magistrate* I, VII (April 1925), p. 79. Mrs Dowson was a Liberal Unitarian and served on the NUWSS executive. She was a leading Nottingham philanthropist and later became a city councillor.
31. Freedman, *Their Sisters' Keepers*, p. 130.
32. Dowson, 'The League of Honour in Nottingham'.
33. For example, *NCW News*, January 1926.
34. TNA PCOM9/409, letter from M. Fry to A. Paterson, 18 July 1930.
35. X. Field, *Under Lock and Key: a Study of Women in Prison* (London: Max Parrish, 1963), p. 209. For an alternative, 'insider's' view of a Holloway concert, see J. Henry, *Who Lie in Gaol* (London: Gollancz, 1952), pp. 44–6.
36. *The Times*, 4 November 1947, p. 5.
37. *House of Commons Debates*, written answers, 13 February 1947, columns 90–1.
38. *The Times*, 14 October 1959, p. 7.
39. For an account of women's voluntary work in the Griffins Society during the last 40 years, see J. Rumgay, *Ladies of Lost Causes: Rehabilitation, women offenders and the voluntary sector* (Cullompton: Willan, 2007).
40. *Daily Mail*, 10 August 1976, p. 10, emphasis in the original.
41. M. Ryan, *The Acceptable Pressure Group* (Farnborough: Saxon House, 1978), pp. 34–5.
42. For example in the *Howard Journal*, IV, 3 (1936), pp. 282–6.
43. Gordon, *Penal Discipline*.
44. Forsythe, 'Gordon, Mary Louisa'.
45. Gordon, *Penal Discipline*, p. 36. For Pethick Lawrence's view, see E. Pethick Lawrence, *My Part in a Changing World*, (London: Gollancz, 1938), pp. 221–3.
46. Gordon, *Penal Discipline*, pp. 37–8. It may be that Gordon had campaigns led by the WFL and WSPU regarding individual cases such as Daisy Lord's in mind (see section below on the death penalty). However she was a strong supporter of the Duchess of Bedford's work.
47. McCall, *They Always Come Back*. For the views of Holloway inmates, see K. Lonsdale et al., *Account of Life in Holloway Prison for Women* (Chislehurst: Prison Reform Council, 1943); Henry, *Who Lie in Gaol*; D. Crisp, *A Light in the Night* (London: Holborn Publishing, 1960); J. Buxton and M. Turner, *Gate Fever* (London: Cresset Press, 1962). For a governor's perspective, see J. Kelley, *When the Gates Shut* (London: Longman, 1967); Size, *Prisons*.
48. McCall, *They Always Come Back*, p. xi. For details of the friendship of McCall and Delafield, see V. Powell, *The Life of a Provincial Lady: A Study of E. M. Delafield and her Works* (London: Heinemann, 1988), which also contains a photograph of McCall.
49. McCall, *They Always Come Back*, p. 40. For a brief account of reform in the prison system during this period, see W. J. Forsythe, 'Reformation and Relaxation in the English Prisons', *Social and Political Administration*, 23, 2 (1989), 161–8.
50. Forsythe, 'Reformation', p. 166.

51. B. D. Grew, *Prison Governor*, (London: Herbert Jenkins, 1958), p. 86. The buildings at Maidstone dated from 1819.
52. See P. Carlen, *Women's Imprisonment: A Study in Social Control* (London: Routledge and Kegan Paul, 1983), p. 18. For an alternative perspective, see Zedner, *Women, Crime and Custody*, pp. 99–100.
53. McCall, *They Always Come Back*, p. 137.
54. A. Brown, 'The Amazing Mutiny at the Dartmoor Convict Prison', *British Journal of Criminology*, 47, 2, (2007), 276–92.
55. Holloway became a women-only prison in 1902. By 1937 the only other local prisons in England and Wales that continued to house women were Manchester, Durham, Birmingham, Cardiff and Exeter.
56. *House of Commons Debates*, written answers, 13 February 1947, columns 90–1.
57. See W. A. Elkin, *The English Penal System* (Harmondsworth: Penguin Books, 1957), p. 146.
58. G. Hudson, 'Lonsdale, Dame Kathleen (1903–1971)', *Oxford Dictionary of National Biography* (online edn: Oxford University Press, 2004, accessed 18 February 2008).
59. K. Lonsdale, 'Women in Science', *Proceedings of the Royal Institution of Great Britain*, 43 (1970), 295–317.
60. As a mother of young children she was exempt from having to undertake war work, which she was anyway prepared to do. She simply objected to the principle of registration.
61. Lonsdale, *Account of Life in Holloway*.
62. Herbert Morrison quoted in *The Times*, 5 November 1943, p. 8.
63. C. Blackford, 'Evans, Dorothy (1888–1944)', *Oxford Dictionary of National Biography* (online edn: Oxford University Press, 2004, accessed 19 February 2008).
64. LMA/3613/01/079, PSMC minutes, 11 April 1946.
65. WUMRC MSS16B/1/3/1, HLPR executive minutes, 9 December 1943 and 22 February 1944.
66. G. Rose, *The Struggle for Penal Reform* (London: Stevens, 1961), p. 306. Two, including Sybil Morrison, were elected in 1945 after two previous unsuccessful attempts.
67. WUMRC MSS16B/1/4, HLPR executive minutes, 25 January 1945.
68. Ryan, *The Acceptable Pressure Group*, p. 37.
69. WUMRC MSS16B/1/4, HLPR executive minutes, 25 January 1945. Mrs Holman was a member of the PRMC as well as the HLPR and NCW.
70. Ibid., executive minutes 1945–9, passim.
71. For the later history of the PRC, see Ryan, *The Acceptable Pressure Group*, pp. 99–100.
72. Rose, *The Struggle for Penal Reform*, pp. 241–2.
73. *Howard Journal*, VI, 1 (1941).
74. University College London Special Collections (UCLSC), Lonsdale papers, G116.
75. For her views on the position of women, see Lonsdale, 'Women in Science'.
76. UCLSC, Lonsdale papers, G118–145.
77. WUMRC MSS16B/1/5, HLPR minutes, 17 October 1952.
78. Ryan, *The Acceptable Pressure Group*, p. 86.

79. Gordon, *Penal Discipline*, pp. 155, 170, 159.
80. Ibid., pp. 179, 187.
81. Ibid., p. 160.
82. *Woman's Leader*, 2 March 1923.
83. Gore, *The Better Fight*, pp. 92–3. The Central Committee for Women's Training and Employment included Lady Crewe, Violet Markham, Gertrude Tuckwell, Marion Phillips, May Tennant, Margaret Bondfield and Lady Cynthia Colville, who were all JPs. Barker also later became a magistrate.
84. For Paterson's education and career, see S. K. Ruck (ed.), *Paterson on Prisons*, (London: Frederick Muller, 1951), pp. 10–15.
85. Ibid., p. 96.
86. *The Times*, 5 April 1923, p. 7.
87. *The Vote*, 22 August 1924, p. 267; Gore, *The Better Fight*, pp. 167–8.
88. S. Whybrow, 'Borstals were for Girls Too: A Study of the First Girls' Borstal, c. 1909–35' (unpublished dissertation, University of Kent, 2006), p. 33.
89. Gore, *The Better Fight*, p. 133.
90. McCall, *They Always Come Back*, p. 6; Henry, *Who Lie in Gaol*, p. 61.
91. HRO 23M57/1, HWMA minutes, 13 April 1942.
92. Barker quoted in *The Magistrate*, II, XXI (April 1929), p. 290.
93. HRO 23M57/1, HWMA minutes, 13 April 1942.
94. For a discussion of the medicalisation of women's deviancy within criminology in the 1950s and 60s, see Rock, *Reconstructing a Women's Prison*, pp. 71–5.
95. Gordon, *Penal Discipline*.
96. WUMRC MSS16B/1/5 HLPR minutes, 17 February 1950.
97. Ibid., 16 March 1951.
98. A member of the HLPR executive and of ACTO, Mrs Creech Jones was a JP and the wife of a Labour MP, a former conscientious objector.
99. WUMRC MSS16B/1/5 HLPR minutes, 21 May and 18 June 1954.
100. D. Wills, 'Marjorie Franklin', *British Journal of Criminology*, 15, 2 (1975), 109–10.
101. WUMRC MSS16B/1/5 HLPR minutes, 31 January 1955.
102. R. Crichton (ed.), *The Memoirs of Ethel Smyth* (Harmondsworth: Penguin, 1987), p. 299.
103. The Dowager Marchioness of Reading, *It's the Job That Counts* (Colchester: privately printed, 1973), p. 127. The quotation is from a speech made in the House of Lords.
104. See, for example, letter from Madeleine Robinson to Lord Templewood, 9 February 1950, Cambridge University Library (CUL) Templewood Papers, Chapter XVI, file 6.
105. They also had strong objections to the regimes of the new detention centres for young offenders set up following the 1948 Criminal Justice Act.
106. Kelley, *When the Gates Shut*, p. 152.
107. Prochaska, *Women and Philanthropy*, p. 167.
108. Ibid., p. 173.
109. Size, *Prisons I Have Known*. pp. 115–6.
110. Ibid., p. 114.
111. Kelley, *When the Gates Shut*, pp. 160–1; Rumgay, *Ladies of Lost Causes*, p. 12.
112. Gordon, *Penal Discipline*, p. xi.

113. Ibid., p. 147.
114. Ibid., p. 205.
115. For the RAP Holloway campaign, see Ryan, *The Acceptable Pressure Group*, pp. 101–9.
116. Gordon, *Penal Discipline*, p. 204.
117. *Woman's Leader*, 2 March 1923.
118. *The Vote*, 28 March 1930, p. 97.
119. *The Magistrate*, II, XXXI (December 1930/ January 1931), p. 463; MA annual report, 1938, p. 16.
120. WMRC MSS16B/1/4 HLPR minutes, 16 June 1945.
121. Margery Fry Papers (MFP), paper on the habitual criminal, n.d., c. 1950, emphasis in the original. Fry made similar points, in more measured tones, in the *Sunday Times*, 13 April 1952, p. 4.
122. J. Bowlby, *Child Care and the Growth of Love* (Harmondsworth: Penguin Books, 1953). For a recent discussion of 'Bowlbyism' and reactions to it, see D. S. Wilson, 'A New Look at the Affluent Worker: The Good Working Mother in Post-War Britain', *Twentieth Century British History*, 17, 2 (2006), pp. 206–29.
123. MFP, radio script for 'London Calling Asia: Personal Call', 13 February 1954.
124. *Howard Journal*, VIII, 3 (1952), p. 187.
125. Quoted in Crisp, *A Light in the Night*, p. 100.
126. B. Wootton, *Social Science and Social Pathology* (London: George Allen & Unwin, 1959), p. 154.
127. A. Ballinger, *Dead Women Walking*, (Aldershot: Ashgate, 2000), p. 1. For a discussion of some murder cases involving women defendants – none of whom were executed – while the 1957 Homicide Act was in force, see E. Seal, 'Women, Murder and the Construction of Gender in the Criminal Justice System of England and Wales, 1957–1962' (unpublished PhD thesis, University of Bristol, 2007).
128. E. O. Tuttle, *The Crusade Against Capital Punishment in Great Britain* (London: Stevens & Sons, 1961) barely mentions the case. A more recent account, B. P. Block and J. Hostettler's *Hanging in the Balance* (Winchester: Waterside Press, 1997) presents a lot of detail on the Thompson-Bywaters case but does not suggest very explicitly the ways in which it influenced subsequent abolitionist campaigns.
129. Block and Hostettler, *Hanging in the Balance*, p. 88.
130. D. J. R. Grey, 'Representations of Infanticide in England, 1880–1922' (Unpublished PhD thesis, Roehampton University, 2008), p. 31.
131. Ibid., pp. 50–2.
132. *The Times*, 14 September 1908, p. 10.
133. D. J. R. Grey, 'Representations of Infanticide in England, 1880–1922' (Unpublished PhD thesis, Roehampton University, 2008), pp. 96–8.
134. Ibid., p. 91.
135. Ibid., pp. 122–4.
136. *The Times*, 7 January 1922, p. 7.
137. D. J. R. Grey, 'Representations of Infanticide in England, 1880–1922' (Unpublished PhD thesis, Roehampton University, 2008), p. 131.
138. *The Vote*, 23 January 1931, p. 28; WUMRC MS16B/4/1/11 NCADP 11th Annual Report, 1935–6, p. 7–8.
139. Ballinger, *Dead Women Walking*, p. 89.

140. This seems to have been the assumption of Cicely Hamilton. See *Daily Sketch*, 13 December 1922, p. 2.
141. *Daily Sketch*, 13 December 1922, p. 2.
142. Ballinger, *Dead Women Walking*, p. 222.
143. Ibid., pp. 233–40.
144. Ibid., p. 240.
145. F. Tennyson Jesse, *A Pin to See the Peepshow* (London: Heinemann Ltd, 1934); J. Colenbrander, *A Portrait of Fryn* (London: Andre Deutsch, 1984), pp. 191–2.
146. E. M. Delafield, *Messalina of the Suburbs* (London: Macmillan, 1924).
147. Delafield, *Messalina*, p. v.
148. Ballinger, *Dead Women Walking*, p. 223; Delafield, *Messalina*, p. 234. Edith and Elsie both say, 'I must tell the truth.'
149. Delafield, *Messalina*, p. 248.
150. *Daily Sketch*, 13 December 1922, p. 2.
151. *Lloyds Sunday News*, 14 January 1923, p. 10.
152. *The Vote*, 19 January 1923, p. 20.
153. WUMRC MSS16B/5/1/7, C. Dane, 'Women Voters and the Death Penalty', pamphlet reprinted from *Good Housekeeping* by the NCADP, n. d. (c.1923–4).
154. MFP, radio script, 'The Most Important Things', 12 May 1957.
155. MFP, undated speech notes.
156. Huws Jones, *Margery Fry*, p. 124.
157. *Howard Journal*, I, 2 (1922), p. 18.
158. Ibid., I, 3 (1924), p. 112.
159. Huws Jones, *Margery Fry*, p. 123; letter from Theodora Calvert to Barrow Cadbury, 5 February 1941 (private collection).
160. See Calvert's obituary in the *Howard Journal*, III, 4 (1933), pp. 20–2.
161. For example, T. Calvert, *Capital Punishment: Society Takes Revenge, An examination of the necessity for Capital Punishment in Britain To-day* (London: National News-letter, 1946).
162. Block and Hostettler, *Hanging in the Balance*, p. 106.
163. It is worth comparing the attention given to Ruth Ellis compared with that for the 53 year-old Styllou Christophi who was executed only six months before Ellis' trial. See Ballinger, *Dead Women Walking*, p. 160. Styllou's case seems to have interested women on the HLPR executive more than Ellis'.
164. *Spectator*, 13 January 1923, quoted in Tuttle, *The Crusade against Capital Punishment*, p. 29.
165. *The Vote*, 19 January 1923, p. 20.

5   Feminism and the Care of Victims

1. *The Vote*, 27 June 1913 (front page).
2. J. Young, 'Radical Criminology in Britain: The Emergence of a Competing Paradigm', *British Journal of Criminology*, 28, 2 (1988), p. 171.
3. S. Schafer, *Restitution to Victims of Crime* (London: Stevens, 1960), p. 7; J. Shapland, J. Willmore and P. Duff, *Victims in the Criminal Justice System* (Aldershot: Gower, 1985), p. 1.
4. See Introduction.

5. WL NVA minutes, 29 December 1897.
6. A. Brown and D. Barrett, *Knowledge of Evil: Child Prostitution and Child Sexual Abuse in Twentieth-century England* (Cullompton: Willan, 2002), p. 58.
7. CCRO RS84/91, 'A Survey of Fifteen Years' Work of the Cambridge NCW', (1928).
8. CKS CH94/6, 'NCW Tunbridge Wells Branch: the First Seventy-Five Years', (1970).
9. *NCW News*, September 1925, p. 241 (emphasis added).
10. Departmental Committee on Sexual Offences against Young Persons, *Report* (London: HMSO, 1925) Cmd 2561, paragraph 62.
11. *Time and Tide*, 13 February 1925, reproduced in Spender, *Time and Tide Wait for No Man*, pp. 168–71.
12. *The Vote*, 13 February 1925, p. 52.
13. For example, Mrs Fawcett: see D. Rubinstein, *A Different World for Women* (Columbus: Ohio State University Press, 1991), pp. 91–2.
14. L. A. Jackson, *Child Sex Abuse in Victorian England* (London: Routledge, 2000), p. 83.
15. C. Smart, 'A history of Ambivalence and Conflict in the Discursive Construction of the "Child Victim" of Sexual Abuse', *Social and Legal Studies*, 8 (1999), p. 393.
16. S. Walklate, 'Can there be a feminist victimology?', in P. Davies, P. Francis and V. Jupp (eds), *Victimisation: Theory, Research and Policy* (Basingstoke: Palgrave Macmillan, 2003), p. 33.
17. Jackson, *Child Sex Abuse*, pp. 100, 108.
18. Ibid., p. 111.
19. Smart, 'A History', p. 394.
20. Ibid.
21. All these suggestions were supported in the *Report* of the Departmental Committee on Sexual Offences against Young Persons, paragraphs 31–2, 53, 630. One of the women on the Committee, Mrs Rackham, opposed the extension of powers of courts of summary jurisdiction.
22. J. Tosh, 'What Should Historians do with Masculinity: Reflections on Nineteenth-century Britain', *History Workshop Journal*, 38 (1994), 179–202.
23. M. J. Wiener, *Men of Blood: Violence, Manliness, and Criminal Justice in Victorian England* (Cambridge: Cambridge University Press, 2004), pp. 3, 192.
24. J. S. Mill, *The Subjection of Women* (New York: Dover Publications, 1997, originally published 1869).
25. Hammerton, *Cruelty and Companionship*, p. 41.
26. A. V. John, 'Between the Cause and the Courts: The Curious Case of Cecil Chapman', in C. Eustance et al. (eds), *A Suffrage Reader* (London: Leicester University Press, 2000), p. 148.
27. C. Beaumont, 'Moral Dilemmas and Women's Rights: The Attitude of the Mothers' Union and Catholic Women's League to Divorce, Birth Control and Abortion in England, 1928–1939', *Women's History Review*, 16, 4 (2007), p. 469.
28. L. A. Jackson, 'Women professionals and the regulation of violence in interwar Britain', in S. D'Cruze (ed.) *Everyday Violence in Britain, 1850–1950* (Harlow: Longman, 2000), p. 126.
29. For example, Geraldine Cadbury: see TNA HO45/13777.

30. L. A. Jackson, 'Women professionals and the regulation of violence in interwar Britain' in S. D'Cruze (ed.) *Everyday Violence in Britain, 1850–1950* (Harlow: London, 2000), p. 127.
31. For nineteenth-century court discussions concerning provocation in cases of violence against women, see Wiener, *Men of Blood*, pp. 175–200.
32. Jackson, *Child Sex Abuse*, p. 99.
33. A. Clark, 'Domesticity and the Problem of Wifebeating in Nineteenth-Century Britain', in D'Cruze, *Everyday Violence in Britain.*
34. S. Jeffreys, *The Spinster and her Enemies: Feminism and Sexuality 1880–1930* (London: Pandora Press, 1985), p. 56.
35. Departmental Committee on Sexual Offences against Young Persons, *Report*, paragraph 38.
36. *Vigilance Record*, April–June 1930, quoted in Smart, 'A History', p. 400.
37. General welfare measures were seen as relevant to achieving reductions in violent crime, including better housing and higher living standards.
38. B. Campbell, *Iron Ladies* (London: Virago, 1987), pp. 67–8.
39. *Howard Journal*, IV, 1 (1934) p. 35; GCRO 06156/1 GWMS minutes, 14 April, 1931.
40. This was seen as more effective than short prison sentences. See D. Garland, *Punishment and Welfare* (Aldershot: Gower, 1985), p. 149.
41. For the influence of psychiatry over British criminology in the early twentieth century, see D. Garland, 'British Criminology Before 1935', *British Journal of Criminology*, 28, 2 (1988), 1–17.
42. *Howard Journal*, X, 1 (1958), p. 20.
43. CCRO 789/Q68, W.A. Potts, *Pioneering Days of the NCW in Birmingham* (1950).
44. R. I. Mawby and S. Walklate, *Critical Victimology* (London: Sage, 1994), p. 71.
45. E. Huws Jones, *Margery Fry: The Essential Amateur* (Oxford: Oxford University Press, 1966), pp. 232–3.
46. M. Ryan, *Penal Policy and Political Culture: Four Essays on Policy and Process* (Winchester: Waterside Press, 2003), p. 28.
47. T. Morris, 'British Criminology: 1935–1948', *British Journal of Criminology*, 28, 2 (1988), p. 23.
48. P. Rock, *Helping Victims of Crime: the Home Office and the Rise of Victim Support in England and Wales* (Oxford: Clarendon Press, 1990), p. 50.
49. Huws Jones, *Margery Fry*, p. 232.
50. Rock, *Helping Victims*, p. 54.
51. Huws Jones, *Margery Fry*, p. 147.
52. See, for example, Margery Fry Papers (MFP), scripts for 'The Single Woman' (6 December 1952); 'Reflections on an Indian Summer' (3 April 1957).
53. M. Fry, *Arms of the Law* (London: Gollancz, 1951), p. 26.
54. Ibid., pp. 124–6.
55. Ibid., p. 126.
56. WUMRC MSS16B/1/4, HLPR Executive minutes, 7 February 1945.
57. Fry, *Arms of the Law*, pp. 21–2.
58. Huws Jones, *Margery Fry*, p. 233.
59. *Howard Journal*, III, 2 (1931), pp. 101–2.
60. A prison earnings scheme, strongly supported by the HLPR, had been introduced from 1929 (see Chapter 4) but the amounts paid were low.

61. CUL, Templewood Papers, Chapter XVI, File 1, letter from SMF, 26 March 1954, emphasis in the original.
62. C. H. Rolph, *Living Twice*, (London: Gollancz, 1974), p. 174; Rock, *Helping Victims*, p. 61. Rolph was the pseudonym of Hewitt (see Chapter 3).
63. M. Ryan, *The Acceptable Pressure Group* (Farnborough: Saxon House1978), p. 79.
64. CUL, Templewood Papers, Chapter XVI, File 1, letter from Hugh Klare 26th September 1956; File 7, letter from Klare, 8 June 1956.
65. WUMRC MSS16B/1/5, HLPR Executive minutes, 15 May 1953.
66. Rock, *Helping Victims*, pp. 54, 89.
67. MFP, radio script, 'Ought we to compensate victims of violence?', 20 November 1956.
68. TNA HO291/135/AC181. Parts of this file remain closed under an exemption to the Freedom of Information Act until 2049. The author was able to see a redacted version with summary details of victims' occupations, injury, cause, any disability, number of days absent from work and occupation of assailant.
69. SMF papers, radio script, European Service, 22 November 1950.
70. MFP, Radio script, 20 November 1956.
71. Huws Jones, *Margery Fry*, p. 235.
72. Rock, *Helping Victims*, p. 83.
73. Ibid., pp. 57–9.
74. TNA HO291/19, ACTO minutes, 27th May 1954. Despite its scepticism, the Home Office did commission some research on the issue, which suggests that the octogenarian Fry was still able to influence officials.
75. TNA HO291/20, notes for Home Secretary's speech to ACTO, 26 June 1958. Butler had also addressed the previous meeting, but attended the second one specifically because of the deaths of Fry and ACTO chairman, Lord Drogheda.
76. TNA HO291/135, memorandum by the Home Secretary to Cabinet Home Affairs Committee.
77. Ibid.
78. Ibid.
79. R. A. Butler, *The Art of the Possible: the Memoirs of Lord Butler* (London: H. Hamilton, 1971), p. 200.
80. *The Times*, 13 October 1961, p. 6. Howe was involved in the production of a report by the Conservative Political Centre on victims' compensation in 1962.
81. Butler, *Art of the Possible*, p. 200.
82. P. Duff, *Left, Left, Left: A Personal account of six protest campaigns, 1945–64* (London: Allison & Busby, 1971), p. 106.
83. Campbell, *Iron Ladies*, p. 67.
84. Ibid., p. 68.
85. *The Times*, 13 October 1961, p. 12.
86. TNA HO291/20, letter from Butler to Heathcoat-Amory, 16th November 1958.
87. Ibid., letter from Heathcoat-Amory to Butler, 24 November 1958.
88. Rock, *Helping Victims*, p. 70.
89. S. Walklate, 'Can there be a Feminist Victimology?', in P. Davies, P. Francis & V. Jupp (eds), *Victimisation: Theory, Research and Policy* (Basingstoke: Palgrave Macmillan, 2003), p. 33.
90. *The Times*, 6 June 1958, p. 7.
91. LMA/3613/01/079, PSMC minutes, 16 October 1952; 19 February 1953.

92. *The Times*, 17 October 1956, p. 13; D. Glick, *The National Council of Women of Great Britain: The First One Hundred Years* (London: National Council of Women, 1995), p. 61.
93. *The Times*, 19 October 1961, p. 6. However, the NCW does not appear to have made the compensation scheme a focus of its campaigning at that time.
94. *The Times*, 5 June 1959, p. 18.
95. TNA HO291/135, memorandum by the Home Secretary to Cabinet Home Affairs Committee.
96. HO291/135; Hull University, 'Justice' archive, cutting from the *Star*, 22 July 1960.
97. 'Justice', *Compensation for Victims of Violence* (London: Stevens, 1962), paragraphs 41–2.The report discusses the possibility of a 'woman' being pregnant, not a 'girl'.
98. Brown and Barratt, *Knowledge of Evil*, p. 83.
99. Hull University, 'Justice' archive, cutting from *Parade*, 5 October 1963, pp. 10–12.
100. Ibid. The supporters of 'Justice' named in the article were Dr Brian Abel-Smith, Louis Blom-Cooper, Emlyn Hooson QC, Dr Nigel Walker, Patrick O'Connor QC and Lord Longford.
101. Ibid.
102. Wiener, *Men of Blood*, p. 177.
103. *House of Lords Debates*, 5 December 1962, column 307.
104. 'Justice', *Compensation for Victims of Violence*, paragraph 20.
105. *The Times*, 5 May 1958, p. 11.
106. Rock, *Helping Victims of Crime*, p. 76.
107. LMA /3613/01/079, PSMC minutes, 15 November 1962.

Conclusion

1. M. Colquhoun, *Woman in the House* (Shoreham by Sea: Scan Books, 1980), p. 5.
2. Quoted in M. Humm (ed.), *Feminisms: A Reader* (London: Harvester Wheatsheaf, 1992), p. 40.
3. J. Kelly, 'The Social Relation of the Sexes: Methodological Implications of Women's History' in J. Kelly, *Women, History and Theory* (London: University of Chicago Press, 1984), p. 3.
4. L. Gelsthorpe and A. Morris, 'Feminism and Criminology in Britain', *British Journal of Criminology*, 28, 2 (1988), p. 93.
5. N. H. Rafter and F. Heidensohn, *International Feminist Perspectives on Criminology: Engendering a Discipline* (Buckingham: Open University Press, 1995), p. 7.
6. Reprinted in P. Carlen et al., *Criminal Women: Autobiographical Accounts* (Cambridge: Polity Press, 1985), pp. 187–8.
7. Fawcett Society Press Release, 31 March 2004.
8. Fawcett Society, *Report*, pp. 43–8.
9. Ibid., p. 51.
10. C. Law, *Suffrage and Power: The Women's Movement 1918–1928* (London: I. B. Tauris, 1997), p. 4.

11. MFP, radio script for European Service, 'general news talk, 1900–1950', 22 November 1950.
12. *Woman's Leader*, 8 February 1924, p. 22.
13. *The Magistrate*, I, XVI (January 1928), p. 215.
14. B. Wootton, *In a World I Never Made* (London: George Allen & Unwin, 1967), p. 172.
15. Ibid., pp. 157–8.
16. Law, *Suffrage and Power*, p. 2.
17. K. Daly and M. Chesney-Lind, 'Feminism and Criminology', *Justice Quarterly*, 5, 4 (1988), p. 497.
18. Humm, *Feminisms*, p. 53.
19. E. B. Freedman, *No Turning Back: The History of Feminism and the Future of Women* (London: Profile Books, 2002), p. 10.

Bibliography

Official sources

The National Archives (TNA)
Home Office Papers: HO45, HO73, HO144, HO291 series.
Papers of the Lord Chancellor's Office: LC02 series.

Official Reports (Command Papers)
Departmental Committee on Sexual Offences against Young Persons *Report* (London: HMSO, 1925), Cmd 2561.
Departmental Committee on the Treatment of Young Offenders, *Report* (London: HMSO, 1927), Cmd 2831.
Departmental Committee on Street Offences, *Report* (London: HMSO, 1928), Cmd 3231.
Departmental Commission on Corporal Punishment, *Report* (London: HMSO, 1938), Cmd 5684.
Departmental Committee on Jury Service, *Report* (London: HMSO, 1965), Cmnd 2627.
Parliamentary Debates (Hansard): House of Commons and House of Lords.
Royal Commission on the Selection of Justices of the Peace, *Evidence* (London: HMSO, 1910), Cd 5358.
Royal Commission on Justices of the Peace, *Report* (London: HMSO, 1948), Cmd 7463.

Unofficial archive sources

Organisations
AMSH records: Women's Library (WL).
GWMS: Gloucestershire County Record Office (GCRO).
HLPR papers (including NCADP and PRL records): Warwick University Modern Records Centre (WUMRC).
HWMA: Hampshire Record Office (HRO)
'Justice' archive: Hull University.
NCW national archives: London Metropolitan Archives (LMA).
NCW Cambridge Branch: Cambridge County Record Office (CCRO)
NCW Tunbridge Wells Branch: Centre for Kentish Studies (CKS)
NUWSS records: WL.
NVA records: WL.
NWCA papers: WL.
SPG papers: WL.

Individuals

Amelia Scott papers: WL.
Gertrude Tuckwell Papers: TUC library (London Metropolitan University).
Helena Normanton papers: WL.
Kathleen Lonsdale Papers: University College London Special Collections (UCLSC).
Margery Fry Papers (MFP): Somerville College, Oxford.
Templewood Papers: Cambridge University Library (CUL).

Newspapers and Periodicals

Common Cause
Daily Mail
Daily Sketch
Howard Journal
Kent and Sussex Courier
Labour Woman
The Magistrate
NCW News
The Times
The Townswoman
The Vote / WFL Bulletin
Votes for Women
Woman's Leader

Books

J. Alberti, *Beyond Suffrage: Feminists in War and Peace 1914–1928* (London: Macmillan, 1989).

M. Andrews, *The Acceptable Face of Feminism: The Women's Institute as a Social Movement* (London: Lawrence and Wishart, 1997).

V. Bailey, *Delinquency and Citizenship: Reclaiming the Young Offender, 1914–1948* (Oxford: Clarendon Press, 1987).

A. Ballinger, *Dead Women Walking* (Aldershot: Ashgate, 2000).

O. Banks, *Faces of Feminism: A Study of Feminism as a Social Movement* (Oxford: Martin Robertson, 1981).

P. Bartley, *Prostitution: Prevention and Reform in England, 1860–1914* (London: Routledge, 2000).

L. Bland, *Banishing the Beast: English Feminism and Sexual Morality 1885–1914* (Harmondsworth: Penguin, 1995).

B. P. Block and J. Hostettler, *Hanging in the Balance* (Winchester: Waterside Press, 1997).

D. Bochel, *Probation and Aftercare: Its Development in England and Wales* (Edinburgh: Scottish Academic Press, 1976).

J. Bowlby, *Child Care and the Growth of Love* (Harmondsworth: Penguin Books, 1953).

A. Brown and D. Barrett, *Knowledge of Evil: Child Prostitution and Child Sex Abuse in Twentieth Century England* (Cullompton: Willan, 2002).

E. Burney, *Magistrate, Court and Community* (London: Hutchinson, 1979).

J. Bush, *Women Against the Vote: Female Anti-Suffragism in Britain* (Oxford: Oxford University Press, 2007).

R. A. Butler, *The Art of the Possible: the Memoirs of Lord Butler* (London: H. Hamilton, 1971).

J. Buxton and M. Turner, *Gate Fever* (London: Cresset Press, 1962).

G. Cadbury, *Young Offenders: Yesterday and Today* (London: George Allen and Unwin Ltd, 1938).

B. Caine, *Victorian Feminists* (Oxford: Oxford University Press, 1992).

B. Campbell, *Iron Ladies* (London: Virago, 1987).

P. Carlen, *Women's Imprisonment: A Study in Social Control* (London: Routledge and Kegan Paul, 1983).

P. Carlen (ed.), *Criminal Women: Autobiographical Accounts* (Cambridge: Polity Press, 1985).

P. Carlen and A. Worral (eds), *Gender, Crime and Justice* (Milton Keynes: Open University Press, 1987).

B. Castle, *Fighting all the Way* (London: Macmillan, 1993).

J. Colenbrander, *A Portrait of Fryn* (London: Andre Deutsch, 1984).

M. Colquhoun, *Woman in the House* (Shoreham by Sea: Scan Books, 1980).

P. Cox, *Gender, Justice and Welfare: Bad Girls in Britain, 1900–1950* (Basingstoke: Palgrave Macmillan, 2003).

E. Crawford, *The Women's Suffrage Movement 1866–1928: A Reference Guide* (London: UCL Press, 1999).

R. Crichton (ed.), *The Memoirs of Ethel Smyth* (Harmondsworth: Penguin, 1987).

D. Crisp, *A Light in the Night* (London: Holborn Publishing, 1960).

P. Davies, P. Francis and V. Jupp, (eds), *Victimisation: Theory, Research and Policy* (Basingstoke: Palgrave Macmillan, 2003).

S. D'Cruze (ed.), *Everyday Violence in Britain 1850–1950* (Harlow: Longman, 2000).

E. M. Delafield, *Messalina of the Suburbs* (London: Macmillan, 1924).

P. Duff, *Left, Left, Left: A Personal account of six protest campaigns, 1945–64* (London: Allison & Busby, 1971).

C. Dyhouse, *Feminism and the Family in England 1880–1939* (Oxford: Blackwell, 1989).

J. P. Eddy, *Justice of the Peace* (London: Cassell, 1963).

W. A. Elkin, *The English Penal System* (Harmondsworth: Penguin Books, 1957).

C. Eustance, J. Ryan and L. Ugolini (eds), *A Suffrage Reader* (London: Leicester University Press, 2000).

X. Field, *Under Lock and Key: a Study of Women in Prison* (London: Max Parrish, 1963).

C. Frankenberg, *Not Old Madam, Vintage: An Autobiography* (Lavenham: Galaxy Books, 1975).

E. B. Freedman, *Their Sisters' Keepers: Women's Prison Reform in America 1830–1930* (Ann Arbor: University of Michigan Press, 1981).

E. B. Freedman, *Maternal Justice: Miriam Van Waters and the Female Reform Tradition* (Chicago: University of Chicago Press, 1996).

E. B. Freedman, *No Turning Back: The History of Feminism and the Future of Women* (London: Profile Books, 2002).

M. Fry, *Arms of the Law* (London: Gollancz, 1951).

J. Gaffin, and D. Thoms, *Caring and Sharing: The Centenary History of the Co-operative Women's Guild* (Manchester: Co-operative Union Ltd., 1983).

D. Garland, *Punishment and Welfare* (Aldershot: Gower, 1985).

D. Garland, *The Culture of Control* (Oxford: Oxford University Press, 2001).

D. Glick, *The National Council of Women of Great Britain: The First One Hundred Years* (London: National Council of Women, 1995).

L. Gordon, *Heroes of their Own Lives: the Politics and History of Family Violence, Boston 1880–1960* (London: Virago, 1989).

M. Gordon, *Penal Discipline* (London: George Routledge and Sons Ltd, 1922).

E. Gore, *The Better Fight: The Story of Dame Lilian Barker* (London: Geoffrey Bles, 1965).

B. D. Grew, *Prison Governor* (London: Herbert Jenkins, 1958).

A. J. Hammerton, *Cruelty and Companionship* (London: Routledge, 1992).

B. Harrison and P. Hollis (eds), *Pressure from Without* (London: Edward Arnold, 1974).

B. Harrison, *Prudent Revolutionaries: Portraits of British Feminists between the Wars* (Oxford: Oxford University Press, 1987).

H. Hendrick, *Images of Youth: Age, Class and the Male Youth Problem* (Oxford: Clarendon Press, 1990).

J. Henry, *Who Lie in Gaol* (London: Gollancz, 1952).

J. Hinton, Women, *Social Leadership and the Second World War* (Oxford: Oxford University Press, 2002).

P. Hollis, *Ladies Elect: Women in English Local Government, 1865–1914* (Oxford: Oxford University Press, 1987).

M. Humm, *Feminisms: A Reader* (Hemel Hempstead: Harvester Wheatsheaf, 1992).

E. Huws Jones, *Margery Fry: The Essential Amateur* (Oxford: Oxford University Press, 1966).

L. A. Jackson, *Child Sex Abuse in Victorian England* (London: Routledge, 2000).

L. A. Jackson, *Women Police: Gender, Welfare and Surveillance in the Twentieth Century* (Manchester: Manchester University Press, 2006).

S. Jeffreys, *The Spinster and her Enemies: Feminism and Sexuality 1880–1930* (London: Pandora Press, 1985).

H. Jones, *Women in British Public Life 1914–50: Gender, Power and Social Policy* (Longman: Harlow, 2000).

J. Jordan, *Josephine Butler* (London: John Murray, 2001).

J. Kelley, *When the Gates Shut* (London: Longman, 1967).

J. Kelly, *Women, History and Theory* (Chicago: University of Chicago Press, 1984).

S. Kemp and J. Squires (eds), *Feminisms* (Oxford: Oxford University Press, 1997).

H. Kennedy, *Eve Was Framed: Women and British Justice* (London: Random House, 1993).

S. K. Kent, *Making Peace: The Reconstruction of Gender in Interwar Britain* (New Jersey: Princeton University Press, 1993).

S. Koven and S. Michel (eds), *Mothers of a New World: Maternalist Politics and the Origins of Welfare States* (London: Routledge, 1993).

C. Law, *Suffrage and Power: The Women's Movement 1918–1928* (London: I. B. Tauris, 1997).

G. Lewis, *Eva Gore Booth and Esther Roper: A Biography* (London: Pandora Press, 1988).

J. Lewis (ed.), *Labour and Love: Women's Experience of Home and Family, 1850–1940* (Oxford: Blackwell, 1986).

J. Lewis, *Women and Social Action in Victorian and Edwardian England* (Aldershot: Edward Elgar, 1991).

J. Liddington, *The Road to Greenham Common: Feminism and Anti-Militarism in Britain since 1820* (London: Virago, 1989).

J. Liddington and J. Norris, *One Hand Tied Behind Us* (London: Virago, 1978).

C. Lytton, *Prison and Prisoners* (London: Virago, 1988, originally published 1914).

E. Macadam, *The Equipment of the Social Worker* (London: George Allen and Unwin, 1925).

E. Macadam, *The Social Servant in the Making* (London: George Allen and Unwin, 1945).

N. and J. MacKensie (eds), *The Diary of Beatrice Webb Volume 2* (London: Virago, 1983).

M. Maguire, R. Morgan and R. Reiner (eds), *Oxford Handbook of Criminology*, 4th edition (Oxford: Oxford University Press, 2007).

L. Mahood, *Policing Gender, Class and Family: Britain 1850–1940* (London: UCL Press, 1995).

H. Mannheim, *Juvenile Delinquency in an English Middletown* (London: Kegan Paul, 1948).

J. Manton, *Mary Carpenter and the Children of the Streets* (London: Heinemann, 1976).

L. Martindale, *A Woman Surgeon* (London: Gollancz, 1951).

R. I. Mawby and S. Walklate, *Critical Victimology* (London: Sage, 1994).

C. McCall, *They Always Come Back* (London: Methuen, 1938).

J. S. Mill, *The Subjection of Women* (New York: Dover Publications, 1997, originally published 1869).

D. Mitchell, *Queen Christabel* (London: MacDonald and Jane's, 1977).

N. Naffine, *Feminism and Criminology* (Cambridge: Polity Press, 1997).

Newnham College Register, Volume I (Cambridge: Newnhan College, 1979).

S. Oldfield (ed.), *This Working Day World: Women's Lives and Culture(s) in Britain 1914–45* (London: Taylor and Francis, 1994).

G. Pearson, *Hooligan: A History of Respectable Fears* (London: Macmillan, 1983).

A. Perkin, *Red Queen* (London: Macmillan, 2003), p. 379.

E. Pethick Lawrence, *My Part in a Changing World* (London: Gollancz, 1938).

A. Platt, *The Child Savers* (Chicago: University of Chicago Press, 1969).

V. Powell, *The Life of a Provincial Lady: A Study of E .M. Delafield and her works* (London: Heinemann, 1988).

F. Prochaska, *Women and Philanthropy in Nineteenth-Century England* (Oxford: Clarendon Press, 1980).

M. Pugh, *Women and the Women's Movement in Britain 1914–1959*, 2nd edition (Basingstoke: Macmillan, 2000).

M. Pugh, *The March of the Women* (Oxford: Oxford University Press, 2000).

J. Purvis and S. Holton, (eds) *Votes for Women* (London: Routledge, 2000).

N. H. Rafter and F. Heidensohn, *International Feminist Perspectives on Criminology: Engendering a Discipline* (Buckingham: Open University Press, 1995).

Reading, Dowager Marchioness of, *It's the Job That Counts* (Colchester: privately printed, 1973).

M. Richards and P. Light, *Children of the Social World* (Oxford: Blackwell, 1986).

P. Rock, *Helping Victims of Crime: the Home Office and the Rise of Victim Support in England and Wales* (Oxford: Clarendon Press, 1990).

P. Rock, *Reconstructing a Women's Prison* (Oxford: Oxford University Press, 1996).

C. H. Rolph, *Living Twice* (London: Gollancz, 1974).

G. Rose, *The Struggle for Penal Reform* (London: Stevens, 1961).

J. Rose, *The Intellectual Life of the British Working Classes* (New Haven: Yale University Press, 2001).

D. Rubinstein, *A Different World for Women: The Life of Millicent Garrett Fawcett* (London: Harvester Wheatsheaf, 1991).

S. K. Ruck (ed.), *Paterson on Prisons* (London: Frederick Muller, 1951).

J. Rumgay, *Ladies of Lost Causes: Rehabilitation, Women Offenders and the Voluntary Sector* (Cullompton: Willan, 2007).

M. Ryan, *The Acceptable Pressure Group* (Farnborough: Saxon House, 1978).

M. Ryan, *Penal Policy and Political Culture: Four Essays on Policy and Process* (Winchester: Waterside Press, 2003).

S. Schafer, *Restitution to Victims of Crime* (London: Stevens, 1960).

H. J. Self, *The Fallen Daughters of Eve: Prostitution, Women and Misuse of the Law* (London: Frank Cass, 2003).

J. Shapland, J. Willmore and P. Duff, *Victims in the Criminal Justice System* (Aldershot: Gower, 1985).

M. Size, *Prisons I Have Known* (London: Allen & Unwin, 1958).

T. Skyrme, *History of the Justice of the Peace Volume 2* (Chichester: Barry Rose, 1991).

C. Smart, *Women, Crime and Criminology* (London: Routledge Kegan Paul, 1977).

A. D. Smith, *Women in Prison: A Study in Penal Methods* (London: Stephens, 1962).

H. L. Smith (ed), *British Feminism in the Twentieth Century* (Aldershot: Edward Elgar, 1990).

H. Sommerlad and P. Sanderson, *Gender, Choice and Commitment: Women Solicitors in England and Wales and the Struggle for Equal Status* (Aldershot: Ashgate, 1998).

S. Spencer, *Gender, Work and Education in Britain in the 1950s* (Basingstoke: Palgrave Macmillan, 2005).

D. Spender, *There's Always Been A Woman's Movement This Century* (London: Pandora Press, 1983).

D. Spender (ed.), *Time and Tide Wait For No Man* (London: Pandora Press, 1984).

J. Springhall, *Youth, Empire and Society: British Youth Movements 1883–1940* (London: Croom Helm, 1977).

J. Springhall, *Coming Of Age: Adolescence in Britain 1860–1960* (Dublin: Gill & Macmillan, 1986).

C. Sykes, *Nancy: The Life of Lady Astor* (London: Collins, 1972).

D. Taylor, *Crime, Policing and Punishment in England 1750–1914* (Basingstoke: Macmillan, 1998).

F. Tennyson Jesse, *A Pin to see the Peepshow* (London: Heinemann Ltd, 1934).

M. Tims, *Jane Addams of Hull House, 1860–1935: A Centenary Study* (London: Allen and Unwin, 1961).

E. O. Tuttle, *The Crusade Against Capital Punishment in Great Britain* (London: Stevens & Sons, 1961).

J. Walkowitz, *Prostitution and Victorian Society* (Cambridge: Cambridge University Press, 1980).

J. Whitney, *Geraldine S. Cadbury 1865–1941 – A Biography* (London: Harrap, 1948).

M. J. Wiener, *Men of Blood: Violence, Manliness, and Criminal Justice in Victorian England* (Cambridge: Cambridge University Press, 2004).

E. Wilson, *Only Halfway to Paradise: Women in Postwar Britain*, 1945–1968 (London: Tavistock, 1980).

B. Wootton, *Social Science and Social Pathology* (London: George Allen & Unwin, 1959).

B. Wootton, *In A World I Never Made: Autobiographical Reflections* (London: George Allen & Unwin, 1967).

L. Zedner, *Women, Crime and Custody in Victorian England* (Oxford: Oxford University Press, 1991).

Pamphlets

N. Adler, *Separate Courts for Children* (London: Women's Industrial Council, 1908).

T. Calvert, *Capital Punishment: Society Takes Revenge, An examination of the Necessity for Capital Punishment in Britain To-day* (London: National News-letter, 1946).

Howard League for Penal Reform, *Making Amends: Criminals, Victims and Society – Compensation, Reparation, Reconciliation: a Discussion Paper* (London: Howard League for Penal Reform, 1977).

'Justice', *Compensation for Victims of Crimes of Violence: A Report* (London: Stevens, 1962).

K. Lonsdale, *Account of Life in Holloway Prison for Women* (Chislehurst: Prison Reform Council, 1943).

J. Lovat Fraser, *Child Offenders* (London: State Children's Association, 1928).

J. B. Thompson, *Justice of the Peace in Juvenile Courts* (London: Labour Research Department, 1944).

Articles

J. C. Albisetti, 'Portia Ante Portas: Women and the Legal Profession in Europe, c. 1870–1925', *Journal of Social History*, 33, 4 (2000) 825–57.

C. Beaumont, 'Citizens not Feminists: The Boundary Negotiated Between Citizenships and Feminism by Mainstream Women's Organisation in England 1928–39', *Women's History Review*, 9, 2 (2000) 411–29.

C. Beaumont, 'Moral Dilemmas and Women's Rights: The Attitude of the Mother's Union and the Catholic Women's League to Divorce, Birth Control and Abortion in England, 1928–1939', *Women's History Review*, 16, 4 (2007) 463–85.

K. Bradley, 'Juvenile Delinquency, the Juvenile Courts and the Settlement Movement, 1908–1950: Basil Henriques and Toynbee Hall', *Twentieth Century British History*, 19, 2 (2008) 133–55.

A. Brown, 'The Amazing Mutiny at the Dartmoor Convict Prison', *British Journal of Criminology*, 47, 2 (2007) 276–92.

C. A. Corcos, 'Portia Goes to Parliament: Women and their Admission to Membership in the English Legal Profession', *Denver University Law Review*, 75, 2 (1997) 307–417.

E. Crawford, 'Police, Prisons and Prisoners: The View from the Home Office', *Women's History Review*, 14, 3/4 (2005) 487–505.

K. Daly and M. Chesney-Lind, 'Feminism and Criminology', *Justice Quarterly*, 5, 4 (1988) 497–538.

W. J. Forsythe, 'Reformation and Relaxation in the English Prisons', *Social and Political Administration*, 23, 2 (1989) 161–8.

D. Garland, 'British Criminology Before 1935' British Journal of Criminology, 28, 2 (1988), 1–17.

L. Gelsthorpe and A. Morris, 'Feminism and Criminology in Britain', *British Journal of Criminology*, 28, 2 (1988) 93–110.

S. Innes, 'Constructing Women's Citizenship in the Interwar Period: The Edinburgh Women Citizens' Association', *Women's History Review*, 13, 4 (2004) 621–47.

J. Lewis, 'Gender, the Family and Women's Agency in the Building of "Welfare States": The British Case', *Social History*, 19, 1 (1994) 37–55.

A. Logan, "A Suitable Person for Suitable Cases": The Gendering of Juvenile Courts in England, c. 1910–39, *Twentieth Century British History*, 16, 2 (2005) 129–145.

A. Logan, 'Professionalism and the Impact of England's First Women Justices, 1920–1950'. *Historical Journal*, 49, 3 (2006) 833–50.

A. Logan, 'In Search of Equal Citizenship', *Women's History Review*, 16, 4 (2007) 501–18.

K. Lonsdale, 'Women in Science', *Proceedings of the Royal Institution of Great Britain*, 43, (1970) 295–317.

T. Morris, 'British Criminology: 1935–1948', *British Journal of Criminology*, 28, 2 (1988) 20–34.

P. Polden, 'The Lady of Tower Bridge: Sibyl Campbell, England's First Woman Judge', *Women's History Review*, 8, 3 (1999) 505–26.

J. Purvis, 'The Prison Experiences of the Suffragettes in Edwardian Britain', *Women's History Review*, 4, 1 (1995) 103–33.

M. Rendel, 'Legislating for Equal Pay and Opportunity for Women in Britain', *Signs*, 3, 4 (1978) 897–908.

C. Smart, 'A History of Ambivalence and Conflict in the Discursive Construction of the "Child Victim" of sexual abuse', *Social and Legal Studies*, 8, 3 (1999) 391–409.

L. Schwarz, 'Professions, Elites and Universities in England, 1870–1970', *Historical Journal*, 47, 4 (2004) 941–62.

J. Tosh, 'What Should Historians do without Masculinity? Reflections on Nineteenth-Century Britain', *History Workshop*, 38 (1994) 179–202.

D. Wills, 'Marjorie Franklin', *British Journal of Criminology*, 15, 2 (1975) 109–10.

D. S. Wilson, 'A New Look at the Affluent Worker: The Good Working Mother in Post-War Britain', *Twentieth Century British History*, 17, 2 (2006) 206–29.

J. Young, 'Radical Criminology in Britain: The Emergence of a Competing Paradigm', *British Journal of Criminology*, 28, 2 (1988) 159–83.

Unpublished Works

C. Eustance, 'Daring to be Free!' (Unpublished D Phil. thesis, University of York, 1993).

D. J. R. Grey, 'Representations of Infanticide in England, 1880–1922' (Unpublished PhD thesis, Roehampton University, 2008).

A. Logan, 'Making Women Magistrates: Feminism, Citizenship and Justice in England and Wales, 1918–1950' (Unpublished PhD thesis, University of Greenwich, 2002).

E. Seal, 'Women, Murder and the Construction of Gender in the Criminal Justice System of England and Wales, 1957–1962' (unpublished PhD thesis, University of Bristol, 2007).

M. Takayanagi, 'Widening Opportunities for Women: The Passage of the Sex Disqualification (Removal) Act 1919' (unpublished paper, 2007).

S. Whybrow, 'Borstals were for Girls Too: A Study of the First girls' borstal, c. 1909–35' (unpublished dissertation, University of Kent, 2006).

Online sources

Fawcett Society www.fawcettsociety.org.uk

J. Laite, 'Paying the Price Again: Prostitution Policy in Historical Perspective', (2006) www.historyandpolicy.org/papers/policy-paper-46.html

National Council of Women of Great Britain http://fp.ncwgb.f9.co.uk/index.htm

Oxford Dictionary of National Biography (online edn).

Index